CW00506650

PAUL

Apostle of the Living God

PAUL

Apostle of the Living God

Kerygma and Conversion in 2 Corinthians

MARK J. GOODWIN

TRINITY PRESS INTERNATIONAL
Harrisburg, Pennsylvania

Trinity Press International, P.O. Box 1321, Harrisburg, PA 17105
Trinity Press International is a division of the Morehouse Group.

Cover design: Jim Booth

Library of Congress Cataloging-in-Publication Data

Goodwin, Mark.
    Paul, apostle of the living God : kerygma and conversion in 2 Corinthians / Mark Goodwin.
       p. cm.
    Includes bibliographical references (p.)
    ISBN 1-56338-318-7 (alk. paper)
    1. Bible. N.T. Corinthians, 2nd – Theology. 2. God – Biblical teaching. I. Title.
    BS2398 .G66 2001
    227'.306 – dc21

                                          00-052744

Printed in the United States of America

01   02   03   04   05   06   10 9 8 7 6 5 4 3 2 1

Contents

𝕫𝕫𝕫𝕫𝕫𝕫𝕫𝕫𝕫𝕫

Abbreviations

🔲🔲🔲🔲🔲🔲🔲🔲🔲🔲

AB	Anchor Bible
ABD	*Anchor Bible Dictionary*
BNTC	Black's New Testament Commentaries
CBQ	*Catholic Biblical Quarterly*
CBQMS	Catholic Biblical Quarterly Monograph Series
CRINT	Compendia rerum iudaicarum ad Novum Testamentum
EKKNT	Evangelisch-katholischer Kommentar zum Neuen Testament
EvT	*Evangelische Theologie*
FRANT	Forschungen zur Religion und Literatur des Alten und Neuen Testaments
HNTC	Harper's New Testament Commentaries
HTKNT	Herder's theologischer Kommentar zum Neuen Testament
HTR	*Harvard Theological Review*
HUCA	*Hebrew Union College Annual*
ICC	International Critical Commentary
JBL	*Journal of Biblical Literature*
JSJ	*Journal for the Study of Judaism in the Persian, Hellenistic, and Roman Periods*
JSNT	*Journal for the Study of the New Testament*
JSNTSup	Journal for the Study of the New Testament: Supplement Series
JSOTSup	Journal for the Study of the Old Testament: Supplement Series

LCL	Loeb Classical Library
LEC	Library of Early Christianity
LXX	Septuagint
MeyerK	H. A. W. Meyer, Kritisch-exegetischer Kommentar über das Neue Testament
MT	Masoretic Text
NIGTC	New International Greek Testament Commentary
NovT	*Novum Testamentum*
NTS	*New Testament Studies*
RB	*Revue biblique*
RQ	*Römische Quartalschrift für christliche Altertumskunde und Kirchengeschichte*
SBL	Society of Biblical Literature
SBLDS	Society of Biblical Literature Dissertation Series
SBLSBS	Society of Biblical Literature Resources for Biblical Study
SBT	Studies in Biblical Theology
SNTSMS	Society for New Testament Studies Monograph Series
StBibTh	*Studia Biblica et Theologica*
TDNT	*Theological Dictionary of the New Testament.* Ed. G. Kittel and G. Friedrich. Trans. G. W. Bromiley. 10 vols. Grand Rapids: Eerdmans, 1964–76.
TGI	*Texbuch zur Geschichte Israels.* Ed. K. Galling. 2d ed. Tübingen, 1968.
WBC	Word Biblical Commentary
WMANT	Wissenschaftliche Monographien zum Alten und Neuen Testament
WUNT	Wissenschaftliche Untersuchungen zum Neuen Testament
ZNW	*Zeitschrift für die neutestamentliche Wissenschaft und die Kunde der älteren Kirche*

Acknowledgments

I completed this book with the encouragement and support of many people to whom I am deeply indebted. The book began as a Yale dissertation in 1992, inspired by the teaching of Abraham J. Malherbe in his course on Paul's Macedonian correspondence. I gratefully acknowledge his seminal insights on the living God that remain foundational in this book.

In revising the dissertation, I have also benefited from dialogue with my colleagues at the University of Dallas, including Rev. Dennis Farkasfalvy, Rev. Enrique Nardoni, and the late Dr. William Farmer. A special word of thanks is due to Dr. Farmer, who helped with suggestions on revising and enriching the manuscript for publication. His input was most valuable. Further, I must also express gratitude to Rev. David Balas, who was steadfast in his encouragement of this project over a period of years. My editor at Trinity Press, Henry Carrigan, contributed in matters of style and substance, and Matthew London helped in preparing the bibliography.

Finally, scholarly work is never simply the product of scholarship alone, but also reflects the nurturing support of friends and family. This book could not have been completed without the support of three people in my life, my parents, Ann and William Goodwin, and my wife, Jean, who provided me with valuable assistance in the completion of this manuscript. She not only did the work of computer formatting and proofreading, but has also been a true companion in her love and support during the years it took to bring this project to completion. It is with great joy that I dedicate the book to her and to my daughter, Sarah.

Introduction

⌈⌉⌈⌉⌈⌉⌈⌉⌈⌉⌈⌉⌈⌉

The Significance of the Living God for Paul

With the recent upsurge in interest in Paul's God-talk,[1] it is surprising that New Testament scholars have paid so little attention to the living God epithet in Paul's letters. Paul's use of the epithet carries a specific and well-defined kerygmatic significance and plays a significant role in his epistolary discourse. The four Pauline uses are: 1 Thess 1:9–10; 2 Cor 3:3 and 6:16; and Rom 9:25–26.[2] The first of these uses, 1 Thess 1:9–10, suggests the epithet's function in Paul's monotheistic kerygma and its significance in designating the living God as life-giving creator. In addition to these four uses, the living God also occurs in post-Pauline sources such as Acts 14:15; 1 Tim 3:10; 4:10; and the *Acts of Paul*, passim. These occurrences are relevant to an understanding of the Pauline living God, since they confirm the epithet's kerygmatic function. These Pauline and post-Pauline sources thus suggest that the living God has a kerygmatic significance associated with the theme of Gentile conversion. Gentiles convert to the living God in response to Paul's kerygma.

There is, however, more to the Pauline significance of the epithet "living God" than its function in Paul's kerygma. The

---

1. Neil Richardson, *Paul's Language about God* (JSNTSup 99; Sheffield: Sheffield Academic Press, 1994), 9–25. Also see Halvor Moxnes, *Theology in Conflict: Studies in Paul's Understanding of God in Romans* (Leiden: E. J. Brill, 1980); J. M. Bassler, *Divine Impartiality* (SBLDS 59; Chico, Calif.: Scholars Press, 1982); and Larry Hurtado, *One God, One Lord: Early Christian Devotion and Ancient Jewish Monotheism* (Philadelphia: Fortress Press, 1988).

2. Other uses of the living God epithet in the New Testament are found in Matt 16:16; 26:63; Heb 3:12; 9:14; 10:31; 12:22; Rev 7:2; 4:9–10; 15:7. See also 1 Pet 1:23 and John 6:57 for probable uses.

epithet also has a rich biblical significance that is reflected in Rom 9:26; 2 Cor 3:3 and 6:16. The living God, for Paul, is also the covenantal God of Israel who formed Israel at Mount Horeb and promised a new covenant. A major aim of this book, then, will be to explore this biblical and Jewish background of the living God, highlighting its relevance for interpreting the Pauline use of the epithet. Specifically, I will focus on exploring the epithet construction "living God," which is found in Hebrew and Greek sources. In linguistic terms, the epithet construction consists of a term for God ("God" or "Lord"), which is modified by the participle "living" in the attributive position, functioning as an adjective.[3] This construction is related to two other linguistic forms in the Hebrew Bible and the LXX, the oath and pronouncement formulas.[4] There is no use of the pronouncement formula in the New Testament, but the oath formula occurs in several New Testament writings, including Rom 14:11.[5] In the oath formula, God swears "as I live" or, in other instances, an Israelite swears, "As the Lord lives." In some New Testament sources, the epithet and the oath formula are used interchangeably, suggesting a close relationship between the two constructions.[6] However, the significance of the oath formula for Paul is minimal in comparison with the epithet construction, since the latter is central in Paul's missionary preaching. For these reasons, then, the epithet construction will receive primary attention in the following discussion.

A complex background informs Paul's use of the living God and is attested in scriptural, Jewish, and early Christian sources.

---

3. In Hebrew, there are three basic constructions: (1) אל חי; (2) אלהים חי; and (3) אלהים היים: In Greek, the basic constructions are: (1) θεὸς ζῶν/ζῶν θεός; (2) ὁ θεὸς ζῶν/ὁ ζῶν θεός; and (3) ζῶν κύριος/κύριος ζῶν.

4. Examples of the oath formula are found in Num 14:21; Jer 22:34; Isa 49:18; Hos 4:15; and 1 Sam 14:39. The pronouncement formula is found in Ps 18:47 (=1 Sam 22:47), "The Lord lives; and blessed be my rock." Henry Everding, "The Living God: A Study in the Function and Meaning of Biblical Terminology" Ph.D. diss., Harvard University Press, 1968, 18–28, 97–98, 102–14.

5. This is Paul's only use of the oath formula. Everding, "The Living God," 285–86.

6. Both Daniel and Revelation make use of both types of construction, suggesting a close relation between them. For example, Dan 4:19 (23) LXX; 5:23 LXX; 6:27 LXX/MT; and 12:7 LXX/MT. However, there is little or no discussion clarifying the nature of this relation between the two constructions.

This background of the epithet falls into three clearly recognizable patterns of association, which this book will refer to as "living God traditions." These traditions consist of the epithet living God used in connection with recurring patterns of thematic association, the latter representing three distinctive facets that are attested in biblical, Hellenistic Jewish, and early Christian sources. While each of these facets is closely interrelated to the others, they each represent a distinct and identifiable aspect inherited by Paul. I will therefore refer to these three facets as biblical, Hellenistic Jewish, and early Christian traditions of the living God. For example, the biblical tradition of the living God tradition is represented in both the Hebrew Bible and the LXX. It consists of the epithet used in repeated connection with covenantal motifs, e.g., the giving of the Decalogue, God's indwelling of the Jerusalem temple, and Hosea's prophecy of a new covenant (Hos 2:1 LXX [1:10 MT]). There is also a distinctive Hellenistic Jewish tradition of the living God consisting of its own pattern of associations surrounding the epithet. In Hellenistic Jewish sources the living God is used repeatedly in connection with the motifs of monotheistic propaganda and idol polemic. Of special significance here is the epithet's function in stylized formulations of idol polemic, which place the living God in antithesis to idols, thus stressing the uniqueness and superiority of the living God in contrast to pagan gods. Living God tradition, then, is recognizable in a complex combination of thematic and linguistic associations of the epithet found in a wide range of literary sources, which Paul himself inherited in the first century B.C.E.

To grasp, then, the full significance of the living God in Paul's letters requires an exploration into the background of the living God in biblical, Jewish, and early Christian sources. Living God tradition goes back to biblical roots that present the living God as the covenantal God of Israel who spoke as a voice out of fire on Mount Horeb, founding the covenant and giving the Decalogue. These roots are attested in a variety of biblical sources, including Hos 2:1 (LXX; 1:10 MT); Deut 4:33 (LXX); 5:26 (LXX; MT); 1 Sam 17:26, 36 (LXX; MT); Josh 3:10–11 (LXX; MT); 2 Kgs 19:4, 16 (LXX; MT); Ps 41:3 LXX [42:3];

83:3 LXX [84:3]; Jer 10:10 (MT only); etc.[7] The latter texts portray God as "living" in the sense of being active and dynamic in the affairs of Israel, delivering in times of crises, and "dwelling" in the Jerusalem temple as a sign of covenantal faithfulness.

The biblical tradition of the living God also presents the living God in association with the new covenant, through the prophecy of Hos 2:1 LXX [1:10 MT]: "Yet the number of the people of Israel shall be like the sand of the sea, which can be neither measured nor numbered; and in the place where it was said to them, 'You are not my people,' it shall be said to them, 'sons of the living God.'" In this prophecy, the living God promises to restore an idolatrous Israel to covenantal sonship following a time of judgment and exile (cf. *Jub.* 1:25). This prophecy about the "sons of the living God" was later taken up and reinterpreted in postexilic Jewish circles, as seen in 3 Macc 6:28; Esth 8:12q LXX; *Jub.* 1:25; and *Jos. Asen.* 19:8. In these texts, "sons of the living God" comes to designate the future eschatological Israel (*Jub.* 1:25), the Jewish community in its identity as the restored covenantal people (3 Macc 6:28; Esth 8:12q LXX), and also Gentile proselytes converting to monotheism (*Jos. Asen.* 19:8). Paul's use of Hos 2:1 LXX [1:10 MT] in Rom 9:26 has affinities with this Jewish interpretive tradition and can be illumined in connection with it.

These biblical roots of living God tradition serve as the basis for further development in subsequent Jewish tradition. Jews of the Hellenistic Diaspora retained the biblical view of the living God as the covenantal God of Israel; however, they also developed their own distinctive traditions of the living God which built upon traditional biblical views. Jews in the Hellenistic Diaspora lived in a polytheistic milieu that prompted the need for new ways of speaking about their living God in contrast to other gods. They therefore developed stylized formulations of idol polemic that set the living God in antithesis to dead idols

---

7. Many occurrences of the living God are common to both the Hebrew Bible and the LXX. However, some occurrences are limited to only one of the latter sources; for example, the living God in Jer 10:10 has no corresponding LXX use, while the use of the living God in Deut 4:33 LXX has no corresponding use in the MT.

(Dan 5:23 and 6:27 LXX; *Jos. Asen.* 8:5; *Sib. Or.* 3:762–66; Bel and the Dragon Theodotion 5–6). These stylized formulations served to stress both the uniqueness and the superiority of the living God in contrast to other idol-gods of the Diaspora. Jews in the Hellenistic Diaspora therefore adjusted living God tradition to the new circumstances of the Diaspora and placed their distinctive stamp upon biblical traditions of the living God.

It was this Jewish tradition of the living God, with its stylized formulations of idol polemic, that exercised a powerful influence on Paul and other early Christians in the first century C.E. Evidence in the New Testament shows that early Christians inherited Jewish traditions of the living God for use in their monotheistic kerygma to Gentile audiences. Paul's letters reflect early Christian (pre-Pauline) kerygmatic traditions of the living God and suggest that early Christians adopted Jewish formulations of the living God in preaching monotheism (1 Thess 1:9; Acts 14:15; 2 Cor 6:16; and *Acts Paul* 7:2; cf. Heb 9:14). Paul, then, like other early Christian missionaries, stands in continuity with Jewish monotheism by proclaiming the one true God to Gentiles and promoting the superior character of the living God in contrast to idols.

However, the living God in early Christian kerygma was more than simply the proclamation of Jewish monotheism. Early Christian kerygma also shows the modification of Jewish monotheism by asserting that the living God has raised Jesus from the dead. Paul proclaimed a God whose "living" character had manifested itself powerfully in the resurrection of Jesus, an act which signaled the prospect of coming judgment and deliverance (1 Thess 1:9–10; Acts 14:15–17; cf. 2 Cor 3:3; 1 Tim 4:10). For Paul and other early Christians, the living God came to be redefined in connection with the resurrection of Jesus as the definitive event of divine life-giving power. Paul's monotheistic kerygma, then, was not a simple continuation of Jewish monotheism, but rather, represents a novel Christian development of earlier living God tradition.

Further, this act of God in raising Jesus provides the analogy for further acts of divine life-giving in the creation of Christian communities of faith. The resurrection-life of the living God

manifests itself in the preaching of the gospel and the resulting missionary foundation of Gentile communities, "churches
of the living God" (1 Tim 3:15; cf. 2 Cor 6:16). Paul's proclamation of the living God to Gentiles was an expression of life-giving
power that resulted in conversion and brought new life to the
converts as God's children. This life-giving power of the living
God also manifests itself in the activity of the Spirit, whom Paul
calls the "Spirit of the living God" (2 Cor 3:3). This Spirit accompanies and confirms Paul's preaching and represents divine
life-giving power in the establishment of Gentile communities.
Further, the deeper theological significance of this community formation is expressed in the language of new covenant
prophecy. The creation of Gentile communities fulfills scriptural promises of a future Israel restored to covenantal relation
with God, promises found in the prophets Hosea, Jeremiah,
and Ezekiel. In his ministry, then, Paul could see the working
of the same living God who had founded Israel at Sinai, and
who was now acting to create a new covenant people out of
Jews and Gentiles through conversion. Called by the living God
as an apostle, Paul himself became a vehicle of the living God's
creative power in forming this new covenant people.

Paul inherited and used a rich biblical and Jewish theology
of the living God, but he was also innovative in appropriating
these traditions for his own epistolary purposes. Paul, therefore,
was more than a passive recipient of living God tradition; he
placed his own distinctive stamp upon that tradition for his own
pastoral and epistolary purposes.

Scholarly Neglect of the Living God
in Paul's Letters

A perusal of the scholarly literature on Paul's four uses of
the epithet in 1 Thess 1:9–10; Rom 9:25–26; and 2 Cor 3:3
and 16 shows that New Testament scholarship has done little
to clarify the rich significance of the living God in Paul's letters. Interpreters generally assume that Paul's use of the "living
God" is equivalent to the Old Testament notion of "God" and
lacks in any special significance of its own. Working with this

assumption, many commentators are content to make terse and perfunctory comments about the epithet, if they say anything at all. The general scholarly perception, then, has been that the epithet is lacking in any specialized significance that distinguishes it from other Old Testament expressions for God.

One reason for this lack of scholarly interest in the living God stems from a wider tendency in New Testament scholarship to neglect the importance of God in Paul's theology. In a recent discussion of Paul's God-talk, Neil Richardson discusses this state of neglect, observing that New Testament scholars ignore Paul's God-talk in favor of christology, eschatology, and other topics.[8] He observes how interpreters tend to assume that Paul's thinking about God, from his conversion onwards, "is perceived to have become more christocentric"; also Paul's God-talk is not distinctive, but rather "moves entirely within lines already laid down by the tradition."[9] The prevailing assumption is that there is nothing new or distinctively Christian in Paul's God-talk. As a result, then, the topic of God in Paul's letters is given marginal attention, often in the form of sweeping generalizations that pay little attention to specific forms of Paul's God-talk.

Another factor contributing to scholarly neglect of the living God is a dearth of knowledge about the epithet's Jewish background. While there are numerous studies of the living God in the Hebrew Bible,[10] there are correspondingly few studies of the epithet in postexilic Jewish sources. The prevailing assumption here is that the epithet's Old Testament roots are sufficient by themselves for understanding the living God in Paul, thus

---

8. Neil Richardson, *Paul's Language about God*, 12–18.

9. Ibid., 15, 16. Richardson here acknowledges the influence of A. Lindemann, "Die Rede von Gott in der paulinische Theologie," *TGI* 69 (1979): 358–59.

10. Helmer Ringgren, *Israelite Religion* (trans. David Green; Philadelphia: Fortress Press, 1966), 87–88; Hans Joachim Kraus, "Der lebendige Gott," *EvT* 27 (1967): 169–201; Jacques Guillet, S.J., "Le Titre Biblique *Le Dieu Vivant*," *L'Homme Devant Dieu: Mélanges offerts au Père Henri De Lubac* (Études publiées sous la direction de la faculté de théologie S.J. de Lyon-Fourvière 56; Paris: Aubier, 1963), 11–23; and Horst Dietrich Preuss, *Old Testament Theology* (2 vols.; trans. Leo G. Perdue; Louisville: Westminster/John Knox, 1991), 1:243–44. A fuller listing can be found in Everding "The Living God," 1–2.

undermining scholarly interest in the Jewish living God.[11] Although there is no denying here the relevance of the epithet's Old Testament background, the living God in Paul cannot be sufficiently grasped by appealing solely to this background. Paul's use of the living God is deeply influenced by Jewish traditions attested in the Pseudepigrapha, the Septuagint, and its additions.

At present, then, there are almost no works that explore the Jewish background of the living God. The one notable exception is Henry Everding's Harvard dissertation of 1968.[12] This remains an important work on the subject, although it is unpublished and consequently has not had a major impact in New Testament studies. By exploring a wide range of literary sources, Everding's work represents an important first step toward understanding the biblical living God and it provides especially useful insights into the Jewish background of the epithet. The problem with Everding's work, however, is related to its scope, which was necessarily sweeping in its examination of a wide range of occurrences in a wide variety of sources. As a result, his individual treatments of the epithet are sometimes cursory and atomistic, tending to look at individual occurrences of the epithet in isolation from other occurrences. Therefore, while Everding's work remains useful, it needs to be supplemented by further investigation.

Further, the nature of the Pauline evidence itself leads many interpreters to the conclusion that the living God is incidental and not deserving of any special treatment. Of Paul's four uses of the epithet, three of these uses would, indeed, seem to be incidental. For example, in Rom 9:26 the epithet occurs as

---

11. For example, Hans Joachim Kraus, "Der lebendige Gott," 195–200, assesses New Testament uses of the living God and concludes that they are largely in continuity with Old Testament occurrences.

12. Everding, "The Living God." In addition to Everding, two articles on the living God are worth mentioning. Kraus, "Der lebendige Gott," 169–201, focuses largely upon Old Testament occurrences with no attention given to Jewish background. W. Stenger, "Die Gottesbezeichnung 'lebendiger Gott' im Neuen Testament," *Trierer Theologische Zeitschrift* 87 (1978): 61–69, discusses New Testament occurrences of the epithet in light of Jewish background; however, the latter is limited to brief comments on parallels. Also note Bultmann's article, "ζάω," *TDNT* 2:855, 858, in which he briefly comments on the Jewish background of the epithet.

part of a scriptural quote from Hos 2:1 LXX [1:10], but it is usually viewed as going along for the ride, so to speak, and is thus extraneous to Paul's argument. In the case of 2 Cor 6:16, the epithet occurs in a passage (6:14–7:1) considered to be a non-Pauline interpolation, which is inserted awkwardly into its present epistolary setting. Such a use is viewed as having little relevance to "genuine" Pauline occurrences of the living God. Further, even though 1 Thess 1:9–10 attests an important kerygmatic function of the epithet, the material in these verses is marked by traditional pre-Pauline features, suggesting that Paul adopts the epithet from early Christian tradition. Here the living God is inherited as a "traditional" item, reflecting little that is characteristically Pauline.

Also hampering any advance in understanding the Pauline living God is the sheer uniqueness of the epithet's use in 2 Cor 3:3 and 6:16. Both uses represent formulations that are *hapax legomena,* "Spirit of the living God" (2 Cor 3:3) and "temple of the living God" (2 Cor 6:16). These expressions remain difficult to interpret because they have no exact parallels in biblical or Jewish tradition. Interpreters do not know what to make of them, assuming, for example, that "Spirit of the living God" translates into the more common Pauline expression "Spirit of God." Such, then, are the factors that have led to the current state of neglect regarding Paul's use of the living God epithet, and so Paul's use of the living God remains an enigma in New Testament scholarship.

The following discussion will redress this state of neglect by following an integrated approach, that is, an approach that interprets the Pauline living God in a manner closely integrated with the epithet's biblical and Jewish background, taking full advantage of the range of evidence in biblical, Jewish, and early Christian sources. This background, when applied to the Pauline living God, furnishes a significant interpretive context for shedding light upon the meaning and function of the Pauline epithet. Further, taking an integrated approach also means examining each occurrence of the Pauline epithet in relation to other occurrences. There is much to be learned, for example, about the enigmatic "Spirit of the living God" in

2 Cor 3:3 by interpreting it in connection with the better understood 1 Thess 1:9–10. In fact, the four genuine occurrences of
the living God in 1 Thess 1:9–10; Rom 9:25–26; 2 Cor 3:3 and
6:16 provide a significant interpretive context within which any
single occurrence can be interpreted.

Aims, Methods, and Organization

The primary aims of this book are: (1) to reconstruct the background of living God tradition in biblical, Jewish, and early
Christian sources, focusing on those occurrences that are relevant for interpreting the Pauline usage of the epithet (chaps.
1–6); and (2) to apply significant aspects of this living God tradition to an interpretation of Paul's argument in 2 Cor 2:14–7:4
(chaps. 7–9). In other words, the first six chapters will reconstruct key aspects of living God tradition from biblical, Jewish,
and early Christian sources and following this reconstruction,
chapters 7, 8, and 9 will then apply the fruits of the preceding
research to an interpretation of the epithet in 2 Cor 3:3 and
6:16. The method for pursuing these aims will be primarily linguistic and theological, analyzing individual occurrences of the
living God in a wide range of sources and literary contexts and
also investigating the theological significance of the epithet.

In terms of organization, the first six chapters constitute a
background study which is the most extensive part of the book.
The aim of these chapters is to reconstruct living God tradition
from a massive sweep of biblical, Jewish, and early Christian
sources. The scope of this reconstruction, however, will be less
comprehensive and more selective than previous work on the
living God, focusing only on those occurrences that are relevant
for understanding the Pauline living God.[13] Paul's four uses of
the epithet in 1 Thess 1:9; Rom 9:26; 2 Cor 3:3 and 6:16 thus
help in determining the parameters for the initial background
study in the book.

---

13. While the occurrences of the living God in the book of Revelation and in
the Letter to the Hebrews are of marginal significance for this discussion, they still
deserve a full-length study in their own right.

Chapters 1 and 2 begin with an investigation into the biblical roots of the living God. This investigation will focus largely on Hellenistic Jewish sources written in Greek, such as the LXX, the additions to the LXX, and the Greek pseudepigrapha.[14] To be sure, a few non-Greek semitic sources are also important and will be included in the discussion, e.g., Jer 10:10 MT and the book of *Jubilees*. However, primary interest will be in Greek sources of the Hellenistic Diaspora, since these sources have the most direct bearing on the Pauline living God. Paul himself was a Greek-speaking Jew who inherits living God traditions from the Greek-speaking Diaspora and cites the LXX text in his letters. Therefore, Jewish traditions of the living God, as they are attested in the LXX and Greek pseudepigraphical sources, provide the primary interpretive context for understanding the Pauline use of the epithet.

Also, where the traditions of the Hebrew Bible influence Paul in his view of the living God, this influence is mediated to him through the LXX, which, to a large extent, faithfully preserves the Hebrew Bible's picture of the living God as the covenantal father of Israel. Given the LXX's faithful reproduction of the biblical living God, there is no need for a full-fledged investigation of living God tradition in the Hebrew Bible. Further, there already exists ample scholarship on the living God in the Hebrew Bible.[15] By comparison, however, scholarship on the living God in Hellenistic Jewish sources remains almost nonexistent.

Chapters 3 and 4 explore a crucial and distinctive tradition of the living God found among Jews of the Hellenistic Diaspora. This tradition is attested in several Jewish sources, e.g., Dan 4–6 LXX; *Joseph and Aseneth;* Bel and the Dragon Theodotion; and *Sib. Or.* 3. In continuity with traditional biblical roots, Hellenistic Jews developed their own distinctive views of the living God based upon the need to strengthen and defend their monothe-

---

14. The focus on Greek sources of the Jewish Diaspora does not imply a strict separation between a Palestinian and Diaspora Judaism. It does, however, recognize the importance of the Hellenistic Diaspora as a crucial background for interpreting the Pauline living God.

15. See for example, Everding, "The Living God," 34–99; Kraus,"Der lebendige Gott," 169–200; Ringgren, *Israelite Religion*, 87–88; Guillet, "Le Titre *Le Dieu Vivant*," 11–23; and Preuss, *Old Testament Theology*, 243–44.

istic identity in a polytheistic environment. To this end, they employ stylized formulations of idol polemic that set the living God in antithesis to idols and served to highlight the superior character of the living God (Dan 5:23 LXX; 6:26–27 LXX; Bel and the Dragon Theodotion 5; *Sib. Or.* 3:762–63; and *Jos. Asen.* 8:5). Chapters 3 and 4, then, will investigate these stylized formulations of idol polemic and explore how they express a distinctive theology of the living God among Hellenistic Jews.

Chapters 5 and 6 constitute a pivotal section in the book, applying the conclusions of the preceding chapters to an interpretation of Paul's use of the epithet. These chapters provide the crucial bridge to the subsequent discussions of the living God in 2 Cor 3:3 and 6:16. More specifically, they gather up the important insights of the preceding chapters and apply them to Paul's use of the living God in 1 Thess 1:9–10 and Rom 9:25–26. Chapter 5 demonstrates the kerygmatic function of the living God in Paul's missionary preaching to the Gentiles (1 Thess 1:9–10; Acts 14:15; *Acts Paul* 7:2). It establishes that Paul, indeed, was a proclaimer of the living God and suggests that Paul's use of the living God is an inheritance of Jewish and early Christian tradition. Further, the living God, for Paul, was fundamentally the creator, the source and giver of life, who raised Jesus from the dead.

Chapter 6 is an assessment of Paul's innovative use of the living God as conversion language in his epistolary discourse, especially Rom 9:25–26. In this chapter, Paul's use of the epithet as a term that carries the association of Gentile conversion serves to evoke the readers' experience of conversion to the living God. Further, conversion to the living God is an event that Paul viewed theologically, that is, as an initiative of the living God, who was active in converting Gentiles through the gospel and the Spirit. Paul's use of the living God in 2 Cor 3:3 and 6:16 presupposes this theological view of conversion in which the living God brings Gentile converts to new life as sons and daughters of the living God.

The three final chapters in the book (7, 8, and 9) shift attention to Paul's use of the living God in 2 Cor 3:3 and 6:16. The primary task in these chapters is to interpret 2 Cor 3:3 (chap. 7) and 6:16 (chap. 8) against the background of the living God traditions examined in earlier chapters. In chapters 7 and 8, the discussion attempts to contribute a better understanding to the rich but enigmatic expressions, "Spirit of the living God" (2 Cor 3:3), and "temple of the living God" (2 Cor 6:16). I will show that both expressions allude to Paul's missionary preaching in Corinth, as well as the resulting conversion and founding of the Corinthian community. Through conversion, the living God has brought the Corinthians to new life as a "people" of the new covenant. In these chapters, I hope to illumine not only the specific occurrences of the epithet in 2 Cor 3:3 and 6:16, but also to shed light on the wider discourse surrounding these occurrences in 2 Cor 2:14–3:3 and 6:14–7:1.

Finally, chapter 9 will explore the implications of the preceding two chapters for clarifying the coherence of 2 Cor 2:14–7:4. The aim here is to explore the underlying coherence of 2 Cor 2:14–7:4 based upon Paul's uses of the living God in 2 Cor 3:3 and 6:16. I will argue that the placement of the epithet at the beginning and end of 2:14–7:4 suggests a kind of inclusio or framing device in the letter. The use of the epithet as a framing device suggests the importance of living God theology as a fundamental presupposition in the wider discourse of 2 Cor 2:14–7:4. I will argue that 2 Cor 2:14–7:4 works from Paul's basic presupposition that he is an apostle of the living God who is commissioned and sent to bring new life to the Gentiles. Paul incorporates living God theology into his self-presentation in 2 Cor 2:14–7:4 to demonstrate his apostolic credentials and persuade the Corinthians to be reconciled to him.

Note: The LXX quotations come from Rahlfs's *Septuaginta* or from the Göttingen *Septuaginta* series. Quotations of the Greek New Testament are taken from the *Novum Testamentum Graece,* edition 26, and the translations of biblical texts are from the RSV.

Chapter One

The Living God as Covenantal God of Israel

᠊᠊᠊᠊᠊᠊᠊᠊᠊᠊᠊᠊᠊

My reconstruction of the living God's background begins with a discussion of the epithet's traditional biblical significance. Chapter 1 looks at biblical and Hellenistic Jewish sources to uncover the traditional biblical significance of the living God, which expresses the active power of Yahweh in delivering Israel from historic enemies. Interpreters generally agree on this aspect of the epithet's meaning. The epithet traditionally designates God as "living" in the sense of being active on behalf of Israel.[1] The living God is the God who intervenes to deliver Israel in times of crisis. The following discussion, however, will sharpen and refine this consensus view of the living God by showing it to be a function of a more fundamental notion: the living God is the covenantal God of Israel. The living God's power and saving activity, manifested in the history of Israel, are expressions of a divine covenantal faithfulness, which points to the more fundamental identity of the living God as the covenantal God of Israel.[2] This identity of the living God goes back to the root notion of the God who founded and elected Israel on Mount Sinai/Horeb.

Typically, interpreters focus on the living God's power and activity exercised on behalf of Israel, but tend to neglect the epithet's significance in designating Israel's covenantal God.

---

1. Kraus, "Der lebendige Gott," 189–90; Ringgren, *Israelite Religion,* 87; Everding, "The Living God," 75–79; Preuss, *Old Testament Theology,* 243–44; Raymond F. Collins, *Studies on the First Letter to the Thessalonians* (Bibliotheca Ephemeridum Theologicarum Lovaniensium 61; Leuven: Peeters, 1984), 235.

2. Kraus, "Der lebendige Gott," 184–90.

They neglect the fundamental covenantal significance that informs the various uses of the epithet. Numerous episodes in the biblical witness reflect this significance, including the two uses of the living God in Deut 4 and 5 LXX. The living God, in its root biblical meaning, functions to designate the covenantal God of Israel, the God who founded Israel on Sinai/Horeb. The living God was Israel's source of life. Interpreters also fail to notice the significant pattern of association in Hellenistic Jewish sources in which the living God is repeatedly identified as the giver of the Decalogue, again indicating the living God as the covenantal God of Sinai/Horeb. Among Jews of the Hellenistic Diaspora, the living God was the divine source of the Mosaic law, something that defined Jewish identity over against the Gentiles.

This chapter will, therefore, develop a fuller picture of the living God as the covenantal God of Israel. The discussion proceeds in two steps. I will first investigate the evidence that links the living God with the foundation of Israel on Mount Horeb and giving the Decalogue. Second, I will explore the epithet's association with the Jerusalem temple as further evidence of the living God's covenantal character. The living God indwells the temple as a sign of God's covenantal faithfulness. Further, this discussion is not intended as an exhaustive examination of the biblical living God, but rather is selective in two ways. First, it focuses on those occurrences of the living God that are relevant for understanding Paul's use of the epithet in 1 Thess 1:9; Rom 9:25–26; and 2 Cor 3:3 and 6:16. Second, I am interested mostly in biblical (LXX) and Hellenistic Jewish sources written in Greek since they provide the background that is most directly related to the Pauline living God.

The Living God and the Sinai Covenant

Deuteronomy 4–5 LXX

Both Deut 4:33 LXX and 5:26 LXX/MT offer important witnesses of the living God's covenantal significance.[3] Associations

---

3. Deut 32:40 furnishes the oath formula in a context of divine judgment: "For I lift up my hand to heaven, and swear, As I live forever, if I whet my glittering sword, and my hand takes hold on judgment, I will take vengeance on my adversaries. . . ."

of the living God with the Exodus appear in Deut 4:33–34 LXX, and this association is confirmed by Jeremiah's use of the oath formula, "As the Lord lives who brought up the people of Israel out of the land of Egypt" (16:14–15; 23:7–8). However, Deut 4:33 LXX and 5:26 LXX/MT bring the epithet into close association with the traditions of Sinai/Horeb. The living God elects Israel and gives it the Decalogue.

In Deut 5:26 the epithet is found in both Hebrew and Greek texts, the latter faithfully preserving the former. However, Deut 4:33 LXX represents a special usage of the living God found only in the LXX, a usage that is absent from the Hebrew text. Regarding Deut 4:33 LXX, Everding observes that "the presence of the epithet in this statement is late."[4] The late postexilic character of this usage is supported by the observation that Deut 4:33 is part of a wider literary unit (1:6–4:43) that is widely regarded as a later addition that was inserted as an introduction to the book.[5]

Deuteronomy 1:6–4:43 provides the narrative setting for Deut 4:33 LXX, narrating Israel's journey from Sinai to the Transjordan and portraying Israel as idolatrous and unfaithful to God and covenant. Deuteronomy 4:1–43 depicts Moses appealing to the Israelites to obey the laws and statutes of the covenant. He begins by recounting the Baal of Peor incident in 4:3–4, which illustrates that obedience to the covenant leads to life, while apostasy leads to destruction. Obedience involves adherence to the Decalogue, as in Deut 4:13: God "proclaimed to you his covenant, which he commanded you to keep, the Ten Commandments which he wrote to you on two tablets of stone."[6]

---

4. Everding, "The Living God," 68. Everding also observes that the addition of the living God "is probably due to an expansion of Deut 4:33 by anticipation of 5:26."

5. Moshe Weinfeld, "Deuteronomy, Book of," *ABD* 2:171. The postexilic character of Deut 4 is also evident from its content. For example, the monotheistic affirmation of Deut 4:25, 39, "the Lord is God and there is no other," recalls Deutero-Isaiah.

6. τὰ δέκα ῥήματα καὶ ἔγραψεν αὐτὰ ἐπὶ δύο πλάκας λιθίνας. The Greek text quoted is from John W. Wevers, *Deuteronomium* (Septuaginta: Vetus Testamentum Graecum; Göttingen: Vandenhoeck & Ruprecht, 1977), 103–4.

The root problem, as described in Deut 4, is Israel's temptation to idolatry (4:15–18, 19–20, 23–28; cf. 29:22–28). Deuteronomy 4:23–24 expresses the problem in this way: "Take heed, therefore, lest, forgetting the covenant which the Lord your God has made with you, you fashion for yourselves against his command an idol in any form whatsoever. For the Lord, your God, is a devouring fire, a jealous God." Moses thus warns that idolatry will eventually lead Israel to destruction and exile and, scattered among the nations, Israel will serve "gods of wood and stone" (4:25–28). However, there is also hope that Israel will eventually repent and "return" to God, obedient to his commandments (4:30). In response, God will be merciful, forgetting not "the covenant which under oath he made with your fathers" (4:31). A future restoration of Israel is thus envisioned in which God and Israel will be reunited.

As proof of God's mercy and faithfulness to Israel, Moses recalls the theophany on Mount Sinai/Horeb, which resulted in God electing Israel from among the nations (4:32–40). Alone among the nations, Israel had been singled out as the only people to hear the voice of God speaking from the midst of fire and live. The election of Israel was due to God's love of the fathers: "And because he loved your fathers and chose their descendants after them, and brought you out of Egypt with his own presence, by his great power..." (4:37). It is within this context of the Horeb theophany that the Greek version of Deut 4:33–34 uses the epithet living God. Moses addresses Israel:

> [33]"Has any people ever heard the voice of the living God speaking out of a fire, as you have heard and lived? (εἰ ἀκήκοεν ἔθνος φωνὴν θεοῦ ζῶντος λαλοῦντος ἐκ μέσου τοῦ πυρός, ὃν τρόπον ἀκήκοας σὺ καὶ ἔζησας) [34]Or has any god ever attempted to go and take a nation for himself from the midst of another nation, by trials, by signs, by wonders, and by war, by a mighty hand and an outstretched arm, and by great terrors, according to all that the Lord your God did for you in Egypt before your eyes?"[7]

---

7. These verses are similar to Exod 33:20 where God, speaking to Moses, had warned: "you cannot see my face; for man shall not see me and live."

Of note here is the manner in which the living God manifests himself in terrifying power that threatens death.[8] Overwhelming divine power "is clearly indicated by the people's amazement that they heard the 'living God's voice but 'still live.'"[9] This dreadful divine power is an expression of divine transcendence, which is also communicated through the invisibility of the God who speaks from fire. The living God is identified with a voice that speaks from fire but cannot be seen.[10] This spiritualizing feature is given classic expression in 4:12–13, where Moses recalls that "You heard the sound of the words but saw no form; there was only a voice. He proclaimed to you his covenant. . . ."[11] The invisible living God who thus manifests himself in word (cf. Jer 23:36) is characterized by an invisible and spiritual character, which became increasingly typical of Hellenistic Jewish traditions of the living God.

While Everding is virtually silent on the living God's covenantal significance, such a significance is implicit in the overall literary setting of Deut 4. Explicit references to "the covenant" are present in the immediate literary context (4:24, 31, 5:2), and there are references to the giving of the Decalogue (4:40, 44, 5:1, 5:6–22), which is inscribed on two stone tablets (4:13; 5:22). Further, the theme of covenantal election is also found in the chapter, especially in 4:34 ("Or did any god ever venture to go and take a nation for himself from the midst of another nation") and 4:37 ("for love of your fathers he chose their descendants and personally led you out of Egypt by his great power"). That Israel "lived" through the terrifying encounter is a sign of its covenantal election. The living God, then, is identified here as the covenantal God who "elected" Israel through a gracious initiative.

The second occurrence of the epithet in Deut 5:26 LXX/MT appears in a narrative context similar to that of Deut 4:33

---

8. Everding, "The Living God," 70, classifies this use in connection with "the sense of Yahweh's dreadful power in theophany."

9. Ibid., 55.

10. Cf. Deut 5:4–5 and 5:22–23 in which God, in giving the Decalogue, also spoke out of the fire.

11. This manner of describing God is closely associated with the monotheistic theology of Deutero-Isaiah.

LXX. However, the living God in Deut 5:26 LXX/MT stands in explicit association with the giving of the Decalogue in Deut 5:6–21. The epithet occurs in the narrative setting of 5:22–32, which follows immediately upon the giving of the Decalogue and serves as an "epilogue" to the account.[12] The epilogue describes both the fear of the Israelites faced with the terrifying presence of God, as well as the Israelite request that Moses serve as mediator in communicating the divine law to Israel.

After the Decalogue is given (5:6–21), Moses addresses Israel in 5:22: "these words the Lord spoke to all your assembly out of the midst of the fire, the cloud, and the thick darkness, with a loud voice; and he added no more. And he wrote them upon two tablets of stone, and gave them to me" (5:22). In 5:23–27, Moses goes on to recount the fear of the Israelites in encountering such an awesome spectacle of divine "glory and greatness" (5:24); the Israelites fear the "great fire" because it would consume them. Moses then recounts how the Israelites had requested that he mediate between them and God:

> [23]"And when you heard the voice out of the midst of the darkness, while the mountain was burning with fire, you came near to me, all the heads of your tribes, and your elders; [24]and you said, 'behold the Lord our God has shown us his glory and greatness, and we have heard his voice out of the midst of the fire; we have this day seen God speak with man and still live. If we hear the voice of the Lord our God any more, we shall die. [25]Now therefore why should we die? For this great fire will consume us; if we hear the voice of the Lord our God anymore we shall die. [26]For who is there of all flesh that has heard the voice of the living God speaking out of the midst of fire, as we have, and still lived?" (τίς γὰρ σάρξ, ἥτις ἤκουσεν φωνὴν θεοῦ ζῶντος λαλοῦντος ἐκ μέσου τοῦ πυρὸς ὡς ἡμεῖς καὶ ζήσεται). (Deut 5:23–26)[13]

---

12. Moshe Weinfeld, *Deuteronomy 1–11* (AB 5; New York: Doubleday, 1991), 319–27, describes this material as "epilogue to the decalogue."

13. Deuteronomy 5:26 LXX preserves the wording of the Hebrew Masoretic text.

Both the LXX and MT of Deut 5:26 use the living God in formulations that stress God's dreadful power encountered in theophany. Deuteronomy 5:23–26 highlights the awesome transcendence of the living God in contrast to the fearful reaction of the Israelites. As in Deut 4:33 LXX, the living God, again, discloses himself through voice and word but cannot be seen.

Most interpreters neglect the covenantal significance of the living God in Deut 5:26, but this significance is indicated through the association of literary context.[14] Most notably, the living God in Deut 5:26 is the same God in the preceding narrative who revealed himself to Israel, spoke the Ten Commandments out of fire, and "inscribed them upon two tables of stone" (5:22). This event of God writing the commandments upon stone tablets is connected to the formation of the covenant mentioned earlier in the chapter (5:2–3). The living God in Deut 5:26 is the God who elected Israel at Sinai and gave the Decalogue as a sign of the covenant.

Both occurrences of the living God in Deut 4:33 LXX and 5:26 LXX/MT thus suggest the living God's close association with the traditions of Sinai/Horeb. The living God is identified as the "voice" which spoke from fire, electing Israel as a covenantal people and giving the Ten Commandments that serve as stipulations for Israel in the covenant. Deuteronomy 4:33 LXX and 5:26 LXX/MT provide strong indications that the living God is the covenantal God of Israel, something that is confirmed by evidence in Hellenistic Jewish sources.

The Living God as Giver of the Decalogue

The association seen in Deuteronomy between the living God, covenantal election, and the Decalogue is retained by Greek-speaking Jews of the Hellenistic world. For Hellenistic Jews, the living God continues to be the covenantal God of Israel who had elected them and given the commandments. Three Jewish texts, Philo, *Decalogue* 67; 2 Macc 15:4; and *Sib. Or.* 3:763,

---

14. Kraus, "Der lebendige Gott," 187, observes that "in the context of the Sinai-Tradition the designation *elohim hajim* receives this special impression."

mention the epithet living God in explicit connection with individual commandments of the Decalogue, reinforcing the view of the living God as the giver of the Decalogue. The following discussion thus serves to reinforce the preceding discussion of Deut 4–5 by showing that Hellenistic Jews viewed the living God as their covenantal God and giver of the Decalogue.

Philo and *On the Decalogue* 67

Philo's *On the Decalogue* is part of his scriptural exposition on the Mosaic legislation, written sometime in the early to mid-first century C.E.[15] *On the Decalogue* 67 is significant not only because it yields Philo's only usage of the epithet, but also because it supports the covenantal significance of the epithet suggested from Deut 4–5. Philo's use of the epithet recalls the theophanic setting described in Deuteronomy, describing the bestowal of the Ten Commandments accompanied by the divine voice that issued from fire.[16] The Ten Commandments are discussed explicitly in paragraphs 50–153, with the first treated in paragraphs 52–65 (denunciations of polytheism) and the second in 66–76 (denunciations of idolatry).

Philo's use of the living God in *Decalogue* 67 occurs as part of his exposition on the second commandment: "you shall not make for yourself an idol, whether in the form of anything that is in heaven above, or that is on the earth beneath, or that is in the water under the earth"[17] (Exod 20:4–5/ Deut 5:8–9). According to Philo, the second commandment "forbids the making of images or wooden busts and idols in general produced by the baneful craftsmanship of painting and sculpture..." (*Decalogue* 156; cf. *Spec. Laws* 1:21–22). This commandment, of course, would have taken on special significance for Jews who lived in a polytheistic milieu where idolatry prevailed.

---

15. Emil Schürer, *The History of the Jewish People in the Age of Jesus Christ* (175 B.C.–A.D. 135) (ed. G. Vermes, F. Millar, and M. Goodman; Edinburgh: T. & T. Clark, 1986), 3:841.

16. Translations and Greek are taken from F. H. Colson and G. H. Whitaker, *Philo* (10 vols.; LCL; Cambridge, Mass: Harvard University Press, 1956–62).

17. Exodus 20: 4–5 LXX: οὐ ποιήσεις σεαυτῷ εἴδωλον... οὐ προσκυνήσεις αὐτοῖς οὐδὲ μὴ λατρεύσῃς αὐτοῖς.

On the Decalogue 67 uses the epithet living God as part of Philo's criticism of idolatry: "for these idolators cut away the most excellent support of the soul, the rightful conception of the ever-living God" (τὸ γὰρ κάλλιστον ἔρεισμα τῆς ψυχῆς ἐξέκοψαν, τὴν περὶ τοῦ ζῶντος ἀεὶ θεοῦ προσήκουσαν ὑπόληψιν). Here the living God is associated, not only with idol polemic, but also with the "truth" of Jewish monotheism—the ever-living God is the true God who alone is worthy of worship. Philo, however, has adapted the living God for use "to his own theological presuppositions."[18] Idolators, in the Philonic sense, lack the "rightful conception" of God, being ignorant of God's "ever-living" eternal character. This rightful conception of the true God is an "apologetic concern" in Philo, associated with the absurdity and irrational character of idolatry.[19] Idolators worship lifeless things that are the products of human manufacture and thus fail "to perceive even that most obvious truth which even a 'witless infant knows,' that the craftsman is superior to the product of his craft, since he is older than what he makes and in a sense its father" (*Decalogue* 69).

While Philo's usage of the epithet reflects something of his own distinctive concerns, his usage also reflects the living God's traditional association with the Decalogue. It is no coincidence that Philo's use of the living God epithet occurs in his discussion of the Decalogue, reinforcing the association already seen in Deut 4–5. Although Philo does not make an explicit assertion about the living God writing the tablets of the Decalogue, he still associates the living God with the God who prohibited idolatry in the giving of the Decalogue. For Philo, the living God is the God, who, on Sinai, gave the commandment prohibiting the manufacture and worship of idols.

2 Macc 15:4 and the Living Lord of the Sabbath

Second Maccabees offers two uses of the living God epithet in 7:33 and 15:4, the latter being more significant for this

---

18. Everding, "The Living God," 254.
19. Ibid., 252, n. 2. For example, in *Decalogue* 76, Philo observes: "let no one, then, who has a soul worship a soulless thing, for it is utterly preposterous that the works of nature should turn aside to do service to what human hands have wrought."

discussion.[20] Second Maccabees 15:4 reinforces the epithet's association with the Decalogue, portraying the living God as the
God who enjoined the fourth commandment concerning the
need to honor the Sabbath. In literary terms, 2 Maccabees is a
summary (*"epitome"*) of an earlier five-volume work by Jason of
Cyrene (cf. 2 Macc 2:23), who came from Cyrenaica and wrote
in the second century B.C.E.[21] This unknown summarizer interpreted and embellished Jason's work, forming it into a history
according to Hellenistic literary conventions.[22] Interpreters also
suggest that 2 Maccabees " . . . has the common purpose of establishing the annual festival of Hannukah. . . . "[23] Jason wrote in the
period of 160–152 B.C.E. and the summarizer had completed his
task by no later than 124 B.C.E.[24] In terms of provenance, Egypt
is the likely place of writing based upon the two introductory
letters and the identity of Jason in Cyrenaica.

Both 2 Macc 7:33 and 15:4 use a distinctive form of the epi-

---

20. In 7:33, the occurrence of the living Lord (ὁ ζῶν κύριος) comes as part of the
famous martyrdom of the seven brothers. Antiochus IV attempted to entice the last
of the seven brothers to "turn from the ways of his fathers," (7:24) but he refuses
in 7:30–33: "I will not obey the king's command, but I obey the command of the
law that was given to our fathers through Moses. But you who have contrived all
sorts of evil against the Hebrews will certainly not escape the hands of God. For we
are suffering because of our own sins. And if our Living Lord is angry for a little
while, to rebuke and discipline us he will again be reconciled with his own servants.
But you unholy wretch. . . . You have not yet escaped the judgment of the allmighty
all-seeing God. . . . " The English is taken from the RSV.

21. Subsequently, however, Jason's work was abbreviated by an unknown summarizer, who produced an *epitome* of the work found in 2 Macc 3:1–15:36. Sidney
Tedesche, *The Second Book of Maccabees* (ed. S. Zeitlin; New York: Harper & Brothers, 1954), 20–24. Martin Hengel, *Judaism and Hellenism* (trans. J. Bowden; 2 vols.;
Philadelphia: Fortress Press, 1974), 1:95–99. Thomas Fischer, "Maccabees, Books
of," *ABD* 4:442–50.

22. Schürer, *The History of the Jewish People in the Age of Jesus Christ*, 3:532–33.
Jonathan Goldstein, *II Maccabees* (AB 41A; Garden City, N.Y.: Doubleday, 1983),
20–21. Robert Doran, *Temple Propaganda: The Purpose and Character of 2 Maccabees*
(CBQMS 12; Washington, D.C.: Catholic University Press, 1981), 77–109. Chris-
tian Habicht, *Historische und legendarische Erzählungen: 2. Makkabäerbuch* (Jüdische
Schriften aus hellenistisch-römischer Zeit; Gerd Mohn, 1976), 189.

23. Fischer, "Maccabees," *ABD*, 443. Also, see Hengel, *Judaism and Hellenism*, 1:97;
and John J. Collins, *Between Athens and Jerusalem: Jewish Identity in the Hellenistic
Diaspora* (New York: Crossroad, 1986), 78.

24. Schürer, *The History of the Jewish People in the Age of Jesus Christ*, 532; Tedesche,
The Second Book of Maccabees, 27–30; Doran, *Temple Propaganda,* 112–13, concludes
that 2 Maccabees was written during the reign of John Hyrcanus. Goldstein, *II Maccabees,* 83, places the composition and abridgment date in the early first century
B.C.E.

thet "living Lord (ὁ κύριος ζῶν)," about which there has been little or no scholarly discussion.[25] I would like to suggest three possible explanations for why Jason uses "Lord" instead of the more commonly used term, "God." These three explanations are not mutually exclusive and can be taken together. First, the expression "living Lord" may reflect an assimilation to the oath formula, "As the Lord lives," although this explanation does not clarify why this author favors "Lord." Second, "living Lord" in 2 Macc may reflect the influence of "Lord" from Deut 32:36, which is quoted in 2 Macc 7:6: "The Lord God is watching over us and in truth has compassion on us, as Moses declared in his song which bore witness against the people to their faces, when he said, 'And he will have compassion on his servants.' "[26] Third, the use of "Lord," as a reference to the Tetragrammaton revealed to Moses on Sinai/Horeb, may serve as a general designation for Israel's covenantal God.[27] The wider use of the term "Lord" in 2 Macc supports this point. Jason frequently employs the term "Lord" to speak about the God of Sinai, e.g., 2:2, 8; 3:22; 9:5. The "living Lord," then, in 2 Macc likely reflects the traditional God of Sinai/Horeb who gave the law through Moses (7:30).

The use of the epithet "living Lord" in 2 Macc 15:4 occurs in the wider literary unit of 2 Macc 14:1–15:36, which describes the campaign against the Jews and their temple in Jerusalem instigated by Alcimus. It is Nicanor who takes military action against Judah and threatens to destroy the temple as part of his plan to capture Judas Maccabee. In planning his assault, Nicanor attempts to take advantage of the Jewish Sabbath (15:1–5) by attacking Judas and his men "on the day of rest" (15:1).

---

25. Most interpreters pass over the epithet's occurrence in 15:4 in silence. For example, Tedesche, *The Second Book of Maccabees;* 166–67; Habicht, *Erzählungen,* 237; and Goldstein, *II Maccabees,* take the epithet as an echo of 1 Sam 17:26, 36 and Jer 10:10.

26. The use of "servants" in 2 Macc 7:6 and 7:33 strengthens the link between the living Lord in 7:33 and Deut 32:36. The oath formula is found, for example, in Deut 32:40.

27. Everding, "The Living God," 130, notes that "the similarity between this unique formulation of the epithet and the construction of the oath formula confirms that God is here designated 'living Lord' to call attention to his power to punish and vanquish."

The Jewish soldiers in Nicanor's army refused to fight and break the Sabbath law:

> [2]And when the Jews who were compelled to follow him said, "do not destroy so savagely and barbarously, but show respect for the day which he who sees all things has honored and hallowed above other days," [3]the thrice-accursed wretch asked if there were a sovereign in heaven who had commanded the keeping of the sabbath day. [4]And when they declared, "it is the living Lord himself the Sovereign in heaven (ἔστιν ὁ κύριος ζῶν αὐτὸς ἐν οὐρανῷ δυνάστης), who orders us to observe the seventh day," he retorted, "And I am a sovereign also, on earth, and I command you to take up arms.... " (15:2–5)

Here the living Lord is described as the Sovereign in heaven who "commanded" the observance of Sabbath, a day that is described as "honored and hallowed above other days" (15:2). This language clearly recalls the command to honor the Sabbath (Deut 5:12–15; Exod 20:8–11) and reflects the book's wider stress on obedience to the Mosaic legislation. As God's special people, Jews are distinguished from other people by their obedience to God's laws and commandments (2 Macc 2:2–3; 3:15; 6:23; 28; 7:1–2). Specifically, they are distinguished by their special type of worship which prohibits any work on the Sabbath (2 Macc 5:25; 6:6, 11; 15:4).

Second Maccabees 15:4 thus identifies the living Lord as the all-seeing God who commands observance of the Sabbath, thus linking him to the giving of the Decalogue.[28] The living Lord is presented as Israel's lawgiver and the founder of a Sabbath day that sets Israel apart from other nations.

Sib. Or. 3:763: Worship the Living One!

Sibylline Oracles 3:763 offers another instance of the living God employed in association with the Decalogue.[29] The date and

---

28. Everding, "The Living God," 134, in commenting on this passage is primarily interested in the epithet's designation of God "in his power and strength as the victorious divine king."

29. Everding, "The Living God," 156–63, discusses the epithet's connection to

provenance of the *Third Sibyl* are generally agreed upon as Egypt of the second century B.C.E.[30] The literary form of the *Third Sibyl* has affinities with the prophetic oracles of the Hebrew scriptures, but the author also employs a Hellenistic literary form that was common in the Graeco-Roman milieu.[31] The *Third Sibyl* addresses a Jewish readership in the Diaspora, serving to reinforce Jewish identity in a polytheistic milieu. Jews are praised as "a race of most righteous men" (3:219), who are "sons of the great God" (3:702). To the Jewish people alone "...did the great God give wise counsel and faith and excellent understanding in their breasts" (3:585). However, the *Third Sibyl* also addresses a Gentile readership, as is suggested from certain exhortations that urge the readers to abandon idolatry and serve God.[32] The message of the Sibyl, then, "is explicitly directed to the Gentiles but no doubt was intended for Jewish readers as well."[33]

In literary terms, the *Third Sibyl* consists of five oracles, the last of which (3:657–808) contains the epithet "living One." This last oracle is arranged as an alternating sequence of warnings about eschatological judgment and exhortations to Gentiles to abandon idolatry. The exhortations in 3:762–66 follow immediately upon the threat of divine judgment in 3:760–61 ("For he himself alone is God and there is no other, and he him-

---

the second commandment, but he does not discuss the covenantal association. Everding's general conclusion is that "it is impossible, however, to determine if ὁ ζῶν had any special meaning. Most probably it was used as a synonym of ἀθάνατος which occurs in III. 766..." (262).

30. The date is fixed by three references to the king of Egypt in 3.193, 318, and 608. John J. Collins, *The Sibylline Oracles of Egyptian Judaism* (SBLDS 13; Missoula: University of Montana Press, 1972), 28–33; see also Collins's more recent treatment in J. J. Collins "Sibylline Oracles," in *The Old Testament Pseudepigrapha* (ed. James H. Charlesworth; 2 vols.; Garden City, N.Y.: Doubleday, 1983), 1:354–56; Nickelsburg, *Jewish Literature* 162; and Schürer, 3:635–37, ca. 50 B.C.E. to 50 C.E. The Greek text comes from Johannes Geffcken, *Die Oracula Sibyllina* (GCS; Leipzig: J. C. Hinrichs, 1902), 87.

31. Collins, *Between Athens and Jerusalem*, 63.

32. Peter Dalbert, *Die Theologie der hellenistisch-jüdischen Missionsliteratur unter Ausschluss von Philo und Josephus* (Hamburg: Herbert Reich, 1954), 116, notes both "apologetic and missionary tendencies" in these exhortations. Also Nickelsburg, *Jewish Literature,* 165, observes that "Book 3 shows a remarkable openness to the Gentiles and may well have been written to be read by them."

33. Collins, "Sibylline Oracles," 1:357.

self will burn with fire a race of grievous men").[34] The latter
thus furnishes the ground for the exhortations in 3:762–66. The
one God, who alone is God, will hold Gentiles accountable for
their sins:

> [762]But urge on your minds in your breasts,
>
> [763]and shun unlawful worship (φεύγετε λατρείας ἀνόμους).
> Worship the living One (τῷ ζῶντι λάτρευε).
>
> [764]Avoid adultery and indiscriminate intercourse with
> males.
>
> [765]Rear your own offspring and do not kill it,
>
> [766]For the Immortal is angry at whoever commits these
> sins.[35]

There are several points of interest in this passage, some of
which will be taken up in the next chapter. For this discussion,
however, the most important points concern the form and function of the epithet within the framework of 3:762–66, as well as
the epithet's association with the language of the Decalogue.

In terms of the epithet's form, an unusual liturgical style
occurs. Instead of the usual construction "living God," 3:763 utilizes the term "living One," based upon the use of the participle
with the definite article (ὁ ζῶν) but without any corresponding
use of the noun "God." The participial formulation "living One"
is paralleled elsewhere in Jewish liturgical formulations, e.g.,
Tob 13:1 ("Blessed is God who lives forever, and blessed is his
kingdom"); Sir 18:1 ("He who lives forever created the whole
universe . . . "); and Dan 4:34 ("and I blessed the Most High, and
praised and honored him who lives forever . . . "). The latter are

---

34. Dalbert, *Die Theologie*, 111, observes that "almost every expression about the
character of God stands in an internal connection with the judgment theme. The
eternal, immortal, immutable God . . . is the giver of law and his judgment confronts
those who violate his laws (III, 257f.)."

35. These verses may have existed independently of their present context, since
they interrupt the flow of thought in 741–61 and 767–808. There is also a shift
from third person singular (755–61) to the imperative second plural (762–66).
Further redactional activity is evident from the plural and singular verb forms in
762, 763a (κατασπεύσαντες, φεύγετε) that alternate with the singular imperatives of
763b–65 (λάτρευε, πεφύλαξο, τρέφε, φόνευε). Cf. Everding, "The Living God," 262;
and Geffcken, *Die Oracula Sibyllina*, 87.

similar to *Sib. Or.* 3:763 in referring to God through the use of the participial form "living One" or "One who lives," without explicit use of the noun "God." That the "living One" of *Sib. Or.* 3:763 refers to an eternally living God is supported from the divine appellation of 3:766, "the immortal."

In terms of its function, the epithet "living One" is part of a dual exhortation in 3:763: "shun unlawful worship; worship the Living One." Taken together the exhortations in 3:763 have a stylized character visible in their chiastic arrangement, which, in Greek, rendered literally, yields: "shun unlawful worship; the living One worship." A chiastic symmetry arises in the way that imperative forms frame the two exhortations at the beginning and end, "shun . . . worship." Also, and more generally, chiasm is present in how "[the Living One] functions in adverse relation to [unlawful worship] in the two antithetical commands about worship."[36] The exhortation to worship the living One counterbalances the need to avoid "unlawful worship," a probable reference to idolatry.

Several observations support the claim that the phrase "unlawful worship" constitutes an allusion to idolatry. First, the exhortation of 3:762 begins with the command, "But urge on your minds in your breasts. . . . " The reference to "your minds in your breasts" recalls similar formulations in *Sib. Or.* 3 that express the idea of idolatry beginning with a person, e.g., 3:548, 3:721–22. Second, the expression "unlawful worship" refers to idolatrous worship widely denounced throughout this writing.[37] Unlawful worship denotes idolatry as counter to God's law and is specifically prohibited by the first two commandments. Idolatry is against God's express will in the Decalogue. Unlawful worship, then, is set in antithesis to idolatry and "the Greeks are exhorted to break away with idolatry and offer a cultic worship to the living God who is life (Fr III, 34). . . . "[38]

---

36. Everding, "The Living God," 256.

37. The term ἀνομία is used of idolatry in biblical and Jewish tradition, e.g., Isa 1:4; 31:6–7; 48:5; Wis 15:17; and *Jos. and Asen.* 11.10. *Sib. Or.* 3:686–87 speaks of Gentiles knowing neither "the law nor the judgment of the great God."

38. James Yeong-Sik Pak, *Paul as Missionary: A Comparative Study of Missionary Discourse in Paul's Epistles and Selected Contemporary Jewish Texts* (Frankfurt: Peter Lang, 1991), 73. Cf. *Sib. Or.* frg. 3:25–34.

Sibylline Oracles 3:763 thus exhorts the Gentile readers to abandon idolatry and take up a proper worship of the one true God and it does so using the traditional language of the Decalogue. The language of 3:763 alludes to the Decalogue, not only in the reference to idolatry as "lawless," but also in reference to the Greek terms for "worship" (λατρείας, λάτρευε). The latter recall Exod 20:5/Deut 5:9 and the second commandment, prohibiting the "worship" of idols: "you shall not bow down to them or serve (λατρεύσῃς) them; for I the Lord your God am a jealous God."[39] Therefore, the exhortations "flee unlawful worship" (3:762) and "worship the living One" (3:763) reflect the second commandment reinterpreted for monotheistic propaganda in the Hellenistic world.[40]

Further, Gentile worship of the living One " . . . has to be substantiated by the avoidance of idolatry, adultery, sodomy, and infanticide. . . . "[41] The moral exhortations in *Sib. Or.* 3:764–65 to avoid adultery, sodomy, and infanticide, also allude to commandments in the Decalogue.[42] *Sibylline Oracles* 3:762–66, in other words, links the "living One," the one true God, with monotheistic worship that is grounded in the Decalogue and moral behavior derived from the Decalogue. The references to avoiding adultery and "killing" offspring constitute specific allusions to Exod 20:13 LXX/Deut 5:17 LXX; and Exod 20:15 LXX/Deut 5:18 LXX. *Sibylline Oracles* 3:762–66, then, likely alludes to three commandments—the second commandment in direct association " . . . with the verbs [to commit adultery] and [to kill] used in the seventh and sixth commandments."[43] Once again, the epithet living God/living One stands in association with language and themes drawn from the Decalogue, suggesting the identity of the living One as the God of Israel who gave the Ten Commandments.

---

39. Exod 20:5 LXX and Deut 5:8 LXX read: οὐ προσκυνήσεις αὐτοῖς οὐδὲ μὴ λατρεύσῃς αὐτοῖς. *Sib. Or.* 3:277 refers to the "errant and unseemly worship (ἐλάτρευσας) of idols." Cf. Everding, "The Living God," 256–63.

40. Everding, "The Living God," 262.

41. Pak, *Paul as Missionary*, 73.

42. In Jewish tradition, sexual immorality is associated with idolatry, e.g., Wis 14:12, 23–24 (Collins, *Between Athens and Jerusalem*, 148).

43. Everding, "The Living God," 258.

The Living God and the Jerusalem Temple

The identity of the living God as the covenantal God of Israel can be extended to include other covenantal associations, such as the living God indwelling the ark of the covenant and later, the Jerusalem temple, e.g., Josh 3:10 LXX (3:10 MT); Pss 41:3 LXX (42:2 MT); 83:3 LXX (84:2 MT); and 2 Kgs 19:4, 16 LXX (19:4, 16 MT). The evidence of Dan 4:19 LXX and 5:23 LXX also illustrates this association of the living God and the temple, both verses employing the expression "house of the living God" in reference to the Jerusalem temple. This temple association indicates the epithet's covenantal significance in that the living God makes himself specially present and accessible to his covenantal people.[44] Through his association with the tabernacle, the living God "walks" in the midst of Israel. In the temple he is addressed with prayer and from there hears the cries of his people. The temple presence of the living God is thus a sign of God's special covenantal relation to Israel, a relation that set Israel apart from the nations.

Again, however, interpreters have generally neglected the association of the living God and the Jerusalem temple, as well as the covenantal significance of this association.[45] This neglect has been especially inhibiting in scholarly attempts at understanding 2 Cor 6:16 and the "temple of the living God." What exactly does it mean to describe the temple as being "of the living God?" The following discussion will address this question by focusing on four biblical texts from the LXX that bear out the living God's special association with the Jerusalem temple: (1) Josh 3:10 LXX (3:10 MT); (2) Pss 41:3 LXX (42:2 MT); (3) 83:3 LXX (84:2 MT); and (4) 2 Kgs 19:4, 16 LXX (19:4, 16 MT). Daniel 4:19 LXX and 5:23 LXX will be discussed in the

---

44. Exod 29:44–45 and Lev 26:11–12 are examples of the indwelling motif expressing divine covenantal faithfulness. Exodus 29:44–45 LXX describes the tabernacle as a dwelling place (τὴν σκηνὴν τοῦ μαρτυρίου) in connection with the covenantal formula "I will be their God." Leviticus 26:12 LXX speaks of God "walking" in the midst of Israel (ἐμπερπατήσω ἐν ὑμῖν), which is followed by the covenantal formula, "and I will be your God and you will be my people."

45. Everding remains silent on the covenantal significance suggested by this association.

next chapter where the focus is on living God traditions unique in Hellenistic Judaism.

Joshua 3:10–11 LXX: The Living God and the Ark of the Covenant

Joshua 3:10–11 offers an important illustration of the living God's association with the theme of divine indwelling as a sign of covenantal faithfulness. These verses portray the living God dwelling and "walking" in the midst of Israel in association with "the ark of the covenant of the Lord of all the earth..." (3:11). The ark contains the two tablets of the Decalogue given by the living God on Sinai/Horeb. Later in Israel's history, Solomon installs the ark in the temple in the holy of holies, the locus of divine indwelling (1 Kgs 8:3–9).

Most interpreters who give attention to the epithet in Josh 3:10–11 stress the active character of the living God, who intervenes on behalf of Israel.[46] This majority view of the living God in Josh 3:10 is clearly supported by the verse itself: "He [Joshua] continued: 'This is how you will know that there is a living God in your midst (ἐν τούτῳ γνώσεσθε ὅτι θεὸς ζῶν ἐν ὑμῖν), who at your approach will dispossess the Canaanites, Hittites, Hivites....'" Joshua reflects deuteronomistic features that express a holy war ideology. The living God is a powerful divine warrior, who fights for Israel and dispossesses the Canaanites. The living God intervenes actively to aid his people and "the ark symbolizes the presence of Yahweh's power which will defeat the enemy."[47] In the conquest of Canaan, the Israelites will know that, where the ark is, so is the living God. This view of a powerful and active living God is also reflected in 1 Sam 17:26, 36, where David fights against the Philistine giant, Goliath, who has "defied the armies of the living God."

However, interpreters of Josh 3:10 do not give much attention to the epithet's covenantal significance, which is expressed in the passage's holy war ideology. The living God is the divine warrior who fights on behalf of his covenantal people and as

---

46. For example, Ringgren, *Israelite Religion*, 87; Kraus, "Der lebendige Gott," 187; and Preuss, *Old Testament Theology*, 1:243.

47. Everding, "The Living God," 47, 49.

an expression of covenantal faithfulness. In Josh 3:11, the ark is explicitly identified as "the ark of the covenant." The ark is a reminder of the covenant and covenantal faithfulness. Also, in 3:10 the living God is said to be "in your midst" or "among you," an expression that recalls the covenantal motif in Exod 29:45 ("And I will dwell among the people of Israel and will be their God") and Lev 26:11–12 ("And I will make my abode among you.... And I will walk among you, and will be your God..."). As a sign of divine faithfulness, God dwells among his people. In Joshua, then, the living God "in your midst" reflects God's continuing faithfulness to his special people and his presence is closely linked to the ark of the covenant, the receptacle of the Decalogue. Joshua 3:10–11 LXX expresses the living God's covenantal faithfulness concretely through the use of the ark and dramatically in the miraculous crossing of the Jordan, which follows in the narrative.

Pss 41:3 LXX and 83:3 LXX [42:2 MT and 84:2 MT]

The epithet "living God" occurs twice in the Psalms, at the beginning of the elohistic Psalter (Ps 42) and in the psalm after the elohistic Psalter (Ps 84).[48] Both occurrences indicate Israel's worship of the living God in the Jerusalem temple. Interpreters describe Pss 41:3 LXX and 83:3 LXX as psalms of pilgrimage, which express the pilgrim's longing to see the face of God in worship.[49] Although these psalms may have had original pre-exilic settings in sanctuaries of the northern kingdom, they were eventually adapted for use in the Jerusalem temple in the second temple period. Both psalms functioned in postexilic worship settings associated with the Jerusalem temple. The "house of God" mentioned in 41:5 LXX could have had no other reference for postexilic Jews than the Jerusalem temple (cf. Dan

---

48. Ps 18:46 (MT) employs the pronouncement formula "the Lord lives" as part of a hymnic statement directed to God (18:46–50).

49. Michael D. Goulder, *The Psalms of the Sons of Korah* (JSOTSup 20; Sheffield: JSOT Press, 1982), 23–50. Goulder argues that the speaker in Ps 42–43 "is not wishing to worship at Jerusalem but at Dan. As a national leader... he is going to the national shrine." In its original preexilic setting, Psalm 42 may recall a worship slogan from the tribe of Dan, also found in Amos 8:14: "those who swear by Ashimah of Samaria, and say 'As thy God lives O Dan' and 'As the way of Beer'sheba lives' they shall fall and never rise again."

4:19; 5:23 LXX). As one commentator puts it: "all the longing of the thirsty and languishing petitioner is directed to Zion, to the place Yahweh has chosen to bear witness to his presence there."[50]

These two psalms, therefore, offer evidence that supports my study in two ways. First, they reflect the belief that the living God indwells the temple sanctuary, thus reinforcing the association between the living God and the temple. Second, Israelite and Jewish prayers are directed to the living God as the source of life and deliverance. The living God is the source of life for whom the psalmist thirsts. I therefore do not agree with Everding when he says that the epithet in the psalms functions merely as an "honorific title," observing that the attribute "living" conveys "no descriptive interpretation of God (e.g., as 'active' or the source of 'life')...."[51]

Pss 41:3 LXX; 83:3 LXX

Psalms 41–42 LXX [42–43 MT] constitute a single psalm unit, as is clear from a number of features, including the common refrain in 41:6, 12; 42:5 LXX [42:5, 11; 43:5 MT]. The epithet occurs at the beginning of the psalm (41:3 LXX [42:2 MT]) in the first of three strophes:

> [2]As a hind longs for springs of waters,
>> so my soul longs for you, O God.
> [3]My soul thirsts for the living God (ἐδίψησεν ἡ ψυχή μου
>> πρὸς τὸν θεὸν τὸν ζῶντα);
>> when shall I go and be seen in the presence of God?
> [4]My tears are my food day and night,
>> as they say to me day after day, "where is your God?"
> [5]These things I recall as I pour out my soul within me,
>> when will I go to the place of marvellous dwelling,
>> unto the house of God,

---

50. Hans J. Kraus, *Psalms 1–59: A Commentary* (trans. H. C. Oswald; Minneapolis: Augsburg, 1988), 441. Everding, "The Living God," 72, observes that the epithet in Ps 42 "may represent the reflection of a general consciousness of the inner experience of God gained in the cultus."

51. Everding, "The Living God," 71.

> Amid the sound of joy and thanksgiving with the
> multitude keeping festival.
> [6]Why are you so downcast, O my soul and why do you sigh
> within me?
> Hope in God, for I shall again praise him, in the
> presence of my Savior, my God. (41:2–6 LXX)[52]

The psalmist's "thirst" for the living God is a "thirst" for the living God who dwells in the temple.

Indications of the temple setting abound in the strophe and elsewhere in the psalm. For example, in 41:5 LXX the psalmist will go to "the house of God, place of marvelous dwelling (ὅτι διελεύσομαι ἐν τόπῳ σκηνῆς θαυμαστῆς ἕως τοῦ οἴκου τοῦ θεοῦ)." The temple is the place of divine "dwelling," a likely allusion to the holy of holies. At the end of 41:5 LXX, the psalmist recalls a temple procession, "the sound of joy and thanksgiving with the multitude keeping festival." Further, a most important allusion to the temple occurs in 41:3 LXX immediately following the mention of the epithet: "when shall I go and be seen in the presence of God?"[53] (The latter is a technical expression for visiting the temple and standing before the sanctuary, the locus of divine presence [Deut 31:11; Ps 118:19].[54])

Further, the image of the psalmist thirsting for the living God, as for water, may constitute an allusion to life-giving waters that flow from the temple, as in Ezek 47 and Ps 46:4. More generally, however, the image of the psalmist "thirsting" for the living God suggests the living God as the source of the psalmist's life.[55] This idea is expressed in Jer 17:13, where God is "the fountain of living water."[56] Also, in Ps 36:9, God is "the fountain of life," who can quench the psalmist's thirst. In Amos 5:6, the prophet tells the Israelites to "seek the Lord and live, lest he break out like fire in the house of Joseph..." (cf. 8:14), and in Ps 18:46

---

52. My own translation of the LXX.
53. 41:3 LXX: πότε ἥξω καὶ ὀφθήσομαι τῷ προσώπῳ τοῦ θεοῦ.
54. Kraus, *Psalms 1–59*, 439.
55. Kraus, "Der lebendige Gott," 194–95. Psalm 41:9 LXX uses an expression that resembles the epithet: "By day the Lord commands his steadfast love; and at night his song is with me, a prayer to the God of my life" (προσευχὴ τῷ θεῷ τῆς ζωῆς μου; Everding, "The Living God," 71).
56. Kraus, "Der Lebendige Gott," 190–95.

the psalmist praises the Lord who lives as the one who delivers from death.

Psalm 83 LXX is a song of Zion and, like Ps 41 LXX, it also illustrates the Jerusalem temple as the place where the living God dwells. As a song of pilgrimage, Ps 84 has much in common with Ps 41 LXX, including the psalmist's longing for God's sanctuary.[57] The psalm begins with a joyful exclamation in the sight of Zion and the temple:

> ²How lovely is your dwelling place (ὡς ἀγαπητὰ τὰ σκηνώματά σου), O Lord of hosts!
> ³My soul yearns and pines for the courts of the Lord,
>   my heart and my flesh exult in the living God (ἡ καρδία μου καὶ ἡ σάρξ μου ἠγαλλιάσαντο ἐπὶ θεὸν ζῶντα).
> ⁴Even a sparrow finds a home
>   and the swallow a nest in which she puts her young,
>   your altars, O Lord of Hosts, my king and my God!
> ⁵Happy those who dwell in your house, ever and ever
>   praising you! (Ps 83:2–5 LXX)

Once again, the temple setting is evident in numerous allusions. In the opening verse, the temple is described as "your dwelling place," (v. 2).[58] Also there is reference to the "courts of the Lord" (83:3), to "your altars" (83:4), and to "your house" (83:5). Like Ps 41 LXX, this psalm also views the Jerusalem temple as the house of the living God, the place of divine indwelling wherein Israel worships its God. The psalmist, then, expresses a prayer of longing to be in the temple in the presence of the living God.

The theme of the living God as the source of the psalmist's life is evident in numerous motifs. Those who "dwell" in God's house and praise the living God will receive divine blessing (83:5–6 LXX). Along these lines, the concentration of divine epithets in the psalm, "living God," "lord of hosts," and "my king," draws attention "to Yahweh's power and strength to vin-

---

57. Goulder, *The Psalms of the Sons of Korah*, 38, observes that "like all other psalms in the psalter, 83 was in the end used at the Jerusalem temple."

58. Cf. Ps 41:5 LXX.

dicate the true Israelite."[59] The living God will vindicate those who worship him. In Pss 41:3 LXX and 83:3 LXX, then, the worshiping community in the temple testifies to life-giving power of the living God. Kraus puts it this way: "the living God can alone allow life to come, which means deliverance and salvation to men who are languishing and fallen in the realm of death. Yahweh is the Lord and Source of life as the one who is present in Israel and in Jerusalem."[60]

2 Kgs 19:4, 16 LXX=Isa 37:4, 17 LXX

Second Kings 19:4 and 16 provide two occurrences of the living God that function as part of Hezekiah's prayer expressed within the temple setting.[61] The two uses of the epithet appear in the narrative setting of 2 Kgs 18:13–19:37, which recounts the Assyrian threat faced by Jerusalem during Isaiah's lifetime (late eighth century B.C.E.). While Sennacherib, the Assyrian king, was in the process of subjugating Judah, he sent his emissary, the Rabshakeh, to Jerusalem to demand surrender. In 2 Kings 18:28–35 the Rabshakeh delivers a message outside the walls of Jerusalem denouncing the king and his God: "Do not let Hezekiah make you to rely on the Lord by saying, the Lord will surely deliver us ... (18:30). ... And do not listen to Hezekiah when he misleads you by saying, The Lord will deliver us. Has any of the gods of the nations ever delivered his land out of the hand of the king of Assyria?" (18:32–33).

In response, King Hezekiah retreats to the "house of the Lord" (19:1) and summons the prophet Isaiah for counsel. The king's messengers found Isaiah, and conveyed to him the king's message: "Thus says Hezekiah, 'this is the day of distress, of rebuke, and of disgrace. ... Perhaps the Lord, your God, will hear all the words of the commander, whom his master, the king of Assyria, sent to taunt the living God (ὅν ἀπέστειλεν αὐτὸν βασιλεὺς Ἀσσυρίων ὁ κύριος αὐτοῦ ὀνειδίζειν θεὸν ζῶντα), and

---

59. Everding, "The Living God," 73, 74.
60. Kraus, "Der Lebendige Gott," *Evangelische Theologie,* 194–95.
61. Isaiah 37:4 and 17 present identical uses of the epithet found in an identical narrative account. The latter likely derives from 2 Kgs 18:13–19:37. What is said about the living God in 2 Kgs, therefore, applies to the Isaian usages as well.

will rebuke him for the words which the Lord, your God has heard..."'" (19:3-4). Eventually in the narrative, the living God shows that he, indeed, has heard the taunt of Rabshakeh and in response does "rebuke" the Assyrian king in a miraculous deliverance (2 Kgs 19:20-36), thus proving himself victorious over Israel's Gentile adversaries. As in 1 Sam 17:26, the living God is "the Divine Warrior or King who has been reproached but who will be victorious."[62]

However, there is more to the significance of the living God in 2 Kgs 19:4, 16 than portraying his power in delivering Israel from Gentile adversaries. The living God is also the God who indwells the Jerusalem temple. This temple association is evident at the beginning of the chapter, where it is said that Hezekiah "went into the house of the Lord" to pray (19:1). The inference here is that Hezekiah prays to the living God who made the temple his dwelling place. This temple association is even clearer in the second occurrence of the epithet in 2 Kgs 19:16. The narrative recounts a second mission of the Rabshakeh, who again taunts the living God: "Do not let your God on whom you rely deceive you by promising that Jerusalem will not be given into the hand of the king of Assyria" (19:10). Hezekiah receives the message in a letter which he then takes and "spreads" before the Lord in the Jerusalem temple. Hezekiah "went up to the house of the Lord and spread it before the Lord" (19:14).

Hezekiah thus delivers his prayer in the temple:

[15]O Lord, God of Israel, enthroned upon the cherubim! You alone are God over all the kingdoms of the earth. You have made the heavens and the earth. [16]Incline your ear, O Lord, and listen! Open your eyes O Lord and see! Hear the words of Sennacherib which he sent to taunt the living God (οὓς ἀπέστειλεν ὀνειδίζειν θεὸν ζῶντα). [17]Truly,

---

62. Everding, "The Living God," 58–60. 1 Sam 17:26, 36 offers a parallel. The living God is used twice (17:26, 36) in contexts where Goliath, the Philistine, has insulted "the armies of the living God." David asks the Israelites, "for who is this uncircumcised Philistine, that he should defy the armies of the living God?" David's triumph over Goliath is also the living God's victory over Gentile adversaries (H. J. Kraus, "Der lebendige Gott," 185–86).

> O Lord, the kings of Assyria have laid waste the nations and their lands [18]and cast their gods into the fire; they destroyed them because they were not gods, but the work of human hands, wood and stone. [19]So now, O Lord our God, save us, I beseech thee, from his hand that all the kingdoms of the earth may know that you, O Lord, are God alone. (19:15–18)

Hezekiah places the letter, mocking the living God, before the sanctuary where God is "enthroned upon the cherubim," a reference to the ark in the holy of holies (cf. 1 Kgs 8:6–9).

Hezekiah's petition consists of several monotheistic assertions which stand in close association with the epithet. In 19:15, the living God is "alone God over all the kingdoms of the earth" and he "made the heavens and the earth" (19:15). In 19:19, the living God is the "only" God: "So now, O Lord our God, save us, I beseech thee, from his hand that all the kingdoms of the earth may know that you, O Lord, are God alone." What is also distinctive about the living God in 2 Kgs 19:16 is its use in a setting of idol polemic, which marks it as a "deuteronomic formulation which may be exilic or later in date."[63] Here, the living God is used in contrast to idols, who are "no gods" (cf. Deut 32:17, 21; Jer 2:11, 5:7) and the works of men's hands (cf. Deut 4:28; 27:15; 31:29; Isa 2:8, 20; 17:8). Hezekiah's prayer thus "establishes a contrast between Yahweh the 'living God' who can deliver Jerusalem and the inanimate powerless gods which were destroyed by the Assyrians."[64]

The point of the story, then, is twofold. First, the living God is active on behalf of his covenantal people, responding to their prayer in times of crisis, a point widely acknowledged in scholarly treatments on the passage. The living God hears the prayer of Hezekiah and brings about the destruction of the Assyrian host (2 Kgs 19:20–37). Second, appeal to the living God is made by going to the temple where the living God "hears" the prayer

---

63. Everding, "The Living God," 62. Everding notes here that "the appropriation of the epithet within the context of idol polemic is clearly late, perhaps later than the epithet's use in 2 Kgs 19:4."

64. Ibid., 62.

of the king. Second Kings 19, then, along with Josh 3:10–11 LXX and Pss 41:3; 83:3 LXX, attests the close association of the living God and the Jerusalem temple. Second Kings 19:15–16 reinforces the notion that the living God indwelled the temple sanctuary in the ark of the covenant as a sign of covenantal faithfulness to his people.

Conclusions

Both biblical and Hellenistic Jewish sources portray the living God as the covenantal God of Israel. The living God's covenantal character is expressed in numerous ways, including the use of the oath formula in connection with the Exodus event: "As the Lord lives who brought up the people out of the land of Egypt..." (Jer 16:14–15; 23:7–8). In Deuteronomy, the living God is the God who speaks as a voice from fire on Mount Horeb in establishing a covenant with Israel (4:33 LXX; 5:26 LXX/MT; cf. Jer 23:36). The living God is the God who brings Israel into existence as a covenantal people. Further, the sources repeatedly associate the living God with the Decalogue and its commandments (Deut 4:33 LXX; 5:26 LXX; Philo, *Decalogue* 67; 2 Macc 15:4; and *Sib. Or.* 3:762–66). Hellenistic Jews identify their living God as the giver of the Decalogue and it is this divinely given law that distinguishes them from the Gentiles.

Moreover, numerous other biblical episodes express the living God's covenantal faithfulness toward Israel. Israel's God was "living" in divine acts of deliverance and rescue (Josh 3:10 LXX/MT; 2 Kgs 19:4, 16 LXX/MT; 3 Macc 6:28; cf. 1 Sam 17:26, 36). The living God stood by his covenantal people, delivering them from their enemies in times of war and other crises. The living God's covenantal faithfulness also expresses itself in texts that refer to God dwelling in the midst of his people. As a sign of covenantal faithfulness, the living God is specially present to Israel. During the conquest of Canaan, the living God was present in connection with ark-tabernacle (Josh 3:10–11 LXX) and this ark was later installed in Solomon's temple, where Israel came to worship the living God (Pss 41:3, 83:3 LXX; 2 Kgs 19:4, 16

LXX). The Jerusalem temple was aptly called "the house of the living God" (Dan 4:19 LXX; 5:23 LXX) because in it the living God dwelled and in it Jews of the second temple period prayed to the living God as the source of life, the fountain who alone could quench their thirst (Ps 41:3 LXX).

Chapter Two

Hosea 2:1 LXX [1:10 MT], the New Covenant, and Eschatological Sonship

ꙮꙮꙮꙮꙮꙮꙮꙮꙮꙮ

There is another group of biblical and Hellenistic Jewish texts that illustrate the covenantal significance of the living God by showing the epithet's association with the new covenant theme. In biblical tradition, the living God also promises to restore Israel to a new covenant after a time of judgment and exile. Of particular significance is Hos 2:1 LXX [1:10 MT] that associates the living God with a future restoration of Israel as the "sons of the living God." The sonship motif designates covenantal status of future Israel. The living God is not only the God who founds Israel on Horeb and gives the Decalogue, but he is also the God who promises to restore Israel after a time of judgment. These texts thus reinforce the covenantal significance of the living God in biblical and Hellenistic Jewish tradition.

Previous scholarly assessments recognize the remarkable character of this Hosean prophecy, but they do not grasp its full significance as a source of living God tradition for later Jewish and early Christian interpreters.[1] Scholars neglect the recurrence of the Hosean expression "sons of the living God" in several Hellenistic Jewish and Pauline texts. *Jubilees* 1:24–25 utilizes the expression "sons of the living God" to describe that ideal future Israel that renounces idolatry and returns to God.

---

1. Everding, "The Living God," 52–54, for example, discusses Hos 2:1 LXX [1:10 MT] under the rubric of "The Living God: Victorious Over Israel's Enemies"; the prophecy "predicts the future triumph of true Israel," which "will be victorious in the decisive eschatological battle of Jezreel."

3 Macc 6:28 and Esth 8:12q LXX employ "sons of the living God" in application to the postexilic Jewish community as the restored covenantal community. There is also a significant use of the Hosean expression in *Jos. Asen.* 19:8, which applies it to Gentile proselytes who, through conversion, become "sons of the living God." The latter is particularly significant in the interpretation of Rom 9:25–26, where Paul quotes Hos 2:1 LXX. Like *Jos. Asen.* 19:8, Paul also applies "sons of the living God" to Gentile converts.

Hos 2:1 LXX [1:10 MT]

Hosea 2:1–3 LXX is part of a salvation oracle given by Hosea, a prophet of the northern kingdom in the eighth century B.C.E. There is some question about the passage's origins and whether it can be attributed to Hosea or to a postexilic redactor. Some interpreters question the passage's Hosean origins based upon its peculiar wording, its use of passive constructions, and its content that reverses previous judgment oracles.[2] Yet, Hos 2:1 LXX became an important expression of new covenant prophecy among postexilic Jews and early Christians.

Hosea 1:2–9 LXX forms the significant interpretive context for understanding the oracle in 2:1–3 LXX, portraying God's judgment against Israel for its idolatry and worship of Baal. Hosea 1:9 is a judgment oracle that describes the birth of the third of Hosea's children, a son: "Call his name Not My People, for you are not my people and I am not your God."[3] The prophet's son becomes a living sign of impending judgment, warning Israel that its covenant is in jeopardy, as indicated by the reversed covenantal formula. In 1:9, the covenantal affirmation formula, "You are my people and I am your God" (cf. Exod 6:7; Lev 26:12) has given way to "You are not my people and I am not your God."

---

2. Hans W. Wolff, *Hosea* (Hermeneia; trans. G. Stansell; Philadelphia: Fortress Press, 1974), 25.

3. The covenantal formula is also found in 2:25 LXX [2:23 MT], summarizing the idea of the new covenant: "And I will have pity on Not Pitied and I will say to Not My People, 'You are my people'; and he shall say, 'You are my God.'"

Immediately following this pronouncement of judgment comes the promise of future salvation in Hos 2:1–3 LXX:

> ^{2:1}Yet the number of the people of Israel shall be like the sand of the sea, which can be neither measured nor numbered; and in the place where it was said to them, "You are not my people," it shall be said to them, "sons of the living God (οὗ ἐρρέθη αὐτοῖς οὐ λαός μου ὑμεῖς, ἐκεῖ κληθήσονται υἱοὶ θεοῦ ζῶντος)." ^{2:2}And the people of Judah and the people of Israel shall be gathered together, and they shall appoint for themselves one head; and they shall go up from the land, for great shall be the day of Jezreel. ^{2:3}Say to your brother 'you are my people,' and to your sister 'you will be shown mercy.' "(Hos 2:1–3 LXX)

Hosea 2:1–3 LXX is an oracle announcing that the covenantal relation will be restored by God at some indeterminate future time. The oracle envisions "a time of eschatological renewal" in which Israel and Judah would be united under one head and the population would increase in great numbers, fulfilling the promises to the patriarchs (Gen 22:17; 32:13).[4]

Most significant, however, are the covenantal associations of the living God found in the oracle. The "sonship" motif in 2:1 LXX carries covenantal significance that is evident from its scriptural background. In the Pentateuch, for example, Israel is described as God's "son" in the covenantal relationship (e.g., Exod 4:22 and Deut 14:1). Hosea 11:1 is particularly significant in this regard: "when Israel was a child, I loved him, out of Egypt I called my son." Israel's identity as God's elect is described in terms of God's "call" of Israel out of Egypt (cf. Isa 42:6; 43:1; 45:4).

Further, the covenantal significance of "sons of the living God" is evident from its function in reversing the nullification of covenant expressed in 1:9, "you are not my people." The expression "sons of the living God" comes as part of a formulation that parallels and is closely linked to 1:9 LXX: "call his name 'not my people' for you are not my people and I am not your

---

4. Everding, "The Living God," 52–53.

God" (cf. 2:25 LXX); and "in the place where it was said to them 'you are not my people,' it shall be said to them 'sons of the living God' " (2:1 LXX). The expression "sons of the living God," in the reversal scheme, equates to "you are my people," designating a future Israel restored as God's beloved sons.

Originally the covenantal formula "You are my people and I am/will be your God" designated the Sinai covenant (e.g., Exod 6:7; Lev 26:12–13; Deut 4:20; Jer 11:4). The prophets, however, reinterpreted the formula to designate the future (new) covenant beyond judgment, as in Jeremiah and Ezekiel (Jer 24:7; 30:22; 31:1; Ezek 11:20; 14:20; 37:26–27).[5] Hosea 2:25 LXX [2:23 MT] also employs this formula to designate the future covenant, "...and I will say to Not My People, 'You are my people'; and he shall say, 'you are my God.' "[6] The Hosean prophecy of the "sons of the living God" in Hos 2:1 LXX is therefore bound up with a wider network of new covenant language attested in Hos 2:18–25, Jeremiah, and Ezekiel.

Hosea 2:1–3 LXX also describes the future restoration of Israel as "sons of the living God" as a creative life-giving action of the living God. This restoration will be accompanied by a dramatic increase in population, an act implying divine creative action (cf. Hos 6:1–2; 13:14).[7] The image of Israel's abundance, likened to the sand of the sea, recalls God's promises to the patriarchs to multiply descendants (e.g., Gen 22:17).[8] Hans Wolff comments, "since the people of the future promise will exist only because of the life-giving power of Yahweh, they will become immeasurably great in number.... Therefore, they are not renamed 'My-People'..., which would attest only the renewal

---

5. In Jer 24:7 the formula is part of a new covenant promise involving a new heart: "I will give them a heart to know that I am the Lord; and they shall be my people and I will be their God, for they shall return to me with their whole heart."

6. Hos 2:20–25 LXX describes the future covenant that God will establish after Israel's repentance.

7. Wolff, *Hosea*, 27. W. Stenger, "Die Gottesbezeichnung 'lebendiger Gott' im Neuen Testament," 65. However, Everding, "The Living God," 52, does not address the life-giving character of the living God in Hosea: "it is not evident that the epithet was used because of any special interpretive value suggested by the term 'living.' "

8. Wolff, *Hosea*, 26, comments that "the words of the prophet, the promise to the patriarchs, has become a new eschatological promise of salvation." A noteworthy parallel is Ezek 37:15–23, which stresses that the future eschatological restoration of Israel will involve a reunion of Judah and Israel.

of the covenant, but would not explain Israel's future abundance of population."[9] Further, the life-giving character of the
living God is suggested by numerous passages in Hosea that illustrate Yahweh as "the one God of Israel who bestows life in all
its forms" (e.g., Hos 2:8–11; 6:1–2; 9:11–14; 13:14).[10] The living
God is viewed as the true "father" of Israel, in whom alone life
is found.

In Hos 2:1 LXX, then, the living God is also the covenantal
father who will, in the future, restore Israel as covenantal sons.
The expression "sons of the living God" designates an Israel
restored to covenantal relation with its God. The expression is
closely linked to the covenantal formula in Hos 1:9; 2:1, and
2:25 LXX ("I will be your God and you shall be my people") so
that the "sons of the living God" are God's special "people."

Jub. 1:24–25 and Eschatological Sonship

The book of *Jubilees* offers two occurrences of the living God epithet in 1:25 and 21:4, the former of which is more significant for
my discussion.[11] *Jubilees* 1:25 attests that Hos 2:1 LXX [1:10 MT]
was still an important biblical prophecy among Hellenistic Jews
and that Israel's status as the "sons of the living God" was still
anticipated as a future eschatological event. *Jubilees* was written
in Hebrew by a Palestinian Jewish writer in the mid-second century B.C.E., approximately 180–160.[12] While *Jubilees* has a second

---

9. Wolff, *Hosea,* 27.

10. Jerome Quinn, *The Letter to Titus* (AB; New York: Doubleday, 1990), 302,
observes of Hos 2:1 LXX: "The God who gives life is the real father of Israel, and
they find life in worship of him alone."

11. *Jub.* 21:4 comes as part of Abraham's farewell discourse: "I hated idols, and
those who serve them I have rejected. And I have offered my heart and spirit so
that I might be careful to do the will of the one who created me because he is the
living God." The English translation is taken from O. S. Wintermute, "Jubilees," in
The Old Testament Pseudepigrapha (ed. James H. Charlesworth; 2 vols.; Garden City,
N.Y.: Doubleday, 1985), 2:95.

12. Both paleographical evidence and the content of the book support a date of
the second century B.C.E. Schürer, *The History of the Jewish People in the Age of Jesus
Christ,* 3:311–14; G. W. E. Nickelsburg, "Jubilees," *Jewish Writings of the Second Temple
Period* (CRINT; Philadelphia: Fortress Press, 1984), 101–3; and John C. Endres, S.J.,
Biblical Interpretation in the Book of Jubilees (CBQMS 18; Washington, D.C.: Catholic
Biblical Association of America, 1987), 12–13.

century Palestinian provenance, it reflects a diaspora-type situation faced by the Jewish community for which it was written. This situation involved the hellenization activity of Antiochus IV, which brought rampant Jewish apostasy. This situation of apostasy in *Jubilees* is reflected, e.g., in 3:31; 15:31; 20:7–9; 22:16–18. The author's "stringent prohibitions against contact with Gentiles suggest that such contact was not infrequent in the Israel of his time."[13] Faced with apostasy in Judea, the author urges the Jewish people of his day to return to covenantal loyalty, and more specifically, "to return to strict obedience to the law and the proper observance of sacred times in accordance with God's covenant."[14]

Jubilees begins with a divine revelation given to Moses during his forty days on Mount Sinai (cf. Exod 24:18). Chapter 1 narrates a revelation of Israel's future, which will involve a future of apostasy followed by a subsequent eschatological restoration (1:4–29). The account of Israel's restoration served to criticize Judah's apostasy in the writer's own day, teaching that future blessings would be bestowed only with repentance and increased faithfulness to the law. *Jubilees* 1 teaches "that God is now about to restore a proper relationship with his people and to call the readers to obedience."[15]

Chapter 1 begins with a revelation of Israel's apostasy and rebellion against God, following the conquest and settlement of the promised land: "...they will turn to strange gods, to those who cannot save them from any of their affliction...for they will forget all my commandments, everything which I shall command them, and they will walk after the gentiles and after their defilement and shame..." (1:8–9). God will send prophetic witnesses against them, but they will reject these witnesses and murder them (1:12). As a result, God will "hide his face from them" and "give them over to the power of the nations to be captive"; Israel will be scattered among the nations in exile (1:13–14).

---

13. Nickelsburg, "Jubilees," 103.
14. Wintermute, "Jubilees," 2:48.
15. Ibid., 2:47.

However, following exile, Israel "will turn" to God "from among the nations with all their heart and all their soul and with all their might"; and God "shall gather them from the midst of the nations ... " (1:15). God will "transplant them as a righteous plant" and he will "build [his] sanctuary in their midst, and [he] shall dwell with them" (1:16–17). With the re-settlement in the land and the rebuilding of the temple, the covenant relationship will be restored, suggested by the covenant formula in 1:18: "And I shall be their God and they shall be my people truly and rightly." At this point, Moses interjects and pleads with God to have mercy on his people that they not be abandoned (1:19–21).

God, however, "rejects the grounds of Moses' plea. That Israel as God's heritage does not remove her from the circle of judgment" (1:22).[16] But God also offers hope by revealing Israel's future repentance and the promise of restoration (1:23–25). Following Israel's repentance, a new era will begin:

> [1:23]But after this they will return to me in all uprighteous-ness. . . . And I shall cut off the foreskin of their heart and the foreskin of the heart of their descendants. And I shall create for them a holy spirit, and I shall purify them so that they will not turn away from following me from that day and forever. [1:24]And their souls will cleave to me and to my commandments. And they will do my commandments. And I shall be a father to them, and they will be sons to me. [1:25]And they will all be called sons of the living God. And every angel and spirit will know and acknowledge that they are my sons and I am their father in uprightness and righteousness. And I shall love them. (1:23–25)[17]

The material in 1:25 clearly recalls the prophecy of Hos 2:1 LXX [1:10 MT] and "the epithet's function here is similar to Hos 1:10 (2:1)," appearing "in a confessional type statement at the

---

16. G. L. Davenport, *The Eschatology of the Book of Jubilees* (Studia Post-biblica 20; Leiden: E. J. Brill, 1971), 27.

17. Translation from Wintermute, "Jubilees," 2:54.

conclusion of God's discourse (1:22–26) in which he promises the eschatological restoration of his people."[18]

Jubilees 1:25 uses the Hosean prophecy to describe the new eschatological era in which Israel will "turn back" to God from sin, keeping all the commandments. The traditional association of the living God and the commandments is significant here. Perfect obedience to the commandments is an aspect of future Israel's covenantal loyalty. Further, future Israel is able to keep the commandments because God has transformed its heart and created the desire to keep the commandments. As Davenport notes, "the circumcised foreskin of the heart means transformed motives."[19] This transformation of heart had not yet taken place in the writer's own day and so the writer "saw his own day as the time when authentic return from exile was beginning to occur, the time of the return to God."[20]

In speaking about Israel's future eschatological sonship, *Jub.* 1:24–25 combines the Hosean expression, "sons of the living God," with 2 Sam 7:14: "And I shall be a father to them, and they will be sons to me. And they will all be called sons of the living God."(*Jub.* 1:24–25) What links the two prophecies is the motif of sonship applied to future Israel. The sonship motif in 2 Sam 7:14 is found in a modified plural form, "...and they will be sons to me," compared with the original singular form in the biblical text, "I will be his father and he shall be my son." Further, the two prophecies of 2 Sam 7:14 and Hos 2:1 LXX [1:10 MT] are also linked by the motif of God's fatherhood. The motif is explicit in 2 Sam 7:14, "And I shall be a father to them..."; the motif is implicit in Hos 2:1 LXX [1:10 MT], with its reference to "sons," implying the living God's fatherhood. The significance of the divine father motif is clarified at the end of *Jub.* 1:25: "And every angel and spirit will know and acknowledge that they are my sons and I am their father in uprightness and righteousness." *Jubilees* 1:24–25 thus illustrates the "linking of eschatological sonship of Israel with the fulfill-

---

18. Everding, "The Living God," 154.
19. Davenport, *Eschatology of the Book of Jubilees*, 27.

ment of two key scriptural promises: 2 Sam 7:14...and Hos 1:10 [MT]."[21]

In sum, the original eschatological meaning of the Hosean prophecy is retained by the author in a new historical context of the second century B.C.E. As in Hosea, *Jub.* 1:25 envisions a future restoration of Israel as eschatological sons of the living God and thus clarifies the continuing significance of Hos 2:1 LXX [1:10 MT] among Jews of the Hellenistic era. Further, *Jub.* 1:25 also retains the original covenantal association of "sons of the living God." As in the original Hosean prophecy, *Jub.* 1:25 and the sons of the living God designate a future Israel restored to covenant with God.[22] According to *Jub.* 1:22–25, then, future Israel will be characterized by a close covenantal relationship with the living God, who will be covenantal father to his eschatological sons. Finally, *Jub.* 1:25 describes the living God's role in the eschatological era in terms of covenantal fatherhood; the living God, in the future eschatological era, will establish a close and loving relation with his covenantal "sons" who repent of their sins.

3 Macc 6:28; Esth 8:12q LXX; and *Jos. Asen.* 19:8 ...

Hellenistic Jews further employed the expression "sons of the living God" in 3 Macc 6:28 and Esth 8:12q LXX. The latter attest a Jewish tradition in which "sons of the living God" designated the postexilic Jewish community under God's covenantal care. Rather than designating future eschatological sonship, the expression in 3 Macc 6:28 and Esth 8:12q LXX comes to designate the present status of the Jewish community as God's covenantal people. That the Jews are "sons of the living God" indicates the close covenantal relationship enjoyed by them with their living God. Also, *Jos. Asen.* 19:8 represents a tradition in which "sons of the living God" came to be applied to Gentile proselytes who became members in God's covenantal community. In *Jos. Asen.*

---

21. Brendan Byrne, *"Sons of God"—"Seed of Abraham"* (Analecta biblica 83; Rome: Biblical Institute, 1979), 194.

22. Michel Testuz, *Les Idées religieuses du livre des Jubilés* (Paris: Menard, 1968), 69.

19:8, the proselytes as "sons of the living God" come to be numbered among God's elect. Through conversion, then, Gentile proselytes enjoyed covenantal privilege of the Jewish community and again the expression serves to designate a covenantal relationship with the living God.

3 Macc 6:28

Third Maccabees is a product of Egyptian Judaism, addressing the troubles of Alexandrian Jews in the second to first centuries B.C.E.[23] The literary form of 3 Macc is "closest in genre to Hellenistic romance"[24] and is a fiction founded upon the reminiscences of events in the reign of Ptolemy IV (221–205 B.C.E.). The work has multiple aims, the most important of which is to promote Jewish life and values in the Diaspora.[25]

The story of 3 Maccabees begins in Jerusalem, where Ptolemy was afflicted by God temporarily due to his profanation of the temple (2:1–24). Ptolemy eventually recovered and subsequently returned to Egypt "uttering bitter threats" against the Jews (2:24). In Egypt, "he proposed to inflict public disgrace upon the Jewish community" (2:27), eventually decreeing the arrest of all Egyptian Jews (3:1, 11–30), who were then rounded up and brought in chains to Alexandria (4:1–21). The Jewish prisoners were locked up in the hippodrome[26] and elephants were gathered ("five hundred in number") and drugged in order to be turned loose upon the Jews "so that the Jews might meet their doom" (5:2).

---

23. Moses Hadas, *The Third and Fourth book of Maccabees* (Jewish Apocryphal Literature; New York: KTAV, 1953), 22; H. Anderson, "3 Maccabees," in *The Old Testament Pseudepigrapha* (ed. James H. Charlesworth; 2 vols.; Garden City, N.Y.: Doubleday, 1983), 2:510; and C. W. Emmet, "The Third Book of Maccabees," *The Apocrypha and Pseudepigrapha of the Old Testament* (ed. R. H. Charles; Oxford: Clarendon, 1913), 1:161.

24. Schürer, *The History of the Jewish People in the Age of Jesus Christ*, 3:538; Anderson, "3 Maccabees," 2:510.

25. The first century B.C.E. is the commonly accepted date for 3 Maccabees. Hadas, *Maccabees*, 11–12, 19–21; Emmett, "3 Maccabees," 156–57; Collins, *Between Athens and Jerusalem*, 104–5; Schürer, *The History of the Jewish People in the Age of Jesus Christ*, 3:540.

26. The decree is found in 3:12–29 and reflects actual Gentile criticisms. Ptolemy's action was defended as necessary for the stability of the state: "when these have been punished as a body, we anticipate that our state will be perfectly established for all future time . . ." (3:26).

In response to their dire situation, the Alexandrian Jews called upon God for deliverance in prayers reported in 3 Macc 5–6. For example, in the prayer of Eleazar (6:2–15), the Jews petitioned God to deliver his "beloved people" from the vain-minded Gentiles.[27] In response, God miraculously delivered his people from death in a scene described in 6:18–19: "Then the great and glorious almighty and true God revealed his holy face and opened heaven's gates, from which descended two angels... visible to all except the Jews, and they confronted the forces of their adversaries and filled them with confusion and timidity...." Upon experiencing the awesome power of God, the king and his troops were paralyzed with terror. In 6:20–21 "even the king began to shudder bodily and he forgot his sullen insolence. The beasts turned back upon the armed forces following them and began trampling and destroying them." The king's anger turned to pity and he commanded that the Jewish prisoners be released from their chains:

> Loose their unjust bonds, loose them utterly; send them back to their own in peace, when you have begged for-giveness for what has already been done. Set free the sons of the almighty and heavenly living God (τοὺς υἱοὺς τοῦ παντοκράτορος ἐπουρανίου θεοῦ ζῶντος), who from days of our ancestors until now has conferred upon our state unimpaired stability and glory. (6:28)

Several points in this passage deserve comment. The expression "sons of the almighty and heavenly living God" is applied to the Egyptian Jews who are delivered by their God. Their deliverance marks them as God's special people.

Also, in 3 Macc 6:28, the living God epithet occurs as part of an expression from Hos 2:1, which stresses the living God's power by the addition of the attributes "heavenly" and "al-mighty" to the expression "sons of the living God." The living

---

27. In 6:11 Eleazar prays, "...let not the vain-minded praise their vanities at the destruction of your beloved people...." Anderson, "3 Maccabees," 2:514, observes that Eleazar's prayer is a celebration "of sacred history, reminiscent of those psalms (e.g., 78, 80, 106, 114, 135, 136) which sing Yahweh's praises for his former acts of deliverance."

God is "heavenly," stressing a transcendent character that is beyond this world. Further, the term "almighty" reflects the Greek word *"pantokratōr"* (παντόκρατωρ), a common term in 3 Macc for expressing divine power (2:2, 8; 5:7; 6:2, 18). In the Hellenistic world, the Greek term *pantokrator* designated a supreme deity who governed and sustained the world.[28] The expression "almighty living God" thus functions "as a royal epithet for the omnipotent and transcendent king."[29]

Further, 3 Macc 6:28 illustrates that this powerful and active living God was the heavenly "father" of the Jewish people, his covenantal "sons." The covenantal relation between the living God and his "sons" is made explicit in 7:6–7 where Ptolemy acknowledges, once again, the special status of the Jewish people: "We upbraided them severely for this conduct, and barely granted them their lives...and because we knew of a surety that God in heaven protects the Jews, being an ally always as a father to his children (ὡς πατέρα ὑπὲρ υἱῶν διὰ παντὸς συμμαχοῦντα) ... " (7:6–7). The living God, in other words, has acted "as a father to his children," echoing earlier attributions of God's fatherhood in the work (e.g., 2:21, 5:7, 6:3, 8). The living God, then, is the powerful protector and deliverer of his people, active in times of crisis and, recalling the traditional biblical significance of the epithet, he is "their merciful God and Father" (5:7).

In 3 Macc, then, the living God is described as covenantal father of the Jewish people, something that was implicit in the expression "sons of the living God." This divine father is active on behalf of his covenantal people. The description of the Jewish people as "sons of the almighty and heavenly living God" thus reflects a tradition in which Jews following the exile were God's restored covenantal people. The expression designated the covenantal identity of Diaspora Jews and implied a close relationship between God and his covenantal sons.

---

28. The term is παντοκράτωρ consists of two terms, πάντα and κράτειν, which form a single word describing a deity who masters or sustains "the all" (=the world). The term is used in the LXX as a translation of the Hebrew term *sabaoth*. See H. Hommel, *Schöpfer und Erhalter: Studien zum Problem Christentum und Antike* (Berlin: Lettner, 1956), 81–137.

29. Everding, "The Living God," 196.

Finally, it is a Gentile king (3 Macc 6:28) who recognizes the power of the living God and the special covenantal status of the Jewish people. At the climactic point in the narrative, a Gentile king acknowledges the active power and transcendent character of the Jewish God. This recognition, of course, does not reflect an actual historical event of a Ptolemaic king having acknowledged the Jewish God; rather, the king's acknowledgment reflects the apologetic concerns of the Jewish community behind 3 Macc. The king's acknowledgment expresses a Jewish view that the living God is active in the world on behalf of his covenantal people, and is also the source of stability behind Gentile kingdoms. Jews worship a God who supports and sustains Gentile kings. Ultimately, then, 3 Macc 6:28 contributes to the central apologetic aim of the writing by depicting a Gentile recognizing the power of the living God.

Esth 8:12q LXX

Esther 8:12q LXX uses the living God in a formulation similar to that of 3 Macc 6:28, describing the Jewish community as "sons of the mighty most high living God."[30] This use appears in one of the six "Additions," Addition E, which has no equivalent in the Hebrew text and which is also designated as Esth 8:12a–x LXX.[31] The writer who composed Addition E expands the Hebrew text of Esth 8:10–12 (Addition E) as a second royal decree of king Artaxerxes.[32] Addition E rescinds the earlier decree

---

30. A first century B.C.E. setting is generally accepted for the Additions to Esther. Collins, *Between Athens and Jerusalem*, 87–89. While some literary dependence is likely between the Additions and 3 Maccabees, there is no scholarly agreement on the direction of this dependence. Everding, "The Living God," 213, 217–18; and Carey E. Moore, *Daniel, Esther, and Jeremiah: The Additions* (AB 44; Garden City, N.Y.: Doubleday, 1977), 195–99.

31. Another occurrence of the living God is found in Esth 6:13 LXX, but is absent from the Hebrew text: "if Mordecai is of the race of the Jews, and you have begun to be humbled before him, you will assuredly fall, and you will not be able to avenge him, for the living God is with him." For a discussion, see Everding, "The Living God," 208–9.

32. The six Additions to Esther are: A (added at the beginning of Esth LXX); B (added to Esth 3:13 LXX); C (added to Esth 4:17 LXX); D (added to Esth 5:1 LXX; E (added to Esth 8:12 LXX); and F (added to Esth 10:3 LXX). Additions B and E are not translations from a Semitic original, but were originally composed in Greek (Moore, *The Additions*, 154, 165–66).

commanding extermination of Jews in the realm (=Addition B, added to Esth 3:13).[33]

The decree in Addition E begins by denouncing the evil deeds perpetrated by Haman (8:12a–n) and concludes by exonerating the Jewish people and reversing the earlier decree (8:12o–x). In the latter part of the decree, the king acknowledges the Jewish people as a righteous people in his domain:

> But we find that the Jews who were assigned to annihilation by this thrice accursed man are not evildoers but are governed by the most righteous laws and are sons of the most high, most mighty living God (υἱοὶ τοῦ ὑψίστου μεγίστου ζῶντος θεοῦ), who has directed the kingdom for us and our fathers in the most excellent order. (Esth 8:12p–q)

Like 3 Macc 6:28, Esth 8:12q LXX utilizes Hos 2:1 LXX [1:10 MT] to describe the Jewish community in favorable terms as "sons of the most high, most mighty living God."

The Hosean expression "sons of the living God" is here modified through the piling up of epithets "most high" and "most mighty," yielding something like "sons of the highest, greatest living God."[34] This piling up of epithets serves to stress the royal and omnipotent character of the Jewish living God.[35] The Hosean expression "sons of the living God" is modified to stress the powerful active character of the living God, although in Esther LXX no miraculous act of God is explicitly reported. The living God is the "greatest" and "most high." The latter epithet was used in the Hellenistic world in application to the chief deity in the pantheon of Graeco-Roman gods. Zeus was sometimes described as "most high." The epithet "most high" is also applied to God in the biblical tradition (e.g., Gen 14:18–19, 22; 1 Esdr 6:31; 8:19; Jdt 13:18; Pss 57:2; 78:56; Mic 6:6; 3 Macc 7:9).

---

33. Moore, *The Additions,* 153. Moore observes that "Additions B and E deepened for the Greek reader the impression of the story's historicity and authenticity by supplying verbatim copies of those royal edicts..." (159).

34. Everding, "The Living God," 210.

35. Ibid.," 211. Cf. 8:12r and 8:12t.

In Esth 8:12q LXX a Gentile king acknowledges Jews as "sons of the most high, most mighty living God," expressing their status as God's covenantal people. As in 3 Macc 6:28, a Gentile king comes to recognize the close and special relationship between the living God and the Jewish community. Jews are not only sons of the living God, but they are also governed by "the most righteous laws," a likely reference to the Mosaic law and the Decalogue. A few verses later, in 8:12t, they are recognized as God's chosen people: "for the all-powerful God has made this a day of joy and not of ruin for his chosen people." Once again, the expression "sons of the living God" suggests the Jewish community's close covenantal bond with the living God.

Further, the Gentile king's acknowledgment reflects the apologetic aim of Addition E, similar to that of 3 Macc. Carey Moore observes that "although a Persian king could have uttered such an expression of monotheistic faith . . . , and although a Persian king could have referred to the Jews as sons of the living God, it is far more likely that the faith of the Jewish writer is expressing itself here, especially since the phrase 'sons of the living God' occurs in Hos 1:10 and 2:1 of the LXX and since the attribution of monotheistic-sounding speeches is sometimes found in highly improbable circumstances. . . ."[36] The king's acknowledgment in Esth 8:12q LXX is thus, in all likelihood, an expression of Jewish faith placed in the mouth of a Gentile. The apologetic accent in the acknowledgment is particularly clear in the motif of the Gentile king recognizing the power of this living God behind his own throne. The king recognizes that the living God has "directed his kingdom in the most successful way." Such a statement reinforces the belief that the Jewish people are a stabilizing factor within the king's domain since they are "governed by the most righteous laws." As in 3 Macc, then, a Gentile king is made to recognize the positive role played by the Jewish people within his domain, thus giving voice to a theme of Jewish apologetic.

---

36. Moore, *The Additions*, 236.

Jos. Asen. 19:8[37]

Joseph and Aseneth is an important source for any discussion of the living God, since it offers three occurrences of the epithet (8:2; 11:10; 19:8).[38] The present discussion, however, is interested in only one of those occurrences, *Jos. Asen.* 19:8, since it furnishes another example of a Hellenistic Jewish appropriation of the Hosean expression "sons of the living God." In this case, the expression is applied to Jewish proselytes, who have converted and thus have entered into a covenantal relationship with the living God. Once again, the expression "sons of the living God" is employed in association with the covenantal theme, although in *Jos. Asen.* 19:8 the application is to Gentile converts.

Joseph and Aseneth is likely a product of the Egyptian Diaspora[39] and has features of Jewish midrashic interpretation.[40] The Jewish character of *Jos. Asen.* emerges from numerous elements in the text: (1) Joseph's adherence to Jewish dietary and marriage customs in 7:1, 5 and 8:5–6; (2) the book's heavy use of the LXX, which suggests both a Jewish author and audience;

---

37. The longer Greek text of Christoph Burchard will be used in preference to the shorter text published by M. Philonenko. Burchard's text is found in an appendix to A. M. Denis's *Concordance grecques pseudépegraphes d'Ancien Testament* (Louvain: Université Catholique de Louvain, 1987), 851–59. An English translation of this Greek text was made by Burchard and can be found in Charlesworth's *Old Testament Pseudepigrapha*, 2:202–47.

38. *Joseph and Aseneth* has been dated in the period ranging from the first century B.C.E. to the first century C.E. On this see Burchard, "Joseph and Aseneth," 2:187–88; Schürer, *The History of the Jewish People in the Age of Jesus Christ*, 3:549; and Collins, *Between Athens and Jerusalem*, 89–91; and more recently, Randall D. Chestnutt, "From Text to Context: The Social Matrix of *Joseph and Aseneth*," *SBL 1996 Seminar Papers* (Atlanta: Scholars Press, 1996), 286.

39. On this see Burchard, *Untersuchungen zu Joseph und Aseneth* (WUNT 18; Tübingen: Mohr Siebeck, 1965), 99–107. Burchard, "Joseph and Aseneth," 2:187; Schürer, *The History of the Jewish People in the Age of Jesus Christ*, 3:46–50; and Collins, *Between Athens and Jerusalem*, 211–13.

40. Some see *Joseph and Aseneth* as a midrashic expansion of Gen 41:45 that attempts to explain how Joseph could have married the pagan Aseneth. V. Aptowitzer, "Aseneth, The Wife of Joseph: A Haggadic Literary-Historical Study," *HUCA* 1 (1924): 239–306; and Schürer, *The History of the Jewish People in the Age of Jesus Christ*, 3:546. For a discussion of literary form, see Marc Philonenko, *Joseph et Aséneth: Introduction, texte critique, traduction et notes* (Leiden: E. J. Brill, 1968), 43–48; Richard Pervo, "Joseph and Aseneth and the Greek Novel," in *SBL 1976 Seminar Papers* (ed. George MacRae; Missoula: University of Montana Press, 1976), 171–81; and Lawrence M. Wills, *The Jewish Novel in the Ancient World* (Ithaca, N.Y.: Cornell University Press, 1995), 170–84.

(3) the conversion theme that "is constructed along the lines of a pattern, current in hellenistic Judaism";[41] and (4) a pattern of idol polemic that is typical of Hellenistic Judaism. The identity of the Jewish group behind the text, however, remains uncertain. Whatever the group's identity, it is "neither nationalistic nor separatist in its outlook. It sought to see Israel as an inclusive people...."[42]

In terms of its audience, *Joseph and Aseneth* has implications for a Gentile readership as illustrated by the Gentile heroine of the story, Aseneth: "the author has recounted a proselyte's progress from the viewpoint of the proselyte."[43] That the story also has implications for a Jewish readership is suggested from numerous scriptural allusions, as well as allusions to Jewish life and customs.[44] One can thus surmise that *Joseph and Aseneth* "...was composed for Jews, both born and naturalized, including perhaps those 'God-fearing' symphathizers who thought and lived Jewish, but never crossed the line formally and were seldom pressed to do so."[45]

The story of *Joseph and Aseneth* falls neatly into two parts, chapters 1–21 and 22–29. The former is of primary significance here since it furnishes three occurrences of the living God, while the latter has no occurrences. The main figures in *Jos. Asen.* 1–21 appear to be symbolic or allegorical in character, having a representative significance.[46] Joseph, "the son of God" (6:2; 13:10;

---

41. Burchard, "Joseph and Aseneth," *Old Testament Pseudepigrapha*, 2:184.

42. Howard Clark Kee, "The Socio-Cultural Setting of Joseph and Aseneth," *NTS* 29 (1983): 411. He observes that "there is no clue as to the economic or social level of the group...." Collins, *Between Athens and Jerusalem*, 214, 217, has classified *Joseph and Aseneth* under the rubric of "mystic Judaism," characterized by a "nonethnic religion of monotheism."

43. G. W. E. Nickelsburg, "Joseph and Aseneth," in ed., Michael Stone, *Jewish Writings of the Second Temple Period* (CRINT; Philadelphia: Fortress Press, 1984), 70. Philonenko, *Joseph et Aseneth*, 53–61, comments that *Joseph and Aseneth* is a missionary romance, meaning a writing "that will appeal to a questing spirit rather than a militant case for conversion."

44. Dieter Sänger, *Antikes Judentum und die Mysterien* (WUNT 2/5; Tübingen: J. C. B. Mohr Siebeck, 1980), 211–12. Burchard, "Joseph and Aseneth," 2:195, favors a Jewish readership of the work, observing that "as a specimen for introducing Judaism, *Joseph and Aseneth* is remarkably ill suited." See also Collins, *Between Athens and Jerusalem*, 217–18.

45. Burchard, "Joseph and Aseneth," 2:195.

46. Wills, *The Jewish Novel in the Ancient World*, 171.

21:3), represents Israel or the Jewish community, and Aseneth is the paradigmatic Gentile convert who abandons idolatry to become "a city of refuge" (15:7; 16:16; 19:5, 8) and "a bride for his [=God's] first-born son, Joseph" (18:11). Aseneth's conversion culminates in her marriage to Joseph, which symbolizes the convert's "marriage" to Judaism.[47] Aseneth thus "becomes a paradigm for proselytes who can take hope and reassurance from her story."[48]

Joseph and Aseneth 19:8 comes at the climax of the story, which describes the reunion of Aseneth and Joseph after a time of separation that is followed by their marriage (chaps. 20–21). In chapter 19 Aseneth has become a Jewish proselyte after a long process of repentance and conversion. This process begins in chapters 7–8, when Aseneth has her first encounter with Joseph, falling passionately in love with him. Joseph, however, refuses any contact with Aseneth, since she worships idols; he declares that "it is not fitting for a man who worships God, who will bless with his mouth the living God ... to kiss a strange woman who will bless with her mouth dead and dumb idols ... "(8:5).

In response, Aseneth "was cut to the heart strongly and was distressed exceedingly" (8:8). Seeing her distress, Joseph places his hand on her head and pronounces a solemn prayer in 8:9 on her behalf: "Lord God of my father Israel, the Most High, the Powerful One of Jacob, who gave life to all things and called them from the darkness to light, and from error to truth, and from death to life; you, Lord, bless this virgin, and renew her by your spirit and form her anew by your hidden hand and make her alive again by your life (ἀνακαίνισον αὐτὴν τῷ πνεύματι σου καὶ ἀνάπλασον αὐτὴν τῇ χειρί σου τῇ κρυφαίᾳ καὶ ἀναζωποίησον αὐτὴν τῇ ζωῇ σου)." This prayer discloses the author's view of conversion as a new creation of the convert. At the end of the prayer Joseph continues, "and number her among your people that you have chosen before all things came into being, and let her enter your rest which you have prepared for your chosen ones...."

---

47. Burchard, "Joseph and Aseneth," 1:189–90; and Collins, *Between Athens and Jerusalem*, 216–17.

48. Collins, *Between Athens and Jerusalem*, 217.

Significantly, Joseph's prayer in 8:9 anticipates the subsequent action of the story in which Aseneth is formed anew by God's hidden hand and given new life. In chapter 9 Aseneth undergoes the ordeal of repentance: "And she wept with great and bitter weeping and repented of her gods whom she used to worship, and spurned all the idols . . . " (9:2). After renouncing her idolatry, Aseneth then addresses God in prayer and soliloquy (chaps. 11–13), pleading with God to forgive her sins and show compassion. This soliloquizing, in turn, brings an encounter with a mysterious heavenly figure, who announces that "from today, you will be renewed and formed anew and made alive again . . . " (15:5), fulfilling the words of Joseph's prayer. Aseneth's renewal also results in being given a new name, "city of refuge," which is a recurring motif in the narrative (15:7; 16:16; 19:5, 8).

By chapter 19, then, Aseneth is transformed, formed anew, made alive again, and "numbered" among God's chosen people. Her transformation is reflected in a luminous physical state that makes a powerful impression on Joseph. Upon seeing Aseneth, Joseph is stunned by her great beauty. He acknowledges her as the proselyte who is representative of all proselytes, saying:

> "Blessed are you by the Most High God, and blessed is your name forever, because the Lord founded your walls in the highest, and your walls are adamantine walls of life, because the sons of the living God will dwell in your city of refuge (οἱ υἱοὶ τοῦ ζῶντος θεοῦ ἐνοικήσουσιν ἐν τῇ πόλει τῆς καταφυγῆς σου) and the Lord God will reign as king over them forever and ever."

Once again, a Hellenistic Jewish writer draws upon Hos 2:1 LXX, but here the writer applies the expression "sons of the living God" to Gentile converts. Aseneth is the model proselyte whose example typifies and prefigures the existence of future proselytes.[49] As the model of Gentile converts, she is also described with a city motif, "walls of life." Gentile proselytes

---

49. Some interpreters do not accept the notion of a full conversion in this story. For example, Shaye D. Cohen, "Crossing the Boundary and Becoming a Jew," *HTR* 82 (1989): 21.

will dwell within her "walls of life," signifying that conversion is a source of life and a place of refuge. Through conversion, then, Aseneth becomes "the model and prototype of the nations which are converted to the faith of Israel."[50]

The expression "sons of the living God" represents Gentile proselytes, as is evident from several observations. First, God "will reign over them [=sons of the living God] as king forever," indicating God's authority over and protection of the convert. In other words, God's kingly reign is effective over those who have accepted his lordship in conversion. Second, the subsequent marriage of Joseph and Aseneth in chapter 21 is symbolic of Gentile proselytes joining themselves to the Jewish community. What happens to Aseneth symbolizes the fate of Gentile converts. Third, the sonship motif is associated with covenantal status as seen earlier, in connection with Joseph, who is himself a son of God (13:10; cf. 21:3).

Fourth, the motif of the city of refuge is closely associated with the conversion theme.[51] In 15:7 Aseneth is a representative figure of those who "attach themselves" to God[52] and become members of the Jewish community: "And your name shall no longer be called Aseneth, but your name shall be city of refuge because in you many nations will take refuge with the Lord God the Most High . . . and behind your walls will be guarded those who attach themselves to the Most High God in the name of repentance."[53] Gentile proselytes find refuge with God through conversion.[54] Along these lines, Philo de-

---

50. Aptowitzer, "Aseneth, the Wife of Joseph," 296. Burchard, "Joseph and Aseneth," 2:189.

51. The idea of Gentiles or proselytes seeking refuge is also found in Zech 2:15 LXX and Isa 54:15 LXX. The latter reads: "Behold, proselytes (προσήλυτοι) will come to you through me and they will seek refuge (καταφεύζονται) with you."

52. The expression "attaching oneself to God" is a term for proselytes also found in 16:14: "happy are all who attach themselves (προσκείμενοι) to the Most High in the name of repentance." The expression "to attach oneself" (προσκείμενοι) is used of foreigners in Isa 56:3, 6 LXX who attach themselves to Yahweh. Gerhard Delling, "Einwirkungen der Sprache der Septuaginta in 'Joseph und Aseneth,'" *JSJ* 9 (1978): 40, 42.

53. The motif of "walls" in 19:8 serves as "a metaphor for Aseneth's repentance," based upon the close association of the "walls" and repentance in chapter 15. Everding, "The Living God," 223, n. 1.

54. For example, in 11:11–12, Aseneth prays: "therefore I will take courage too

scribes Gentile proselytes as "refugees" fleeing to the camp of piety: "they [proselytes] have left, he says, their country, their kinsfolk and their friends for the sake of virtue and religion. Let them not be denied another citizenship or other ties of family and friendship, and let them find places of shelter standing ready for refugees to the camp of piety"[55] (*On the Special Laws* 1.52).

In *Jos. Asen.* 19:8, then, "the sons of the living God" are proselytes who flee from idolatry and find refuge in the Jewish community through conversion. They attach themselves to the Most High God in the name of repentance and are "numbered" among God's chosen people, becoming members of the covenantal community. Further, through conversion, proselytes receive the covenantal status of sonship as "sons of the living God."[56] In this regard, the sons of the living God in *Jos. Asen.* 19:8 retains that covenantal significance seen in Hos 2:1 LXX; *Jub.* 1:25; 3 Macc 6:28; and Esth 8:12q LXX. The difference with *Jos. Asen.* 19:8, however, is that sonship designates a covenantal status acquired by Gentiles through conversion.

Conclusions

Hosea 2:1 LXX [1:10 MT] defines an important covenantal significance of the living God, which profoundly influences Paul in Rom 9:25–26. The living God in Hosea is the covenantal God of Israel who promises to restore Israel to covenantal status in a future time beyond judgment and exile. This restoration is fundamentally eschatological in character. Hosea looks to a future time when the living God would graciously restore Israel to a new covenantal status as "sons of the living God." The covenantal status of this future Israel is described in terms of eschatological sonship and a close filial relation to the living God

---

and turn to him, and take refuge with him, and confess all my sins to him. . . . Who knows maybe he will see my humiliation and have mercy on me. Perhaps he will see this desolation of mine, and have compassion on me, and see my orphanage and protect me because he is a father to orphans. . . . " See also 12:6 and 13:1–2.

55. *Philo* (trans. F. H. Colson; LCL; Cambridge, Mass.: Harvard University Press, 1984), 7:129. See also *On Dreams* 2:273.

56. Everding, "The Living God," 223.

as divine father. *Jubilees* 1:24–25, written in the second century
B.C.E., retains the basic eschatological thrust of Hos 2:1 LXX
[1:10], stressing God's paternal love for the newly restored sons.
Further, Hosea's vision of this future Israel as "sons of the living God" is the result of God's gracious and life-giving action,
which makes the sons number as "the sands of the sea." God's
role as the creator of Israel is implicit in the Hosean text. The
implication is that the living God is the divine father whose
(pro)creative action results in the generation of "sons."

The importance of Hos 2:1 LXX [1:10] for subsequent Jewish and early Christian tradition is evident from five texts: *Jub.*
1:24–25; 3 Macc 6:28; Esth 8:12q LXX; *Jos. Asen.* 19:8; and Rom
9:25–26. What these five texts hold in common is the use of the
expression "sons of the living God" to designate a close covenantal relation with the living God. The covenantal relation applies
to three distinct groups, beginning with future eschatological
Israel (Hos 2:1 LXX; *Jub.* 1:24–25). It also applies to postexilic Jewish communities in the Hellenistic Diaspora (3 Macc
6:28; Esth 8:12q LXX). Here the status of covenantal sonship
is a present reality and the living God is covenantal father of
Jewish children, watching over and protecting his covenantal
communities. Finally, the Hosean expression applies to Gentile
proselytes who convert to the living God (*Jos. Asen.* 19:8; Rom
9:25–26). The expression "sons of the living God," used as a
designation for Gentile proselytes, is novel within Jewish tradition, but this usage reflects a tradition with which Paul may
have been familiar (Rom 9:25–26). Despite its diversity of application, then, the expression "sons of the living God" commonly
designates a close covenantal relation between the living God
and his "sons."

Finally, while the prophecy of Hos 2:1 LXX [1:10] is unique
in the prophetic literature, it does, in some ways, link up with
other prophetic promises of the new covenant. In Hosea, the
"sons of the living God" (2:1 LXX) is synonymous with God
restoring Israel as "my people" (1:9, 2:25 LXX). The Hosean
prophecy of the "sons of the living God" thus links up with a
wider network of new covenant language, specifically, the promise, "I will be their God and they shall be my people." The latter

is found throughout Jeremiah and Ezekiel designating God's newly restored covenantal people. Therefore, Hosea's vision of a future Israel does not stand in isolation from other prophetic visions of the new covenant, but rather, is bound up with them through the motifs of sonship and peoplehood.

Chapter Three

The Living God in Hellenistic Jewish Monotheism

𝔯𝔢𝔯𝔢𝔯𝔢𝔯𝔢𝔯𝔢𝔯𝔢𝔯𝔢

Chapter 3 explores a crucial and distinctive facet of living God tradition found among Jews of the Hellenistic Diaspora and is represented in a variety of Jewish sources, e.g., Dan 4–6 LXX; *Joseph and Aseneth;* and Bel and the Dragon Theodotion. Greek-speaking Hellenistic Jews retained not only the biblical significance of the living God as the covenantal God of Israel, but they also developed their own distinctive vision of the living God that went beyond earlier biblical notions. For Hellenistic Jews, the living God was no longer simply the covenantal God of Israel, but also the universal lord and creator, who alone created all things and who alone was worthy of worship from all people. Hellenistic Jews developed a more universalistic view of the living God.

Henry Everding refers to this Jewish development of the living God as "the epithet's adjustment to the theological milieu of early Judaism."[1] This adjustment occurred as part of a wider trend among Hellenistic Jews who attempted to construct a bridge between Hellenistic culture and Jewish tradition.[2] One way in which Diaspora Jews attempted to construct this bridge was by translating their traditional biblical faith into terms that

---

1. Everding, "The Living God," 273.
2. Schürer, *The History of the Jewish People in the Age of Jesus Christ* III.1:138–39, observes that Jews of the Diaspora were "compelled by the force of circumstances to try to reconcile and unite Judaism and Hellenism . . ."; also, "the Jew in the Diaspora may have felt himself more strongly directed to place in the forefront his general religious ideas, the notion of a supreme God and of a future reward. Only with this presupposition could he to a certain extent harmonize Jewish and Greek culture. . . ."

were compatible with Hellenistic culture.[3] In this translation
process, Hellenistic Jews developed new ways of speaking about
their God, stressing God in terms that were accessible to both
Jews and Gentiles in the Hellenistic world. For example, they
avoided anthropomorphic expressions in speaking about God;
they expressed God's character in more spiritual terms by promoting his heavenly, invisible, and eternal character; and they
also adapted the language of Hellenistic religion and philosophy to Jewish God-talk.[4] Hellenistic Jews, then, transformed
traditional biblical ways of speaking about God in order to stress
God's transcendent character and universal supremacy.

An important factor behind this hellenizing of Jewish God-
talk was the polytheistic life setting of Diaspora Jewish communities. Jewish life in a polytheistic milieu prompted the need for
new ways of expressing God's unique character in contrast to
other "gods" and for polemicizing against those other gods.[5]
The Diaspora setting of Hellenistic Jewish communities was
replete with idols and idolatrous practices, compelling these
communities to respond with idol polemic and apologetic that
promoted the superiority of their one God. Hellenistic Jews
therefore sought new strategies for defending, clarifying, and
promoting their exclusive monotheism in contrast to idols.[6] In

---

3. Collins, *Between Athens and Jerusalem*, 1–10, characterizes the situation of Diaspora Jews as a "problem of maintaining the identity of the people and its survival as
a distinct entity" (1). Hellenistic Jews were "eager to win the respect of the Greeks
and adapt to their ways," and "yet the Jews were a distinct people with their own
peculiar traditions..." (4). The result was a tension or "dissonance" in which Jews
sought to participate in Hellenistic culture while remaining Jewish. The majority
of Diaspora Jews sought to reduce this tension by promoting "those aspects of Judaism which were most acceptable in the Hellenistic world... since they presented
Judaism in terms which a Greek could understand and appreciate" (9–10).

4. Dalbert, *Die Theologie der Hellenistischen-Jüdischen Missionsliteratur* (Hamburg:
Herbert Reich, 1984), 130–31. See also G. F. Moore, *Judaism in the First Centuries of the
Christian Era* (3 vols.; Cambridge, Mass.: Harvard University Press, 1955), 1:361–62;
Martin Hengel, *Judaism and Hellenism* (Philadelphia: Fortress Press, 1974), 1:255–
67; and Louis Feldman, *Jew and Gentile in the Ancient World* (Princeton: Princeton
University Press, 1993), 51–57; and Collins, *Between Athens and Jerusalem*, 9–10.

5. G. F. Moore, *Judaism in the First Centuries of the Christian Era*, 1:362, observes
that Jews of the Hellenistic Diaspora "lived in the midst of polytheism; they wrote
to exhibit the superiority of Judaism, whether it be considered philosophically, reli-
giously, or morally, and in the endeavor to convert Gentile readers from their vain
idols to serve the living God."

6. Moore, *Judaism in the First Centuries of the Christian Era*, 1:360–61, defines Jew-

this process, they found the biblical living God particularly useful in polemicizing against idols and promoting the superiority of their monotheism.

In the setting of the Jewish Diaspora, a distinctive expression of the living God in stylized formulations of idol polemic emerged that placed the living God in antithesis to "dead" idols. These antithetical formulations are not found in the Bible, although they do have biblical roots, e.g., 1 Sam 17:26, 2 Kgs 19:16–18. In the latter examples, the living God of Israel demonstrates his powerful character by defeating Israel's Gentile adversaries, thus implying his superior character vis-à-vis the gods of other nations. However, the biblical witness lacks stylized formulations of idol polemic that are the product of the Jewish Diaspora with its polytheistic milieu. In such a milieu, Hellenistic Jews had to demonstrate the superiority of their one God over against the many gods. Their polemic and apologetic were based on fundamental notions: the other gods were nothing more than handmade "idols," the product of human manufacture, while the living God was the transcendent Most High God who exercised universal sovereignty. This God was "living" in the sense of being powerful, active, and the source of life for all living creatures. The life-breath of every human being was in his hands and to him alone every person owed allegiance.

Moreover, the superior character of the living God for Hellenistic Jews is rooted in his identity as the creator, who made the world, gave life, and continues to give life in sustaining creation. The living God's identity as creator is not one facet of the epithet's significance among others. Among Hellenistic Jews it is a root idea, and the following discussion will seek to demonstrate that the association of the living God and the creator theme is fundamental to the Jewish understanding of the living God, more fundamental than has been previously recognized. The living God is no longer simply the maker of Israel, the

ish monotheism as "the religious doctrine that there is one God and no other, or, if it must be expressed abstractly, the doctrine of the soleness of God, in contradiction to polytheism, the multiplicity of gods." See also Dalbert, *Die Theologie Der Hellenistischen-Jüdischen Missionsliteratur,* 124–30; Nils Dahl, "The One God of Jews and Gentiles," *Studies in Paul* (Minneapolis: Augsburg, 1977), 178–91; and E. P. Sanders, *Judaism: Practice and Belief 63 B.C.E.–66 C.E.* (London: SCM, 1992), 242–51.

source of life for those within the covenant. The living God is also the creator of all people, Jew and Gentile alike.

The following discussion, then, goes beyond previous studies by focusing on this root significance of the Jewish living God and its functions of polemicizing against idols and promoting monotheism. The failure among New Testament scholars to investigate adequately and grasp the Jewish living God has had an adverse effect on understanding the Pauline use of the epithet. While the significance of this Jewish background of the living God is generally acknowledged,[7] the failure to develop an adequate picture of this background has hampered interpretation of the Pauline living God. With the Jewish background of the living God largely unexplored, New Testament commentators have tended to appeal to the biblical witness alone as the crucial background for interpreting the epithet. Therefore, the Jewish background of the Pauline living God remains an area in need of further investigation.

In conducting such an investigation, this chapter will examine Jewish sources that emanate from the Hellenistic Diaspora, most of which were written in Greek. Some sources were originally composed in Greek, such as *Joseph and Aseneth* and *Sibylline Oracles* 3, while other sources represent Greek translations of Semitic originals, such as Dan 4–6 LXX and Bel Theodotion. In examining these sources, a primary working presupposition is that all of them were addressed to Jewish communities and thus reflect something of the living God's function in those communities.[8] The apologetic function of these sources is evident

---

7. For example, Stenger, "Die Gottesbezeichnung 'lebendiger Gott' im Neuen Testament," 63–64, argues that the living God's use in the New Testament texts is attributable to the influence of "Jewish missionary language"; however, he does little to discuss specific Jewish texts. Victor Furnish, *II Corinthians* (AB 32A; Garden City, N.Y.: Doubleday, 1984), 182, comments on Paul's use of the living God in 2 Cor 3:3, relying heavily on Everding's work and noting that in 1 Thess 1:9 and 2 Cor 6:16, "Hellenistic-Jewish motifs are prominent." However, little is done to clarify these Hellenistic-Jewish motifs. Also, Dom Jacques Dupont, *The Salvation of the Gentiles: Essays on Acts of the Apostles* (trans. J. Keating; New York: Paulist Press, 1979), 70–72, comments on the living God in Acts 14:15, observing that "Christians merely take over the formula that the Jews used to describe the conversion of pagans to the one true God of Israel...."

8. V. Tcherikover observed some years ago that Hellenistic Jewish literature was

in how each of them was "directed toward strengthening the confidence of a Jewish audience in their own heritage."[9]

In terms of organization, this chapter begins by exploring the epithet's function in stylized formulations of idol polemic (Dan 5:23, 6:26–27 LXX; Bel and the Dragon 5 Theodotion; and *Jos. Asen.* 8:5). The second part of the chapter investigates the theological implications of these antithetical formulations. These formulations furnish crucial evidence on living God theology among Hellenistic Jews and the identity of the living God as universal lord and creator. Placed in antithesis to idols, the living God designates the creator who "lives" forever and who gives life.

These stylized formulations of idol polemic also reflect a Jewish tradition of the living God that was inherited by early Christian missionaries, such as Paul. In his monotheistic kerygma, Paul proclaimed the living God in antithesis to idols, following in the footsteps of Diaspora Jews before him. Therefore, the use of the living God in formulations of stylized antithesis constitutes an important traditions-historical bridge to early Christian use of the living God and provides a crucial background to the Pauline usage of the epithet.

The Living God in Antithetical Formulations of Idol Polemic

Among Hellenistic Jews, the living God came to be used in stylized formulations of idol polemic that are absent from the Hebrew Bible. These stylized formulations are clearly attested in five instances: Dan 5:23 LXX and 6:27 LXX; Bel 5 Theodotion; *Jos. Asen.* 8:5; and *Sib. Or.* 3:762–63. In these instances, the living

---

addressed to a Jewish readership and served to strengthen Jewish identity in the Diaspora ("Jewish Apologetic Literature Reconsidered," *Eos* 48 [1956]: 169–93).

9. Schürer, *The History of the Jewish People in the Age of Jesus Christ,* 3:609. Collins, *Between Athens and Jerusalem,* 8–9, observes that much of Hellenistic Jewish literature "is explicitly devoted to defending Judaism in Hellenistic categories," which describes the apologetic aim of this literature. Jewish apologetic "is directed simultaneously to those within and to those outside. If Gentiles could be persuaded to embrace Judaism, clearly, the Jews need not feel social pressure to abandon it. The outward movement of the propaganda simultaneously has the effect of bolstering the faith of the community."

God is "explicitly contrasted with idols in antithetically shaped formulas";[10] and each formulation is characterized by "a compact antithetical structure in which the epithet is juxtaposed with a contrasting designation of the idols."[11] In the antithesis, the living God is directly opposed to idols in a stylized literary manner, often involving a chiastic arrangement. I have already discussed one such example in *Sib. Or.* 3:763: "Flee unlawful worship, the living One worship." The imperatives "flee" and "worship" form an inclusion at the beginning and end of the two clauses and so a chiastic symmetry emerges. This arrangement sets the "worship" of the living One in antithesis to "unlawful worship."

The penchant for antithetically opposing the living God to idols is also reflected in other uses of the epithet in settings that make a general contrast between the living God and other gods. For example, 2 Kgs 19:16–18 LXX/MT; Jer 10:10 MT; Deut 4:33–34 LXX utilize the living God in contrast to the gods of other nations, stressing his superiority with respect to these foreign gods. In these examples, however, the contrast is not direct, but rather implicit by association from literary context.[12] Other examples of this loose and general contrast between the living God and idols are found in Philo, *Decalogue* 67 and *Jos. Asen.* 11:10.[13] In these examples, the living God "is explicitly contrasted with idols . . . in contexts where the epithet alone designates the God who is differentiated from idols."[14] The contrast serves to distinguish the living God from idols, although it is not constructed in a stylized fashion. The use of the living God in stylized formulations of idol polemic thus represents a distinctive and specialized function of the epithet among Jews of the Hellenistic Diaspora. These formulations suggest that Diaspora

---

10. Everding, "The Living God," 276.

11. Ibid., 224.

12. Ibid., 61. These uses lack a neat polemical antithesis. See Everding's discussion on 2 Kgs 19:16 on pp. 61–62.

13. Over against stylized formulations of idol polemic, Everding identifies two other groups in which the living God is contrasted with idols: (1) 2 Kgs 19:16; Jer 10:10; and Deut 4:33 LXX; and (2) *Decalogue* 67 and *Jos. Asen.* 11:10. The former involve a general contrast through context, while the latter involve a direct antithesis, although the antithesis is not formal.

14. Ibid., 276–77.

Jews defined the character of the living God through a process of antithesis vis-à-vis the idol-gods of the Hellenistic world. The significance of the term "living" received its significance in contrast to handmade idols, denoting the living God's transcendent universal character.

Dan 5–6 LXX

Two examples of the living God employed in stylized antitheses appear in Dan 5:23 LXX and 6:27 LXX. Both the MT and LXX versions of Daniel are rich sources of living God tradition, but it is the latter that is of primary interest here.[15] Daniel 4–6 LXX represents a unique textual tradition and stands largely independent of the MT, showing substantial divergences from the latter.[16] The LXX version of Dan 4–6 would seem to involve different textual traditions that reflect distinctive Diaspora concerns.[17] In terms of literary genre, both the MT and LXX of chapters 4–6 reflect the form of court tales[18] that "insist on the importance of fidelity to the Jewish religion and refuse any compromise with idolatry. It is because of (not despite) their fidelity to their own God that the Jews succeed."[19] A Jewish lifestyle for the Diaspora is thus affirmed in these tales. Engagement with the Gentile world is promoted but without compromising Jewish faith.

The two occurrences of the living God in Dan 5:23 LXX are unique to the LXX version and occur in an episode that features the idolatry of a Gentile king. The chapter begins with a preface that summarizes the idolatry of king Belshaz-

---

15. In the MT (Aramaic) the living God epithet is found in Dan 6:20, in which Daniel is called "servant of the living God" after surviving the lion's den. The liturgical style of the epithet, the God "who lives forever," is found in Dan 4:34, 6:26, and 12:7. Daniel Theodotion gives the Greek translation of the Masoretic text.

16. John J. Collins, *Daniel*, Hermeneia (Minneapolis: Fortress Press, 1993), 4–7. Also see L. F. Hartmann and A. A. DiLella, *The Book of Daniel* (AB 23; Garden City, N.Y.: Doubleday, 1978), 76–84.

17. Collins, *Daniel*, 219–20. The date and provenance of Daniel LXX is customarily placed in Egypt in the late second century B.C.E. (135–100) See Hartmann and DiLella, *The Book of Daniel*, 78; Collins, *Daniel*, 7–8; and M. Delcor, *Le Livre de Daniel* (Paris: J. Gabalda, 1971), 21.

18. Collins, *Daniel*, 42–47. See also W. Lee Humphreys, "A Lifestyle for the Diaspora," *JBL* 92 (1973): 211–23.

19. Collins, *Daniel*, 51.

zar, Nebudchadnezzar's son. Belshazzar "praised all the molten and graven gods in his drink and he did not give praise to the Most High God." This preface introduces the main action of the subsequent narrative that revolves around Belshazzar's idolatry. Belshazzar uses sacred Jewish vessels belonging to the Jerusalem temple in his idolatrous rites, thus desecrating them. Belshazzar "gave an order to bring the gold and silver vessels of the house of God, which Nebudchadnezzar, his father, had brought from Jerusalem, and to serve wine in them to his companions" (5:2). Belshazzar's idolatry, then, is especially heinous because he used holy temple vessels in his pagan worship (cf. Isa 52:11). The desecration of such vessels "was an outrage even by pagan standards."[20]

As a result, the idolatrous king incurs the punishing wrath of Daniel's God. Forebodings of this wrath appeared during Belshazzar's banquet. Mysterious fingers appeared and began writing on the wall of the royal palace, striking terror into the king (5:5–6). After the court magicians failed to interpret the mysterious writing, Daniel was summoned (5:13, 16) and he was able to give the interpretation in 5:23, 26–28:

> [23]King, you made a feast for your friends and you were drinking wine, and the vessels of the house of the living God were brought to you (τὰ σκεύη τοῦ οἴκου τοῦ θεοῦ τοῦ ζῶντος ἠνέχθη σοι) and you and your officials drank from them and praised all of the handmade idols of men. You did not praise the living God (καὶ τῷ θεῷ τῷ ζῶντι οὐκ εὐλογήσατε). Your spirit is in his power and he gave you your kingdom, and you neither praised nor lauded him. . . . [26]This is the interpretation of the writing: the time of your kingdom is numbered, your kingdom is coming to an end, [27]it is cut off and it is finished; [28]your kingdom is given to the Medes and Persians.[21] (5:23, 26–28)

By desecrating the sacred temple vessels, Belshazzar offends the living God whose power and activity was not constrained by

---

20. Ibid., 245.
21. The English text is from Collins, *Daniel*, 239.

the destruction of his "house." The living God is thus active in bringing Belshazzar's rule to an end (5:26–28 LXX).

The first occurrence of the epithet comes as part of an expression describing the Jerusalem temple as "the house of the living God," and this recalls the same expression from Dan 4:19 (22) LXX.[22] Following traditional biblical lines, the proper worship of the living God is associated with the temple cult and its sacred vessels. The living God has a special "house" in Jerusalem, which is under his patronage and protection, preserving the traditional biblical view of Pss 41:3 LXX [42:2], 83:3 LXX [84:2], and 2 Kgs 19:4, 16 LXX/MT. However, this traditional notion is coupled with the distinctive Hellenistic Jewish accent that the living God "lives in heaven" (Dan 4:23 [27] LXX) and thus transcends the earthly sphere. Even with his temple in ruins, the living God still exercises universal sovereignty over Gentile kings, exercising divine power to depose those kings who profaned his house and worshiped idols.[23] Daniel 5:23 LXX also employs the living God a second time in a formula of stylized antithesis that sets the epithet in contrast to "handmade idols." This use of the living God is notably absent from the MT and remains unique to the LXX, indicating its distinctiveness as a formulation of Diaspora Judaism.[24] This second occurrence uses the living God in a chiastically styled antithesis: "[you] praised all of the handmade idols of men. The living God you did not bless."[25] In this verse, the chiastic arrangement involves parallel elements that are balanced against one another. The verbs "you praised" and "you did not bless" are balanced against one another at the beginning and end of the two sentences. Also,

---

22. The relation of Dan 4 and 5 LXX is evident from similar content in both chapters. Collins, *Daniel*, 255, observes that both chapters "... are tales of royal hybris. In the first the king is humbled and repents; in the second he fails to learn his lesson. Both stories thus illustrate the divine sovereignty of God over all people, including powerful kings."

23. Everding, "The Living God," 232–33, offers a useful comparison of the LXX text with that of Theodotion, stressing the former's distinctive character within the Greek textual tradition.

24. Everding, "The Living God," 233–36. The Theodotionic version of Dan 5:23 is lacking in the epithet.

25. In Greek the chiasmic arrangement of 5:23 LXX is clearer: ἠνέσατε πάντα τὰ εἴδωλα τὰ χειροποίητα τῶν ἀνθρώπων. καὶ τῷ θεῷ τῷ ζῶντι οὐκ εὐλογήσατε.

the objects of the verbs, "idols" and "God" placed in antithesis to one another, along with their contrasting attributes of "handmade" and "living."[26]

The stylized antithesis of Dan 5:23 LXX thus introduces an important aspect of living God tradition among Jews of the Hellenistic Diaspora. The antithesis between the living God and idols serves to highlight the distinction between proper and improper worship. Belshazzar mistakenly praises handmade idols, rather than blessing the living God, who has ultimate power over his life-breath. The living God should be worshiped because he is the source of human life, as Daniel affirms at the end of 5:23 LXX: "Your spirit is in his power and he gave you your kingdom...." The king's "spirit" is in God's power, meaning that this God "has power over human life."[27] The aim of Dan 5:23 LXX, then, is to expose the error of idolatry as a failure to recognize the one living God who is the source of life for all people.

Another antithetical use of the living God is found in Dan 6:27–28 LXX.[28] The story of Daniel 6 LXX begins with Daniel thrown into the lion's den for having violated king Darius's decree. Darius, who is sympathetic to Daniel, is trapped by the force of his own decree and compelled to order Daniel's execution; but he is hopeful that Daniel will escape death in the lion's den and wishes Daniel well: "Your God whom you worship (σὺ λατρεύεις) three times a day will rescue you from the power of the lions" (6:17 LXX). The next day, Darius returns to learn of Daniel's fate, crying out, "O Daniel, are you alive, and has your God whom you continually serve (ᾧ λατρεύεις ἐνδελεχῶς), saved you from the lions...?" (6:21 LXX).[29] Daniel responds, "O King I am still alive (ἔτι εἰμὶ ζῶν) and God has saved me from the lions as I was found righteous before him" (6:22 LXX).

---

26. Cf. Dan 5:4 LXX: "they [Belshazzar and his feast companions] did not praise the eternal God who had power over their spirit."

27. Everding, "The Living God," 236.

28. Citations from Daniel 6 LXX are given according to Rahlfs's *Septuaginta.*

29. Dan 6:20 MT has a use of the living God not found in the LXX version: "O Daniel, servant of the living God, has your God whom you serve continually, been able to deliver you from the lions?"

In response to Daniel's deliverance, the king makes a bold proclamation, declaring his intent to worship the Jewish God:

> [27]All the people in my kingdom should adore and worship the God of Daniel for he is a living God who endures for generations after generations forever (αὐτὸς γάρ ἐστι θεὸς μένων καὶ ζῶν εἰς γενεὰς γενεῶν ἕως τοῦ αἰῶνος).[30] [28]I Darius will adore and serve him all my days, for the idols made by hand are not able to save as the God of Daniel redeemed Daniel. (6:27–28 LXX)

Daniel 6:27–28 LXX employs an epithet form that stresses God's eternal character in a formulation of stylized antithesis, although the antithesis here is not as sharp as in 5:23 LXX.[31] The antithesis between the living God and idols is present through an interaction of elements in 6:27 LXX and 6:28 LXX. The king's intent to "adore and serve him [the living God]" is balanced against his implied rejection of handmade idols that cannot save ("for the idols made by hand are not able to save as the God of Daniel . . . "). God's living character is stressed as an active saving power that is contrasted with the impotence of idols "that cannot save." The description of Daniel as "living" (6:21, 22) also suggests the living God as the source of Daniel's life and deliverance. Daniel "lives" because the living God acted on his behalf with a saving power that stands in antithesis to handmade idols that "cannot save." This living God, then, is characterized by active power that saves and delivers from death.

Further, God's eternally enduring character is counterbalanced by idols that are "handmade," signifying their perishability as products of human manufacture. Predicating idols as "handmade" stands in stark juxtaposition to the God who lives forever, exposing the utter folly of worshiping the for-

---

30. In Dan 6:27 LXX the placement of ζῶν in second position after μένων allows the traditional liturgical expression to remain intact. Everding, "The Living God," 237, comments that the term "living" functions "less as a epithet per se and more as a description of an attribute of God." Theodotion reverses the participial predicates μένων καὶ ζῶν.

31. Everding, "The Living God," 237.

mer.[32] Daniel's God, "who endures and lives forever," is thus brought into association with handmade idols that cannot save, reflecting the pattern of antithesis discussed earlier in this chapter.

Finally, Dan 6:27–28 LXX is striking in its portrayal of a Gentile king who acknowledges the power of the living God using language drawn from the second commandment:

> [27]"All the people in my kingdom should adore and worship the God of Daniel (προσκυνοῦντες καὶ λατρεύοντες τῷ θεῷ τοῦ Δανιηλ) for he is the living God who endures for generations after generation forever. [28]I Darius will adore and serve him all my days (ἐγὼ Δαρεῖος ἔσομαι αὐτῷ προσκυνῶν καὶ δουλεύων πάσας τὰς ἡμέρας μου), for the idols made by hand are not able to save as the God of Daniel redeemed Daniel."

This language of "adoring and worshiping" (προσκυνοῦντες καὶ λατρεύοντες) and "adoring and serving" (προσκυνῶν καὶ δουλεύων) derives from the second commandment (Exod 20:5/Deut 5:9).[33] In the narrative, Daniel himself is portrayed as a law-abiding Jew who "worships" God three times a day, continually "serving" him (6:17, 21). Both English terms "worship" (6:17) and "serving" (6:20) translate the same Greek term, *latreuein* (λατρεύειν), which also recalls language from the second commandment. Daniel is thus portrayed as a strict monotheist according to the second commandment. Similarly, Dan 6:27–28 LXX suggests that the Gentile king has rejected his handmade idols for an exclusive worship of the one God, who lives forever.

Bel and the Dragon 5 Th and *Jos. Asen.* 8:5

Two more examples of stylized antithesis are found in Bel and the Dragon 5 Theodotion[34] and *Jos. Asen.* 8:5. The former

---

32. Ibid., 238.

33. Exod 20:5 and Deut 5:9 LXX: οὐ προσκυνήσεις αὐτοῖς οὐδὲ μὴ λατρεύσῃς αὐτοῖς.

34. Bel Theodotion was written in the late second or early first century B.C.E. Sidney Jellicoe, *The Septuagint and Modern Study* (Oxford: Clarendon, 1968), 91; Marti J. Steussy, *Gardens in Babylon: Narrative and Faith in the Greek Legends of Daniel* (SBLDS 141; Atlanta: Scholars Press, 1993), 28–37; Schürer, *The History of the Jewish*

consists of two stories (vv. 1–22, 23–42) that have been combined into a single narrative.[35] There is no current consensus on the relationship of Bel LXX and Theodotion. Some argue that Bel Theodotion is a later reworking of the LXX, whereas others argue that Bel Theodotion represents an independent tradition.[36] Whatever the exact relationship between the two versions, Bel Theodotion is significant because it features four uses of the epithet "living God" in verses 5–6, 23–24.

The first episode in Bel 1–22 Th is sharply focused around the theme of idol polemic and serves to expose the folly of worshiping "handmade" idols.[37] The narrative is reminiscent of idol parodies in the Bible, e.g., Isa 44 and Wis 13–15.[38] A Jewish readership of Bel Theodotion is commonly accepted since idol parody, among Diaspora Jews in a polytheistic milieu, served to reinforce Jewish identity and clarify the superior character of Jewish monotheism. Idol polemic functions to counteract the temptations experienced by Jewish communities to participate in the surrounding culture by worshiping other gods.[39]

The narrative of Bel 1–22 Th begins with a conversation between Daniel and the Persian king Cyrus. The latter queries Daniel on why he does not worship the god Bel, to whom the king directs his worship: [5]"When the king asked him, 'why do you not adore Bel?' Daniel replied, "because I worship not idols made with hands, but only the living God who made the heaven and the earth and has dominion over all mankind (ἀλλὰ τὸν ζῶντα θεὸν τὸν κτίσαντα τὸν οὐρανὸν καὶ τὴν γῆν καὶ ἔχοντα πάσης σαρκὸς κυριείαν)." [6]The king then said to him, 'do you

---

People in the Age of Jesus Christ 3:722–30; and Witton Davies, "Bel and the Dragon," *The Apocrypha and Pseudepigrapha of the Old Testament in English* (ed. R. H. Charles; 2 vols.; repr., Oxford: Clarendon, 1983), 1:652–57.

35. Moore, *The Additions,* 121–25, observes that the two stories in Bel were originally independent before being combined in the extant version.

36. Ibid., 119; Steussy, *Gardens in Babylon,* 28–37; and Wills, *The Jewish Novel in the Ancient World,* 130.

37. Collins, *Daniel,* 417. Davies, "Bel and the Dragon," 1:656, concludes here that "what is taught is the absurdity of idolatry and the duty of worshiping the only true God—Yahweh."

38. Moore, *The Additions,* 127. See also Wolfgang Roth, " 'For Life, He Appeals to Death' (Wis 13:18): A Study of Old Testament Idol Parodies," *CBQ* 37 (1975): 21–47.

39. Moore, *The Additions,* 127–28; Everding, "The Living God," 249–50.

not think that Bel is a living God?' Do you not see how much he eats and drinks everyday?' " In response, Daniel goes on to prove that the Bel idol is not "living" or animate in any way. It is not the Bel who eats and drinks food every night, but rather the priests of Bel who sneak into the temple and remove the food items.

More importantly, the term "living" is the object of a word-play in the conversation between Daniel and Cyrus. The king is not only wrong in viewing the Bel idol as "living," but he also misunderstands Daniel's idea of a living God.[40] Daniel's idea is expressed earlier as part of a stylized antithesis in verses 5–6. Daniel asserts, "I worship not idols made with hands but only the living God who created the heaven and the earth and has dominion over all flesh." The expression "I worship not . . . but only . . . " creates an antithesis between the living God and the Bel idol. The Bel idol "made with hands" stands in stark antithesis to the living God who "made the heaven and earth."[41] The antithesis, in other words, places the humanly created idol in contrast with the God who created the world and rules over all humanity. The dual effect of such a formulation is that the king's worship is exposed as utter folly, while Daniel's worship is promoted as more proper and reasonable. Bel is an idol, the product of human manufacture, and therefore not a suitable object of worship. The contrast serves to poke fun at the absurd character of idolatry, while indicating the living God's transcendent status as the creator and lord of all.

Daniel's living God, then, "lives" in the sense of being the world's active creator and sovereign lord in a unique category all his own.[42] The attribute "living" is thus exploited "to explicate the reality and power of Daniel's God in distinction from the idol."[43]

---

40. Everding, "The Living God," 241.

41. The Syriac version of Bel 5 (SyrW) offers a similar polemic to that of the Theodotionic: "I worship not images or sculpted things or idols because they are the work of men's hands."

42. There is a link between God the creator making all things and having authority over all flesh. God rules what he himself has created. Dalbert, *Die Theologie der Hellenistischen-Jüdischen Missionsliteratur,* 125.

43. Everding, "The Living God," 242.

Joseph and Aseneth 8:5 offers another example of the living God used in stylized antithesis. When Aseneth and Joseph first meet, Joseph, scrupulous in his Hebrew piety, refuses a kiss of greeting from the idol-worshiping Aseneth:

> "It is not fitting for a man who worships God who will bless with his mouth the living God (ὅς εὐλογεῖ τῷ στόματι αὐτοῦ τὸν θεὸν τὸν ζῶντα), and eat blessed bread of life and drink a blessed cup of immortality... and anoint himself with blessed ointment of incorruptibility to kiss a strange woman who will bless with her mouth dead and dumb idols (ἥτις εὐλογεῖ τῷ στόματι αὐτῆς εἴδωλα νεκρὰ καὶ κωφὰ) and eat from their table bread of strangulation and drink from their cup a libation of insidiousness and anoint herself with ointment of destruction."[44]

The antithetical structure of 8:5 has a clearly recognizable symmetry. The man who blesses with his mouth the living God is set in antithesis to the women who blesses with her mouth dead and dumb idols. The two acts of blessing performed by Joseph and Aseneth are mirror images of one another, signifying mutually exclusive spheres of life, the Jewish and the pagan.[45] One sphere is defined by its exclusive commitment to the living God, the other by its adherence to the worship of idols. The respective worships of Aseneth and Joseph result in parallel but opposite effects, life for Joseph, and death for Aseneth.[46]

The antithesis also involves the opposition of divine attributes. Joseph's God is "living," while Aseneth's idols are "dead and dumb."[47] Idols are lifeless products of human manufac-

---

44. The Greek text comes from the appendix in A. M. Denis, *Concordance grecque des pseudépigraphes d'Ancien testament* (Louvain-la-Neuve: Université Catholique de Louvain, 1987).

45. Interpreters often take the triadic formula as a narrative device that contrasts two spheres of existence, Jewish and pagan. Burchard, "Joseph and Aseneth," 191; and *Untersuchungen*, 121–33; Collins, *Between Athens and Jerusalem,* 214; and Chestnutt, "From Text to Context," 288–89.

46. Claus Bussmann, *Themen der paulinischen Missionspredigt* (Bern: Peter Lang, 1971), 146.

47. In 11:8, Aseneth confesses to God that she had "worshiped dead and dumb idols" who are also described as "strange gods" (11:7).

ture that do not offer life, nor do they answer the prayer of
the idol worshiper. The worship of idols is associated with "in-
sidiousness" and "destruction," whereas worship of the living
God is associated with "life," "immortality," and "incorruptibil-
ity." Worshiping the living God means "life," which is presented
in numerous ways throughout the narrative of *Joseph and Aseneth*.
For example, the subsequent narrative shows that life comes
through conversion to the living God, who recreates and refashions the convert, calling her to new life as a daughter of
the Most High (8:9). Conversion results in the convert being
numbered among the chosen people and, eventually, living in
God's "eternal life forever" (8:10).

Implications for Living God Theology

What, then, can be concluded from the existence of these
formulations of stylized antithesis? Clearly the living God functioned in stylized antitheses of idol polemic as a weapon in
Jewish attacks on polytheism. This polemical function of the
living God developed from a need in the Hellenistic Diaspora
to counter a polytheistic environment permeated by idolatry.[48]
In the Hellenistic Diaspora, polytheism confronted Jews "as the
worship of a multiplicity of gods represented by images or, as
among the Egyptians, by living animals. Idolatry was the universal concomitant of polytheism and Jews made no difference
between them."[49]

The antithesis between the living God and "handmade idols"
serves the polemical aim of exposing Gentile gods as idols, the
products of human manufacture (Dan 5:23 LXX; 6:27 LXX; Bel
5 Th).[50] This branding of idols as "handmade" (χειροποίητος)

---

48. Moore, *Judaism in the First Centuries of the Christian Era*, 1:362, observes "the
assertions of the soleness of God and the argument against the many gods have
naturally a larger room in the apologetic of Hellenistic Jews than in the Palestinian
schools and synagogues. The authors of the former lived in the midst of polytheism;
they wrote to exhibit the superiority of Judaism...."

49. Ibid.

50. Everding, "The Living God," 272–75, observes of the term "handmade" that
it "functions as a technical term for idol with a definite deprecatory theological
connotation," 273.

goes back to prophetic polemic, as in Isa 44:9–20, which pokes fun at the worship of a statue fashioned by human craftsmanship. Idolators give "to the work of men's hands the honor that belongs to the God that made heaven and earth."[51] In Wis 15 the author asserts: "For they thought that all their heathen idols were gods, though these have neither the use of their eyes to see with, nor nostrils with which to draw breath, nor ears with which to hear. . . . For a man made them and one whose spirit is borrowed formed them; for no man can form a god which is like himself. He is mortal and what he makes with lawless hands is dead, for he is better than the objects he worships, since he has life, but they never have" (15:14–17). Along similar lines, handmade images are also branded as "dead and dumb" (*Jos. Asen.* 8:5) and "all of them are lifeless things" (Philo, *Decalogue* 7).[52] This polemic against idols as "handmade" and "dead" thus attacks the absurdity of worshiping images, which are nothing more than inanimate hunks of wood and stone fashioned by human beings. The stylized formulations of idol polemic also serve to expose the folly of worshiping "handmade" idols by setting them in opposition to a clearly superior object of worship, the living God who is the creator and source of life. By contrasting the living God with "handmade" and "dead" idols, Jews were thereby able to convey the irrationality of idol worship.[53]

These antithetical formulations of idol polemic serve not only to criticize idolatry, but also to highlight the superior character of the Jewish living God, who is set off as unique from the other gods of the Hellenistic world. The antithetical logic of these formulations had a positive thrust in disclosing something of the superior character of the living God. The antithetical formula-

---

51. Moore, *Judaism in the First Centuries of the Christian Era,* 1:363.

52. For similar critiques of idols as "dead things" or "lifeless," see Wis 13:10,17; 15:5; and *Sib. Or.* 3:30–31, 588–90.

53. This criticism of idolatry is also found among Graeco-Roman intellectuals, who ridiculed idol worship as vulgar superstition (e.g., Heraclitus, Cicero, Plutarch, and Lucian). Johannes Weiss, *The History of Primitive Christianity* (trans. F. C. Grant; New York: Wilson-Erickson, 1937), 236–40; Edwyn Bevan, *Holy Images: An Inquiry into Idolatry and Image Worship in Ancient Paganism and Christianity* (London: George Allen, 1940; repr., 1971), 63–83; F. C. Grant, *Hellenistic Religions: The Age of Syncretism* (Indianapolis: Bobbs-Merrill, 1953), 71–104; and Gerhard von Rad, *Wisdom in Israel* (Nashville: Abingdon, 1972), 183–85.

tions concisely demonstrate the superior character of the living God as the proper object of worship. Employed in formulations of stylized antithesis, the living God received a powerful positive accent and came to be defined in contrast to other "gods" in the Hellenistic world. The living God was everything that handmade idols were not—living, active, powerful, invisible, heavenly, and eternal. The living God came to be increasingly portrayed with attributes that stressed superior power and universal authority. In contrast to lifeless handmade idols, the living God was powerfully alive; he lived eternally in heaven, whereas handmade idols had an earthly origin in human manufacture; idols were handmade, but the living God made the heaven and the earth. While the living God had a "house" on earth, he is "the eternal incorruptible Creator who lives in the sky" and "in the golden boundless vault of heaven."[54]

Further, God's superior "living" character is linked to his identity as the biblical creator, something that has not been fully appreciated among interpreters.[55] The creator theme is implicit in the rational criticism of idols and in the antithetical formulations which oppose the living God and idols. Where it is asserted that idol-gods are handmade, the implication is that the living God is, by contrast, uniquely transcendent and does not have origins in human craftsmanship. In contrast to handmade idols, the living God is unique as the creator of all things, who acted alone in creating. In other words, the polemic against "handmade" idols implies the superior character of the living God who was not made by others. Further, the living God's identity as creator is implied through the antithetical logic of opposing the living God and idols. It makes no sense to worship idols because the idolator honors something created in the place of worshiping the creator who made all things. From

---

54. *Sib. Or.* frg. 3:17, 25. The philosophers Hecataeus and Theophrastus thought that Jews worshiped heaven as the highest God. Hengel, *Judaism and Hellenism,* 1:256, observes that the Gentile view of Jews worshiping heaven "was particularly illuminating for Aristotelian philosophy, as in it the firmament was regarded as an expression of divine perfection."

55. Everding observes several instances in which the living God is associated with the creator theme; however, he is hesitant in identifying the living God as the Creator. See, for example, Everding, "The Living God," 278.

a Jewish perspective, the folly of worshiping idols is rooted in a failure to recognize the living God's unique identity as creator; and, by contrast, the superior character of Jewish monotheism is grounded in the recognition that the one living God is the creator who made all things and reigns over all people. Therefore, what is explicitly asserted in Bel 5 Th is implicit in the other antithetical formulations of the living God: "I worship not idols made with hands but only the living God who created the heaven and the earth and has dominion over all flesh" (Bel 5 Th). The living God's identity as creator is a logical correlate of denouncing idolatry as a false worship.

For Hellenistic Jews, then, the living God was fundamentally the creator who made heaven and earth, a view that is expressed in a variety of Jewish texts that identify the living God as the source and giver of life. For example, in *Jub.* 21:4, Abraham declares: "I hated idols, and those who serve them I have rejected. And I have offered my heart and spirit so that I might be careful to do the will of the one who created me because he is the living God."[56] In Dan 5:23 LXX, Daniel asserts that the living God was the source of the life-breath in Gentile kings: "You did not praise the living God. Your spirit (=life-breath) is in his power and he gave you your kingdom, and you neither praised nor lauded him." The theme of the living God giving life is also implicit in *1 En* 5:1: "observe how the verdant trees are covered with leaves and they bear fruit. Pay attention concerning all things and know in what manner he fashioned them. All of them belong to him who lives forever."

That the living God epithet designates the life-giving creator is also suggested from the wordplay on "life" found in the *Letter of Aristeas* 15–16 and Josephus, *Ant.* 12:22, two passages that are frequently overlooked in discussions of the living God. While neither passage makes explicit use of the living God, they both illuminate the significance that the attribute "living" held for Jews in the Hellenistic Diaspora. In the *Let. Aris.* 15–16 and *Ant.* 12:22, "Zeus" is identified with the Jewish creator-God and

---

56. Both texts are taken from Charlesworth's *Old Testament Pseudepigrapha*, 1:14 and 2:95. Also, Sir 18:1 is relevant: "He who lives forever created the whole universe."

his name is interpreted etymologically in terms of life-giving. The Greek term for Zeus (ζῆνα) is interpreted as "life" and associated with divine life-giving. This makes sense etymologically since the name "Zeus" derives from the Greek verb "to live (ζῆν)," thus designating Zeus as the source and giver of life; and so Zeus (ζῆνα) is "the one by whom all live" or the one who "breathes life into all creatures."[57] How is this relevant to the identity of the living God as creator? Both texts show how Hellenistic Jews sought to make their creator God accessible to Gentiles in the Hellenistic world. The Jewish God is like "Zeus," whose name, in Greek, means "life";[58] and "life" also implies the divine action of giving life.[59] Therefore, the implication is that calling God "living" carries the association of divine life giving. Like Zeus, the living God was a most high God whose very name evoked his function in giving life.

Conclusions

This chapter shows that Hellenistic Jews developed their own distinctive living God theology, adjusting the traditional biblical view of the living God to one that was more universalized. The living God was no longer simply the covenantal God of Israel, but also the universal lord of all people, active in the affairs of Gentiles as well as Jews. In contrast to dead idol-gods worshiped by the Gentiles, the Jewish living God had a truly "living" character that manifested itself in concrete acts of deliverance and judgment among Gentiles as well as Jews. Hellenistic Jews thus retained the traditional covenantal notion of the living God, but

---

57. *Let. Aris.* 16: "These people [Jews] worship God the overseer and Creator of all, whom all men worship including ourselves, O King, except that we have a different name. Their name for him is Zeus and Jove. The primitive men, consistently with this, demonstrated that the one by whom all live and are created is the master and Lord of all." Josephus, *Ant.* 12:22: "They and we [Jews] revere the God who has ordered all things, by naming him in an etymologically correct way Zeus and giving him his name on the basis of the fact that he breathes life into all creatures."

58. Everding, "The Living God," 116–18.

59. *Sib. Or.* frg. 3:34: "But he is life and imperishable eternal light." The creator theme is also expressed in *Sib. Or.* 3, God is "the Great Begetter" (3:296) and "the begetter" (3:726); and the Sibyl exhorts the readers "to revere the name of the one who has begotten all" (3:550).

they also extended the scope of the living God's activity to include Gentiles. Bel the Dragon 5 Theodotion encapsulates this distinctive universalistic view of the living God among Hellenistic Jews; the living God " ... created heaven and earth and has dominion over all flesh."

Hellenistic Jews developed this distinctive view of the living God antithetically, that is, in response to the pervasive idolatry in the Diaspora milieu. Confronted with a prevailing culture of polytheism, they developed ways of differentiating their one true God from other gods and expressing his superiority. The living God epithet, placed in antithesis to idols, was perfectly suited for expressing the uniqueness and superiority of the one God. The epithet's use in stylized formulations of idol polemic served to expose the utter folly of worshiping idols, which were "handmade," products of human manufacture, lifeless things, made of perishable materials. It was sheer absurdity to venerate them.

The identity of the living God as life-giving creator is attested in numerous Jewish texts. The use of the epithet in stylized formulations of idol polemic serves to promote the identity of the living God as life-giving creator. In contrast to other gods in the Hellenistic world, the living God was unique as the sole creator and universal lord. The polemical logic of placing the living God in antithesis to idols expresses the folly of worshiping handmade created objects instead of the creator who made them. Idolators fail to recognize the one God who is creator. Also, Hellenistic etymological reflections on the term "Zeus" as a life-giving creator (*Let. Arist.* 15–16; *Ant.* 12:22) indicate that the attribute "living" carries the association of life-giving among Hellenistic Jews. The living God is the God who, by definition, gives life. From all indications, then, Hellenistic Jews viewed the living God as the biblical creator, the source and giver of life who ruled over his creation (Bel 5 Th; *Jub.* 21:4; Dan 5:23 LXX; *1 En* 5:1; Sir 18:1). At the creation of the world, the living God gave life and he continues to sustain life in the present. One Jewish author expresses the point in this way: "But he is life and imperishable eternal light and he pours out a delight sweeter than honey for men ... " (*Sib. Or.* frg. 3:34–35).

Chapter Four

The Living God in Jewish Prayer and Missionary Language

The use of the epithet in antithetical formulations of idol polemic suggests two other important functions of the living God among Hellenistic Jews that have not yet been discussed. First, this use suggests the epithet's function in Jewish liturgical settings and in Jewish prayer, an area in which there has been little or no scholarly discussion. Second, the use of the living God in antithetical formulations suggests the epithet's role in Jewish missionary appeals to Gentiles. The living God to whom Jewish communities prayed was also the God whom they promoted to Gentiles in their missionary appeal.

These two functions of the epithet, both liturgical and missionary, offer important background for understanding the Pauline living God. Paul's use of the living God in a monotheistic kerygma (1 Thess 1:9; Acts 14:15) has its roots in Jewish missionary uses of the epithet. Further, early Christian Gentile communities, like those addressed in Paul's letters, came to be defined as communities whose identity was grounded in monotheistic worship, that is, the worship of the living God. These communities were aptly named "temples" or "churches" of the living God (2 Cor 6:16; 1 Tim 3:15), since they distinguished themselves in a pagan environment by their exclusive commitment to the living God.

The following discussion is arranged into two parts, beginning with an exploration into the liturgical function of the epithet in Jewish prayer and concluding with an investigation into the epithet's missionary function.

Jewish Worship of the God Who Lives Forever

The formulations of stylized antithesis analyzed in the preceding chapter illustrate the living God's association with Jewish prayer language and show the living God to be the object of Jewish worship.[1] In these formulations, the living God is typically the object of praise, blessing, or worship. In some cases, Jews praise the living God (Bel 5 Th; *Jos. Asen.* 8:5). When Daniel, in Bel 5 Th, speaks of "revering" the living God, and when Joseph, in *Jos. Asen.* 8:5, speaks of "blessing with his mouth the living God," a Jewish worship practice is in view. In other cases, however, Gentiles are in view as subjects. Gentiles praise the living God (Dan 6:27 LXX); they are denounced for not praising the living God (Dan 5:23 LXX); or they are exhorted to worship the living One (*Sib. Or.* 3:763). Either way, the living God is presented as the proper object of Gentile worship. Like Hellenistic Jews, Gentiles also should praise the living God.

These portrayals of the living God as the proper object of worship serve a Jewish apologetic aim of promoting the validity of Jewish monotheism as the true and proper worship in the Hellenistic world. The living God is not only the proper object of worship for Hellenistic Jews, but also for non-Jews. True worship is directed to the living God because he is the true God and creator, the heavenly and invisible God who alone is worthy of worship. In promoting the superior character of the living God, Hellenistic Jews were able not only to attract Gentiles to the worship of the one true God, but also to bolster their own monotheistic identity in the Diaspora. Hellenistic Jews therefore promote the worship of the living God for the dual purpose of clarifying the validity of this worship to Gentiles and to themselves.[2]

---

1. Everding, "The Living God," 277, summarizes the various functions of the living God in Hellenistic Jewish tradition, e.g., apologetic, idol polemic, and missionary tract, but he omits any discussion of a liturgical function.

2. Regular communal prayer became a basic component in synagogues of the Hellenistic Diaspora, which were called "houses of prayer." Lee I. Levine, *Judaism and Hellenism in Antiquity: Conflict or Confluence?* (Peabody, Mass.: Hendrickson, 1998), 160–67; D. A. Fiensy and D. R. Darnell, "Hellenistic Synagogal Prayers," in Charlesworth, *The Old Testament Pseudepigrapha*, 2:671–97.

Three types of evidence indicate the epithet's liturgical function within a Jewish worship setting: (1) the repeated use of the living God as the object of praise and blessing in stylized formulations of antithesis; (2) the biblical and Jewish association of the living God with the Jerusalem temple, suggesting the epithet's traditional function in Jewish worship; and (3) the liturgical style of the epithet which describes God as the "One" who lives forever. Beginning with the first type of evidence, one finds the repeated use of the living God as the object of praise and blessing in stylized formulations of antithesis. The epithet's use in recurring association with worship language suggests its use in connection with Jewish prayer.

In *Jos. Asen.* 8:5, for example, Joseph describes his Jewish worship in terms of blessing directed to the living God: "It is not fitting for a man who worships God who will bless with his mouth (ὅς εὐλογεῖ τῷ στόματι αὐτου τὸν θεὸν τὸν ζῶντα) the living God, and eat blessed bread of life and drink a blessed cup of immortality...." Here Jewish existence is defined in connection with the activity of "blessing" God, reflecting the language of Jewish *berakoth*.[3] In Bel 4–5 Th, Daniel's worship-stance is set in stark opposition to the king's idolatry. In verse 4, the king worships his Bel idol while Daniel "worshiped (προσεκυνεῖν)" his own God; and in verse 5, Daniel does not "revere" (σέβομαι) handmade idols, but the living God. The term "worship" (προσκυνεῖν) in verse 4 recalls the prohibition of the second commandment: "you shall not bow down to (προσκυνήσεις) or serve them" (Exod 20:5/Deut 5:9 LXX). Daniel's worship of the living God thus represents Jewish monotheism and its exclusive devotion to the one true God.

Daniel 5:23 LXX reflects the Jewish expectation that Gentiles renounce idolatry and worship the living God. Belshazzar and his companions "praised (ἠνέσατε) all the handmade idols of men... " but they "did not bless (οὐκ εὐλογήσατε) the living God." Daniel 5:23 LXX thus expresses a Jewish view that the living God is the proper object of Gentile devotion and

---

3. Delling, "Einwirkungen der Sprache der Septuaginta in 'Joseph und Aseneth,'" 39–41. Similar blessings are reflected in *Jos. Asen.* 3:3 and 15:12.

expresses the expectation that Gentiles "bless" the living God. Further, *Sib. Or.* 3:762–63 reflects the exhortation of the Jewish writer that Gentiles renounce idolatry and "worship the living One (τῷ ζῶντι λάτρευε)." The imperative, "worship," (λάτρευε) recalls the second commandment's prohibition against serving (λατρεύσῃς) graven images (Exod 20:5/Deut 5:9) and is here transferred to Gentiles. Gentiles are thus urged to adopt a monotheistic stance in worshiping the living One.

Finally, in Dan 6:26–27 LXX Darius confesses the living God as the proper object of worship. In 6:26, the king's subjects are encouraged "to worship and serve (προσκυνοῦντες καὶ λα- τρεύοντες) the God of Daniel, for he is the God who endures and lives forever." In 6:27, the king declares that: "I Darius shall worship and serve (προσκυνῶν καὶ δουλεύων) him all my days, for the idols made by hand are not able to save." Again, the Jewish writer appeals to the language of Exod 20:5/Deut 5:9 (προσκυνήσεις καὶ λατρεύσῃς) in portraying the proper monotheistic worship. The living God, then, is not only the proper object of worship for Hellenistic Jews, but also for non-Jews.

A second body of evidence supports the liturgical function of the living God and is rooted in the epithet's biblical association with the Jerusalem temple. The temple is the place where Israelites addressed their living God in prayer, e.g., Pss 41:2 LXX; 83:3 LXX; and 2 Kgs 19:16 LXX. The Jerusalem temple was also the locus of the living God's divine indwelling, serving as a mark of God's covenantal faithfulness. During the Hellenistic era, the Jerusalem temple remained the central place of worship for Hellenistic Jews and came to be viewed as the place and symbol of true worship over against other false worship in pagan temples. To Hellenistic Jews, there could be only one true temple of worship in the world since there was only one God (*Spec. Laws* 1:67; *Ag. Ap.* 2:193; cf. *Let. Aris.*, 83–120).[4] What marked the superior

---

4. For example, Philo, *Spec. Laws* 1:67, says: "But he provided that there should not be temples built either in many places or many in the same place, for he judged that since God is one, there should be also only one temple." See E. Goodenough, *Jewish Symbols in the Greco-Roman Period* (Princeton: Princeton University Press, 1953), 1:3–32.S; also Safrai, "Relations Between the Diaspora and the Land of Israel," in *The*

character of worship in the Jerusalem temple was its imageless worship of the invisible creator God, which followed the dictates of the second commandment (Exod 20:4–5; Deut 5:8–9). This imageless worship recalls the theophany on Sinai/Horeb when the Israelites "saw no form" on the day that God spoke from the midst of fire (Deut 4:15; cf. 4:33–34). In contrast to pagan temples where images were worshiped, the Jerusalem temple held no visible image of God as the object of worship. Tacitus observes, "the Jews conceive of one God only, and that with the mind alone; they regard as impious those who make from perishable materials representations of god in man's image; that supreme and eternal being is to them incapable of representation and without end. Therefore, they set up no statues in their cities, still less in their temples. . . . "[5]

For Jews in the Hellenistic Diaspora, the temple remained the living God's special "house," the central locus of true worship, even though his activity as universal lord transcended the physical confines of the temple. In Dan 4:19 (22) LXX and 5:23 LXX, the Jerusalem temple is termed "house of the living God," reflecting the epithet's traditional covenantal association with the Jerusalem temple. I turn briefly now to an examination of Dan 4:19 (22) LXX to show this association.[6] The plot of the Dan 4 LXX revolves around God's act of judging, deposing, and eventually restoring the Gentile king, Nebudchadnezzar. The story begins with Nebudchadnezzar receiving a vision of a great tree stretching to heaven, but the tree is subsequently cut

---

Jewish People in the First Century: Historical Geography, Political History, Social, Cultural, and Religious Life and Institutions (CRINT; ed. S. Safrai and M. Stern; Amsterdam: Van Gorcum, 1974), 187.

5. Tacitus, *Histories*, 5:5: "Iudaei mente sola unumque numen intellegent; profanos qui deum imagines mortalibus materiis in species hominum effingant; summum illud et aeternum neque imitable neque interturum. Igitur nulla simulacra urbibus suis, nedum templis sistunt." Hengel, *Judaism and Hellenism*, 1:261, observes that Gentile intellectuals "regarded the 'spiritual' Jewish worship of God, devoid of images, with good will. . . . "

6. In Rahlfs's *Septuaginta,* the verse is found at 4:22, whereas in Ziegler's version of the Greek text, the verse is listed at 4:19. The verse will thus be designated as Daniel 4:19 (22) LXX in the following discussion. Joseph Ziegler, *Daniel, Susanna-Daniel-Bel et Draco* (Societatis Litterarum Gottingensis 16:2; Göttingen: Vandenhoeck & Ruprecht, 1954). Also, Collins, in his commentary on *Daniel,* offers an English translation of the Greek text that I will follow.

down and destroyed (4:14). Daniel is then summoned by the king to interpret the dream, a task that he successfully accomplishes (4:15–24). According to Daniel, the tree in the dream symbolizes the king himself and the judgment that was soon to befall him. The king gives his account of the judgment in 4:30a–34a, recounting a seven-year period in which his "sins and ignorance" led to his punishment by God (4:30a, 30c). After these seven years, Nebudchadnezzar is restored to his throne in an event that one interpreter describes as a "royal conversion."[7]

The expression "house of the living God" occurs in the narrative unit of 4:15–24 LXX, in which Daniel interprets the dream and pronounces impending judgment:

> As for that tree being raised up and approaching heaven, and its trunk touching the clouds: you, O King, have been exalted over all humanity that is on the face of the earth. Your heart was raised up in arrogance and power with regard to the holy one and his angels. Your deeds were seen, how you desolated the house of the living God (καθότι ἐξερήμωσας τὸν οἶκον τοῦ θεοῦ τοῦ ζῶντος) on the occasion of the sins of the holy people (4:19 [22] LXX).

In this verse, the living God is active against a Gentile king because of the latter's arrogance and destruction of the temple. Although the sins of Israel are mentioned, it is Nebudchadnezzar's arrogance in desolating the temple that is singled out as "a defiant challenge to the 'living God.' "[8] The king is thus punished and deposed for his arrogance in destroying "the house of the living God."

This judgment of Nebudchadnezzar serves to indicate the living God's special relationship with the Jerusalem temple. The living God, like other deities of the Graeco-Roman world, has his own "house" as a special place of dwelling.[9] The Jerusalem

---

7. Collins, *Daniel*, 233–34.

8. Everding, "The Living God," 227. The MT never explicitly mentions the Babylonian king being reproached for the destruction of the temple.

9. Doran, *Temple Propaganda*, 102. Doran speaks of a common topos or pattern in which a temple is attacked, the defenders pray to the deity for help, and the attackers are repulsed.

temple is the living God's "house," under the special protection and patronage of the living God. However, in contrast to other deities of the Graeco-Roman world, the living God is active in punishing adversaries who destroy the temple. Daniel's "house of the living God" thus stands in continuity with earlier biblical tradition and reflects the traditional association of the living God with the Jerusalem temple.

Further, while a special relation exists between the living God and his earthly "house," the activity of the living God also transcends the confines of this house and is not in any way limited by it. In this both Dan 4:19 (22) LXX and 5:23 LXX express a distinctive Hellenistic Jewish perspective.[10] Both verses demonstrate the transcendent character and universal authority of the living God, who is active in punishing Gentiles while the temple lies in ruins. Both Dan 4:19 (22) LXX and 5:23 LXX portray an exilic setting in which the Jerusalem temple is in ruins. What is striking, however, is that the living God is still active in exercising judgment on the Gentile king. The destruction of the Jerusalem temple in no way affects the ability of the living God to exercise his authority as heavenly sovereign. With the temple in ruins, the living God is still active in punishing Nebudchadnezzar, thus revealing his character as a universal heavenly lord.

The universal and transcendent character of the living God is further affirmed in Dan 4:23 (27) LXX, which speaks of God "living in heaven" as universal sovereign: "The Lord lives in heaven, and his authority is over all the earth (κύριος ζῇ ἐν οὐρανῷ καὶ ἡ ἐξουσία αὐτοῦ ἐπὶ πάσῃ τῇ γῇ)."[11] The living God "lives" as transcendent lord in heaven, exercising authority over the whole earth. The heavenly dwelling allows him to oversee the earth and all that transpires there.[12] Further, while the living God has an earthly "house" in the Jerusalem temple, and this "house" remains the locus of true spiritual worship, his real

---

10. The expression "house of the living God" in Dan 4:19 (22) and 5:23 LXX is unique to the LXX and not found in the MT of Daniel.

11. This language is peculiar to the Greek version. Ziegler's version lists the verse as 4:23, while Rahlfs's *Septuaginta* lists it at 4:17.

12. Everding, "The Living God," 228.

dwelling is in heaven, transcending the earthly sphere.[13] The living God's real home is a heavenly one and not in a temple made by human hands. The destruction of the temple serves to disclose the transcendent spiritual character of the living God, whose "life" and activity are still exercised against Israel's Gentile adversaries.

Daniel's "house of the living God" thus indicates the character of true spiritual worship in the Hellenistic era, a worship that is directed to the living God, who lives in heaven and who oversees the affairs of all humanity.

Finally, I turn to a third and final body of evidence that reinforces the claim that Hellenistic Jews worshiped the living God in their prayer and synagogal worship. In contrast to Gentiles, Hellenistic Jews venerated a transcendent heavenly God who had no corresponding image and who was incomparable as the eternal creator. Jews prayed to their living God using a liturgically styled construction that stressed God's eternal character. God is he who lives forever and ever. For example, I have already discussed Dan 6:27 LXX, which offers the expression, "a God who endures and lives for generation after generation forever" (θεὸς μένων καὶ ζῶν εἰς γενεὰς γενεῶν ἕως τοῦ αἰῶνας). Another example of this liturgically styled construction occurs in *Sib. Or.* 3:763, a construction that uses only a definite article and a participle (ὁ ζῶν/τῷ ζῶντι), yielding the term "the living one."[14] The term "God" is not explicit, but rather is implied in the definite article. Also, *Sib. Or.* 3.766, with its designation of God as "the Immortal," indicates that "the living One" in 3:763 is the God who "lives" forever. The participial construction, "the living One," is easily adaptable to the liturgical formulations praising God as the "One who lives forever."

Decisive in recognizing this liturgical style of the epithet is its repeated occurrence in prayer language. In Tob 13:1, for

---

13. Sanders, *Judaism: Practice and Belief 63 B.C.E.–66 C.E.*, 71, observes that "Jews did not think that God was there and nowhere else, nor that the temple in any way confined him. Since he was creator and lord of the universe, he could be approached in prayer at any place. Nevertheless, he was in some special sense present in the temple."

14. Cf. Gerhard Delling, "Partizipiale Gottesprädikationen in den Briefen des Neuen Testaments," *Studia Theologica* 17 (1963): 15–42.

example, one finds: "Then Tobit wrote a prayer of rejoicing, and said, 'Blessed is God who lives for ever, and blessed is his kingdom' " (εὐλογητός ὁ θεὸς ὁ ζῶν εἰς τοὺς αἰῶνας). In Sir 18:1 a similar formulation occurs: "He who lives forever created the whole universe; the Lord alone will be declared righteous" (ὁ ζῶν εἴς τὸν αἰῶνα ἔκτισεν τὰ πάντα). Daniel 4:34 MT/Th reads: " . . . I, Nebudchadnezzar, lifted my eyes to heaven and my wits returned to me. I blessed the Most High and gave praise and glory to the One who lives forever, for his dominion is eternal dominion . . . " (καὶ τῷ ὑψίστῳ εὐλόγησα καὶ τῷ ζῶντι εἰς τὸν αἰῶνα ἤνεσα καὶ ἐδόξασα). Other examples occur in Philo, *Decalogue* 67; *2 Bar.* 21:9–10; and *1 En.* 5:1 (cf. Dan 12:7; Rev 4:9–10).

The cumulative weight of three types of evidence thus supports the liturgical function of the living God in Jewish communities of the Hellenistic Diaspora. First, in antithetical formulations of idol polemic, the epithet living God recurs as the object of blessing or reverence. In all cases, Jews or Gentile properly worship the living God. Second, the epithet living God recurs in association with the Jerusalem temple, suggesting the epithet's function in connection with Jewish worship. For Hellenistic Jews, the Jerusalem temple remains the place of true worship rendered to the one God over against other false worships in pagan temples. The living God makes the temple his special "house," but worship is properly directed to a living God who transcends this earthly house and "lives" in heaven. Finally, Hellenistic Jews prayed to a transcendent eternal God, a God "who lives forever." The idea of God living eternally becomes part of a liturgically styled expression that characterized Jewish prayer in the Hellenistic world. In contrast to the idol-gods worshiped by Gentiles, Hellenistic Jews directed their worship to an eternal creator God who alone was worthy of worship.

The Living God, Proselytes, and Gentile Sympathizers

There is another function of the epithet that is crucial for understanding the Pauline living God and it remains largely neglected in the scholarly literature. The living God functioned in missionary appeals to Gentiles to accept Jewish monotheism or, at least, to acknowledge the reality of the Jewish God. This missionary function of the epithet is based upon its theological significance in designating the Jewish God as the universal lord and creator. Since the living God was the true God, who made all people and who reigned supreme over Gentile and Jew alike, he alone was worthy of worship.[15] Gentiles, then, should abandon the folly of idol worship and render worship to the living God who created them. To further strengthen the missionary appeal, Hellenistic Jews also stressed that the living God was active in punishing idolators who refused to recognize him as creator and lord.

This missionary function of the living God evokes a larger, much-debated question about the existence of a Jewish mission to Gentiles in the Hellenistic world.[16] Given the lack of hard evidence supporting an active Jewish mission, it is hard to arrive at any definite conclusions; and while it is clear that Jewish communities did make appeals to Gentiles, the methods and approaches used varied from community to community. What is beyond dispute, however, is the large number of Gentiles in the Hellenistic world who were attracted to Judaism, as is evident from the numerous references to proselytes in Jewish literature.[17] This Gentile attraction to Judaism expressed itself in a variety of forms.[18] Some Gentiles were sympathetic in simply admiring Jewish monotheism without taking any steps toward conversion. Others acknowledged the power and reality of the

---

15. Terence Donaldson, *Paul and the Gentiles: Remapping the Apostle's Convictional World* (Minneapolis: Fortress Press, 1997), 51–74, speaks of "the various patterns of universalism" operative in second temple Judaism and "ways in which Judaism could conceive of the 'salvation' of Gentiles that were consistent with its own covenantal self-understanding."

16. Feldman, *Jew and Gentile in the Ancient World*, 288–341, argues that the evidence supports a widespread Jewish missionary effort. Against this view, however, are Martin Goodman, *Mission and Conversion: Proselytizing in the Religious History of the Roman Empire* (Oxford: Clarendon, 1994) and Scot McKnight, *A Light among the Gentiles: Jewish Missionary Activity in the Second Temple Period* (Minneapolis: Fortress Press, 1991).

17. For example, Jdt 14:10; Tob 1:8; *2 Bar.* 41.4; *Ant.* 20:34–53; Philo, *Virtues* 102; *Spec. Laws* 1:51–52; and Tacitus, *Hist.* 5:5.2.

18. Cohen, "Crossing the Boundary and Becoming a Jew," 13–33. See also McKnight, *A Light among the Gentiles,* 91–100.

Jewish God, while remaining polytheist. Still others approached full conversion by venerating the one God and renouncing polytheism. Full conversion entailed, not only acceptance of exclusive monotheism, but also the adoption of Jewish laws and membership within a Jewish community.[19]

The function of the living God in attracting Gentiles to Judaism is illustrated in several literary portrayals of Gentiles acknowledging the reality and power of the living God, and, in one case, converting to the living God (*Jos. Asen.* 11:10). These literary portrayals will be taken up in two categories: texts already examined in previous chapters (3 Macc 6:28; Esth 8:12q LXX; *Sib. Or.* 3:762–63; Dan 6:27–28 LXX) and texts not yet examined (Bel 23–42 Th; *Jos. Asen.* 11:7–10). While these literary portrayals do furnish insight into living God theology among Hellenistic Jews, they are not historical reports of "what happened," but rather, literary constructions produced for the purposes of Jewish apologetic. They represent an idealized picture of how Gentiles should respond to the Jewish God. As constructs of Jewish apologetic, they reflect an important function of the living God in Jewish missionary appeals. These narrative portrayals illustrate Gentiles accepting the living God as sympathizers or converts and they are suggestive of how Hellenistic Jews promoted the living God in the Hellenistic world and what it was about the living God that appealed to Gentiles.

Specifically, these literary portrayals suggest that Gentiles should worship the living God because he is the universal lord and creator. While the creator theme is not explicit in these portrayals, it is implicit in expressions of the living God's lordship and kingly power. When Gentiles acknowledge the living God as eternal lord, they implicitly acknowledge his identity as creator. Such expressions are implicitly expressions of God's creatorhood. The living God's lordship over the world derives from his role as creator, as indicated by Bel 5 Th: "I worship not idols made with hands, but only the living God who made the heaven and the earth and has dominion over all mankind."

---

19. Cohen, "Crossing the Boundary," 31. Cohen describes some Gentile sympathizers as "adherents" to Judaism, following Arthur Darby Nock.

Gentiles Portrayed Acknowledging the Living God

I have previously examined four Jewish texts that are relevant to this discussion because they portray Gentiles acknowledging the reality and power of the living God. This aspect of the living God, however, was not explored in my previous discussions and so here I wish to draw out and highlight this aspect without going into an extensive analysis. I will simply review their content and identify the ways in which they reflect a missionary function of the living God. In three cases, 3 Macc 6:28; Esth 8:12q LXX; and Dan 6:27–28 LXX, the epithet is placed upon the lips of Gentile kings, who acknowledge the reality and power of the Jewish living God. The acknowledgment comes in response to powerful acts of deliverance witnessed by the king. For example, Gentile kings acknowledge Jews as "sons of the almighty living God of heaven" (3 Macc 6:28) or "sons of the most High and most mighty living God" (Esth 8:12q LXX). In these two cases, the king does not convert, but rather acknowledges the reality of the Jewish God. The acknowledgment implies a Gentile recognition of the living God's reality and power. In 3 Macc 6:28 and Esth 8:12q LXX, then, the living God appeals to Gentiles as a powerful transcendent God who is active on behalf of the Jewish people.

Daniel 6:26–27 LXX offers another portrayal of a Gentile king "acknowledging the power of the god of the Jews."[20] The Gentile king in Daniel LXX represents reverent Gentiles, who respond to "some manifestation of the power of the God of the Jews and as a result venerate the god and acknowledge his power."[21] In Dan 6 LXX Darius responds to Daniel's miraculous deliverance from the lion's den with a decree acknowledging the power and reality of Daniel's living God. Having witnessed firsthand the saving power of Daniel's God, the king commits himself to the worship of this God: "I Darius will adore and serve him all my days, for the idols made by hand are not able

---

20. Cohen, "Crossing the Boundary and Becoming a Jew," 15–17. Cohen observes that reverent Gentiles "do not stand in any special relationship with the god of the Jews. They behave as 'normal' pagans behave when confronted by a foreign god and foreign religion."

21. Ibid., 16.

to save as the God of Daniel redeemed Daniel" (6:28 LXX). Further, the king acknowledges the eternal character of Daniel's God: "All the people in my kingdom should adore and worship the God of Daniel for he is the living God who endures for generations after generation forever" (6:27 LXX). The king's response thus indicates how the Jewish living God appeals to Gentiles. The living God is an active powerful God who intervenes on behalf of his people and he is uniquely eternal in contrast to handmade idols. This eternal character indicates the living God's identity as eternal creator, making him far superior to the other gods.

Finally, *Sib. Or.* 3:762–63 offers an explicit example of how the epithet would have functioned in Jewish missionary appeals to Gentiles. The imperatives of 3:762–63 are in the second person and addressed directly to Gentiles: "flee unlawful worship/ the living one worship" (φεύγετε λατρείας ἀνόμους, τῷ ζῶντι λάτρευε). These imperatives urge Gentiles to renounce idolatry (=unlawful worship) and to direct their worship to the God who is truly living.[22] The motivation for Gentiles to convert to the living God is found in the surrounding context of 3:760–61 and 766. The former introduces the exhortations of 3:762–66 with the following assertions: "for he himself alone is God and there is no other and he himself will burn with fire a race of grievous men" (760–61). An important motive for Gentiles coming over to the worship of the living One is that he alone is God, expressed in standard monotheistic language: "for he himself alone is God and there is no other."

Also motivating Gentile conversion of Gentiles is the threat of divine judgment that brackets the whole unit of 3:762–65. The judgment theme appears in 761, "he himself will burn with fire a race of grievous men...," and in 766, "for the Immortal is angry at whoever commits these sins." These assertions about divine judgment serve to ground the missionary appeals of 3:762–63. Gentiles are exhorted to "worship the living One" on the basis that God is angered by their idolatry and will hold

---

22. Similar is the earlier appeal addressed to Gentiles in 3:732–40 to "turn back, be converted, and propitiate God."

them accountable for it.[23] Based upon the threat of judgment, Gentiles must worship "the living One" and avoid idolatry and immoral practices (3:762–66).

Bel 23–42 Th and *Jos. Asen.* 11:7–10

There are two other texts, not previously examined, that also portray how the Jewish living God appealed to Gentiles in the Hellenistic world. These texts are also suggestive of how Hellenistic Jews promoted the living God in their missionary language. Bel and the Dragon 23–42 Theodotion offers a story of a Gentile king acknowledging the power and reality of the living God, while *Jos. Asen.* 11:10 portrays a Gentile acknowledging the living God as part of conversion.

Bel 23–42 Th

The story in Bel 23–42 Th narrates the conversion of a Gentile king who acclaims Daniel's living God in a standard monotheistic affirmation. The story begins in verses 23–26:

> There was also a great dragon, which the Babylonians revered. And the king said to Daniel, "You cannot deny that this is a living god (θεὸς ζῶν); so worship him." Daniel said, "I will worship (προσκυνήσω) the Lord my God, for he is the living God (ὅτι οὗτός ἐστιν θεὸς ζῶν). But if you O King give me permission, I will slay the dragon without sword or club"[24] (vv. 23–26).

Here the king calls the serpent-god "living" because it is a living animal, perhaps a snake of some kind. Daniel, however, counters that his God is a "living God" in a different sense which is made clear in the subsequent narrative.[25]

To prove that the king's serpent-god is not really a living God, Daniel slays the serpent by feeding it a poisonous concoction that causes it to burst. In the presence of the dead

---

23. On the judgment theme in *Sib. Or.* 3, see Dalbert, *Die Theologie*, 111.

24. There is no reference to the living God in the LXX and the verse sequence proceeds in an order different from that of Theodotion.

25. Wills, *The Jewish Novel*, 61, observes that "the concrete aspect of a 'living' God is anchored in the pagans' sensibilities to the mundane world, instead of being allowed to float upward in the direction that it is pointing."

creature, Daniel then exclaims to the king "See what you have been worshiping!" (v. 27). The serpent is a perishable creature whose mortality renders it inappropriate as an object of worship. Daniel's God, on the other hand, "lives" in a different sense as is indicated by Daniel's assertion, "I will worship (προσκυνήσω) the Lord my God, for he is the living God" (v. 25). The motif of God's Lordship recalls Daniel's earlier assertion that the living God "has dominion over all flesh" (v. 5). The living God is the transcendent universal lord whose activity of exercising dominion over it makes him truly "living."

Beyond this point in the narrative there is no occurrence of the living God. However, the latter part of the story does serve to clarify the "living" character of Daniel's God. In a manner similar to the story in Dan 6, Bel 33–39 Th narrates the deliverance of Daniel from the lion's den, a deliverance that the king attributes to the saving power of Daniel's living God. Following the miraculous deliverance, the king in verse 41 acclaims: "You are great, O Lord God of Daniel, and there is no other besides you" (οὐκ ἔστιν πλὴν σοῦ ἄλλος). This acclamation is the "standard deuteronomic monotheistic affirmation," which recalls the language of Deutero-Isaiah.[26] The king therefore recognizes the activity of Daniel's living God in the miraculous escape from the lion's den. In response, he acknowledges the greatness and uniqueness of Daniel's God.

Is the episode a portrayal of King Cyrus converting to Judaism? Upon witnessing the snake's death earlier in the story, the king apparently converts to Judaism because his subjects rally against him, saying: "the king has become a Jew (Ιουδαῖος γέγονεν ὁ βασιλεύς)"[27] (v. 28). This conversion is further confirmed by the king's monotheistic acclamation at the end of the story. However, a full conversion is unlikely: "the king confesses the God of Daniel and apparently becomes a monotheist, but even then it is not clear that he has become a Jew";[28] also,

---

26. Everding, "The Living God," 247. The expression is a standard monotheistic confession found, e.g., in Isa 45:18; 46:9; Deut 4:35; Jer 10:6; 2 Kgs 19:15; *Sib. Or.* 3:760; etc.

27. Everding, "The Living God," 247. See also Nickelsburg, *Jewish Literature*, 27.

28. Collins, *Daniel*, 415.

"...neither the narrator of the story nor Daniel regard the Persian king as a Jew. He was a Persian king with a peculiar devotion to the Jewish God."[29]

Bel and the Dragon 23–42 Theodotion thus portrays the ways in which the Jewish living God appealed to Gentiles. The Gentile king acknowledges the unique reality and power of the living God on the basis of Daniel's miraculous deliverance from the lion's den. The living God is a powerful divine Lord who is active in delivering those who worship him. Daniel's God is powerfully "alive" in the rescue of Daniel. Further, the king recognizes that Daniel's God is uniquely "living," since he alone is God and "there is no other" (v. 41). No other god is "living," in the manner of Daniel's God.

Jos. Asen. 11:10d

Joseph and Aseneth 11:10 offers a final literary portrayal of a Gentile convert acknowledging the living God. What distinguishes this portrayal from others is its explicit depiction of a Gentile converting to the living God.[30] In *Joseph and Aseneth* conversion consists of three elements: (1) exclusive devotion to the living God accompanied by a renunciation of idols; (2) the convert's acceptance and practice of Jewish laws; and (3) the convert's membership in the Jewish community.[31] These three elements are all present in *Joseph and Aseneth,* either implicitly or explicitly.

For example, in *Jos. Asen.* 8:5, Joseph describes the Jewish life as an exclusive sphere of existence over against pagan existence. Aseneth's exclusive devotion to the living God is implied in her dramatic renunciation of idolatry (chaps. 9–10) and in her decision to "turn" to the God who was living and true (11.7–10).[32] Also, Aseneth's membership in the Jewish community is suggested from Joseph's prayer of 8:9. The convert is

---

29. Cohen, "Crossing the Boundary," 23.

30. Everding, "The Living God," 268.

31. Cohen, "Crossing the Boundary," 26–31, identifies these three points as evidence of conversion.

32. In dramatic fashion, she "took all her gods that were in her chamber...and ground them to pieces and threw all the idols of the Egyptians through the window" (10:12).

"numbered" among God's chosen (8:9).[33] Further, the marriage between Aseneth and Joseph in chapters 20–21 symbolizes the "marriage" between the Gentile proselyte and the Jewish community.[34] Chapter 11, then, portrays a Gentile who not only acknowledges the Jewish living God, but who also intends to convert and take her place in the Jewish community.

At the beginning of chapter 11 Aseneth abandons her ancestral worship and finds herself alone in her upper room, the setting for her long soliloquy. The soliloquy has two parts (11:3–14; 11:15–18) and is followed by Aseneth's prayer (12:1–13:14). The first soliloquy in 11:3–14 expresses Aseneth's desire to "turn" to the living God. In this soliloquy conversion entails not only the abandoning of idols, but also the separation from previous familial and social relations: "What shall I do, miserable (that I am) or where shall I go; with whom shall I take refuge, or what shall I speak, I the virgin and an orphan and desolate and abandoned and hated?" (11:3–4).[35] In short, Aseneth's renunciation of idols leaves her "orphaned," a state that reflects the general plight of Gentile converts who, having abandoned ancestral worship, also withdraw from former social ties and associations.[36]

Aseneth's soliloquy continues:

> [7]And the Lord the God of the powerful Joseph, Most
>   High,
>   hates all those who worship idols,
>   because he is a jealous and terrible God
>   toward all those who worship strange gods.
> [8]Therefore he has come to hate me too,
>   because I worshiped dead and dumb idols
>   and blessed them,

---

33. Cohen, "Crossing the Boundary," 21.

34. Regarding Aseneth's practice of Jewish laws, the narrative is silent. However, it is reasonable to assume that upon her marriage Aseneth adopted those customs already practiced by Joseph.

35. The surrounding narrative never mentions that Aseneth was hated by her family; what Aseneth describes is not present in the surrounding narrative, which suggests that this material was originally independent of its present context.

36. In his writings, Philo also refers to this plight of proselytes in this way, e.g., *Spec. Laws* 1:52.

⁹and ate from their sacrifice,
    and my mouth is defiled from their table
    and I do not have the boldness to call on the Lord God
        of heaven
    the Most High, the Mighty One of the Powerful Joseph,
    because my mouth is defiled from the sacrifice of idols.
¹⁰But I have heard many saying[37]
    that the God of the Hebrews is a true God,
    and a living God (θεὸς ζῶν), and a merciful God,
    and compassionate and long-suffering and pitiful and
        gentle,
    and does not count the sin of a humble person,
    nor expose the lawless deeds of an afflicted person at
        the time of his affliction. (11:7–10)

In this passage, the living God occurs in a literary context where idols are criticized as "dead and dumb" (11:7–8), although the polemic in 11:8 does not represent the stylized form of antithesis found in 8:5.

Aseneth recognizes that the living God "hates all those who worship idols, because he is a jealous and terrible God toward all those who worship strange gods" (11:7). The description of God as "jealous and terrible" recalls the language of the second commandment in Exod 20:5/Deut 5:9: "... For I, the Lord, your God, am a jealous God, inflicting punishment for their father's wickedness on the children of those who hate me..." Aseneth, therefore, recognizes a truth of Jewish monotheism, that God stands opposed to idolatry and punishes those who worship idols.[38] She muses that this jealous and terrible God hates her because she formerly worshiped "dead and dumb idols" (11:8). Later, in 11:17, Aseneth will pose the question:

---

37. This indicates further evidence of source material not fully integrated into the narrative. In 11:10, Aseneth has heard "many" speaking about this God but the "many" appear out of nowhere, so to speak, and are never identified. Locked up in her father's estate, Aseneth had no prior opportunity to hear the "many," who are, presumably, Jewish, since they speak about the Jewish God.

38. Everding, "The Living God," 267, observes that 11:7–10 draws on traditions "derived from Jewish monotheistic propaganda based on the first two commandments." Cf. Chestnutt, "From Text to Context," 293.

"how shall I open my mouth to the Most High...and be sure
that the Lord will not be angry with me...?"

The living God is thus a jealous and terrible God who demands recognition as the only true God and who punishes those
who reject him. A similar notion is expressed in *Sib. Or.* 3:766:
"for the Immortal is angry at whoever commits these sins," referring to immoral practices that were linked to idolatry. In striking
parallel to *Jos. Asen.* 11:7–10, Jer 10:10 predicates God as both
"living" and "true" in connection with divine wrath: "But the
Lord is the true God; he is the living God and the everlasting
King. At his wrath the earth quakes and the nations cannot endure his indignation."[39] As sovereign lord and everlasting king,
the living and true God sees the idolatry of Gentile nations and
is roused to indignation (cf. Jer 49:21; 47–48). As a former idolator, then, Aseneth has much to fear from this "jealous" living
God. The living God is a jealous and terrible God who is active
in holding Gentiles accountable for their idolatry.

In 11:10, Aseneth reflects on how she has heard "many"
speaking about the God of the Hebrews as "a true God (θεὸς
ἀληθινός) and a living God (θεὸς ζῶν) and a merciful God (θεὸς
ἐλεήμων)." This predication of God as living and true is significant since Paul, in 1 Thess 1:9–10, also describes God as living
and true. What, then, did Aseneth mean by a true God? The idol
polemic in 11.7–9 suggests that "true" carries a polemical significance, stressing the reality or "truth" of the one God in contrast
to idols who are false gods or no gods at all. The Jewish God is
"real" in contrast to the falsity or unreality of idol-gods.[40] Hellenistic Jews employed the term to assert God's permanence in
contrast to idols that were handmade and perishable, e.g., *Let.
Aris.* 140; Wis 12:27; 15:1; and the *Sib. Or.* frg. 1:10–11; 1:20–
22; and 3:46–47. Jews are those "who worship the true God"
(*Let. Aris.* 140) and any Gentiles "who honor the true eternal
God inherit life" (*Sib. Or.* frg. 3:45–46). Aseneth's recognition

---

39. Everding, "The Living God," 64–68. Jer 10 LXX has no mention of the living
God. In fact vv. 6–8 and 10 are absent from the LXX. These and other observations
suggest that "verse 10 existed independent of its present context" and "its original
context is now lost" (Ibid., 65).

40. Bussmann, *Themen der paulinischen Missionspredigt*, 174–76.

of Joseph's God as the "true God" thus implies her acceptance of exclusive monotheism that comes with conversion.

In 11:10, Aseneth has also been told "by the many" that the God of the Hebrews is a "merciful God," who forgives idolaters if they renounce idolatry and confess their sins.[41] The God of the Hebrews is "a merciful God and compassionate and long-suffering and pitiful and gentle ... " (11:10). These words recall the language of Exod 34:6, where God shows mercy to Israel after the worship of the golden calf: "The Lord passed before him [Moses] and called, the Lord, the Lord, a God merciful and gracious, slow to anger and abounding in steadfast love and faithfulness ... " (34:6 MT; cf. Exod 20:6).[42] As the living God of Israel was merciful to his own idolatrous people, so too is he merciful to idolatrous Gentiles who repent of their idolatry.

The merciful living God is also the heavenly "father" who embraces proselytes as his children. *Joseph and Aseneth* describes conversion as something which establishes Gentile converts in a filial relation to the living God. Converts become "sons of the living God" (19:8) and Aseneth herself becomes "a daughter of the Most High" (21:4) through conversion. The living God, then, is active as a merciful God who forgive idolators and welcomes them into a close filial relation. In 11.13 Aseneth speaks of taking refuge with God because "he is the father of orphans ... " (11:13; cf. 12:13) and later the proselyte is like "a little child who is afraid" and "flees to his father" (12:8). Conversion in *Joseph and Aseneth* means that not only are converts "numbered among God's people" (8:9), but they are also adopted as children by the divine father.

Conclusions

In Jewish communities of the Hellenistic Diaspora, the epithet "living God" functioned in Jewish missionary appeals to Gentiles and in liturgically styled formulations associated with Jewish

---

41. Everding, "The Living God," 267.

42. This combination of attributes occurs frequently in the Bible as a description of God's saving character, e.g., Num 14:18 LXX; Pss 85:15 LXX; 102:8 LXX; and 144:8 LXX.

prayer. The latter suggest the intra-community function of the living God among Hellenistic Jews who directed their worship to the God who, in contrast to other so-called gods, lives forever. It is therefore no coincidence that the antithetical formulations of idol polemic examined in the preceding chapter (Dan 5:23 LXX; 6:27–28 LXX; Bel 5 Th; *Jos. Asen.* 8:5; and *Sib. Or.* 3:763) utilize the living God in contexts where he is the object of human blessing or reverence. The living God is the proper object of reverence for both Jews and Gentiles alike.

Further, Hellenistic Jews promoted the living God as the proper object of worship in connection with designating the Jerusalem temple as his special "house" (Dan 4:19, 5:23 LXX). For Hellenistic Jews, the Jerusalem temple was the "house of the living God," the locus and symbol of the true worship in the Hellenistic world. The living God makes the temple his "house," but his real dwelling is in heaven (Dan 4:23 [27] LXX; 2 Macc 15:4; 3 Macc 6:28). The living God "lived" in heaven as an eternal and invisible God, transcending the earthly realm. This God was incapable of material representation and was thus properly worshiped without images in the temple and Diaspora synagogues. Hellenistic Jews thus directed their worship to the transcendent heavenly God who lives forever.

Liturgical formulations expressing God's eternal character suggest the Hellenistic Jewish strategy of stressing God's uniqueness and superiority in a polytheistic milieu. Whereas idols were handmade and subject to the ravages of time, the living God was eternal, imperishable, living forever and ever (Esth 8:12q LXX; *Jos. Asen.* 19.8; Philo, *Decalogue* 67; *Sib. Or.* 3:762–66; Sir 18:1; Tob 13:1; Dan 6:27–28 LXX). This uniqueness of the eternally living God is an expression of God's unique identity as sole creator and lord. Describing God as the One who lives forever serves to characterize the uniqueness of the creator who alone made the heaven and the earth with no assistance.[43]

The missionary significance of the epithet emerges in several Jewish texts that portray Gentiles acknowledging the reality of the living God or converting. These examples reflect how

---

43. Dalbert, *Die Theologie*, 124–25.

Hellenistic Jews promoted the living God to Gentiles in their missionary appeals. One way in which Jews promoted the living God was to stress his uniqueness as the only true God; he alone is truly God and there is no other (*Sib. Or.* 3:761; Bel 41 Th; *Jos. Asen.* 11:10). In this way, Hellenistic Jews were able to differentiate the living God from other gods and stress his superior character. As universal creator and lord, the living God alone was worthy of Gentile worship, a point repeatedly made in narrative portrayals of Gentiles who acknowledge the reality and power of the living God (3 Macc 6:28; Esth 8:12q LXX; Dan 6:26–27 LXX; Bel 23–42 Th; and *Jos. Asen.* 11:7–10). Gentiles should give exclusive devotion to the living God because he alone is their creator and lord.

Another way in which Hellenistic Jews promoted their living God to Gentiles was to stress his active character in delivering his people. Gentiles witness firsthand the power of the living God in delivering Daniel or the Jewish people and they respond with acclamations acknowledging the reality of the living God (Dan 6:26–27 LXX; Bel 23–42 Th; 3 Macc 6:28). The Jewish God is thus powerfully alive in contrast to the other gods who are nothing more than lifeless handmade idols.

Finally, Hellenistic Jews promoted a living God who was powerfully alive against idolatrous Gentiles and the missionary appeal here involved the threat of judgment. The living God was a "jealous and terrible God toward those who worshiped strange gods" (*Jos. Asen.* 11:8). The living God is angered by Gentile idolatry and will hold Gentiles accountable for it. God's living wrath was directed against idolators and manifested in the exercise of judgment (*Sib. Or.* 3:762–66; Dan 5:23, 26–28 LXX; and *Jos. Asen.* 11:8). This link between idolatry and the living God's anger is expressed in Jer 10:10: " . . . at his wrath the earth quakes and the nations cannot endure his indignation." Further, the threat of the living God's wrath was countered by the picture of a merciful and compassionate living God, who welcomes repentant Gentiles into a filial relationship. The living God invites Gentiles to flee from the idolatry and divine wrath into the arms of a forgiving divine father.

How does this Jewish background of the living God help in

understanding Paul's use of the epithet? This background represents a significant influence upon Paul and his proclamation of the living God. As a missionary, Paul proclaimed the living God as the eternally living creator God who alone was the proper object of Gentile worship. In response, he converted Gentiles and founded Gentile communities whose identities were bound up with the living God in churches or temples of the living God (1 Tim 3:15; 2 Cor 6:16).

Chapter Five

The Living God in Paul's Monotheistic Kerygma

In this chapter, I will establish and clarify Paul's missionary preaching of the living God, which was his primary means of introducing monotheism to Gentile audiences. Three texts will serve as the evidential base that illustrates Paul as proclaimer of the living God: 1 Thess 1:9–10 and two post-Pauline texts, Acts 14:15; and *Acts Paul* 7:2. While interpreters widely acknowledge living God's function in Paul's kerygma, little has been done to gather up and explore the full range of evidence supporting this function. Previous studies have therefore suffered from an incompleteness that the following discussion hopes to correct.

A second and related task of this chapter is to explore what Paul taught his Gentile converts about the living God. Going beyond the brief excerpts of kerygma found in 1 Thess 1:9–10; Acts 14:15; and *Acts Paul* 7:2, one wonders how Paul would have explained the living God to his Gentile converts. In what ways was God "living"? I will attempt to answer this question by amplifying the excerpts of Paul's kerygma, using Paul's own God-talk (Rom 1:18–25 and 1 Cor 8:4–6) and the Jewish background of the living God. The latter is particularly useful in filling out the Pauline picture of the living God. Paul followed in the footsteps of Hellenistic Jews in promoting the living God as the one God and creator of all people, Jew and Gentile alike. However, Paul's teaching on the living God was no simple continuation of Jewish views since, for Paul, the living God had also raised Jesus from the dead. Paul's teaching on the living God thus repre-

sents something new and distinctive with respect to the earlier
Jewish tradition.

Paul as Proclaimer of the Living God

1 Thess 1:9–10[1]

First Thessalonians 1:9–10 is one text affirming that Paul was
a missionary who customarily proclaimed the living God in his
monotheistic kerygma to Gentiles. First Thessalonians 1:9–10
occurs in the letter's thanksgiving period, a period that is un-
usually long, stretching from 1:2 to 3:13, making it a lengthy
section in the letter.[2] Within the framework of this extended
thanksgiving period, 1 Thess 1:2–10 serves to remind the Thessalonians of their missionary origins, as well as serving to ground
Paul's subsequent exhortation in the letter.[3] First Thessalonians
thus begins "... by looking back on a process that began with
the 'turning' or 'conversion' of the addressees from idols to
serve a living and true God."[4]

Numerous kerygmatic and conversion motifs are found in
1 Thess 1:4–10, thus providing important evidence for establishing the kerygmatic character of 1:9–10. The latter is part
of a wider network of allusions to kerygma and conversion in
1 Thess 1. For example, an allusion to conversion appears in
1 Thess 1:4 in reference to the community's divine "election."
Paul says, "for we know, brethren beloved by God, that he has

---

1. Acts 17:1–9 describes Paul's visit to Thessalonika, but it remains silent on
his founding of a Gentile community. Luke's account, while valuable as a reminiscence of events in Thessalonika, has been shaped to serve Luke's purposes
(Abraham Malherbe, *Paul and the Thessalonians: The Philosophic Tradition of Pastoral
Care* [Philadelphia: Fortress Press, 1987], 12–17).

2. Paul Schubert, *Form and Function of the Pauline Thanksgivings* (Berlin: Töpelmann, 1939), 16–27. In this view, the thanksgiving period begun in 1:2–5 is brought
to its formal conclusion in 3:10–13. See also Ernest Best, *The First and Second Epistle
to the Thessalonians* (BNTC; repr., London: A. & C. Black, 1986), 33–35, 65.

3. 1:2–10 is sometimes described as philophronetic in function, serving to pre-
pare for the subsequent exhortations in chaps. 4–5. B. Rigaux, *Saint Paul: Les épîtres
aux Thessaloniciens* (Paris: Librairie Lecoffre/J. Gabalda, 1956), observes that "the
apostle engages in a long explication of his relations with the Thessalonians at the
foundation of the church."

4. Wayne Meeks, *The Moral World of the First Christians* (Philadelphia: Westminster, 1986), 125–26.

chosen you" (εἰδότες ἀδελφοὶ ἠγαπημένοι ὑπὸ τοῦ θεοῦ, τὴν ἐκλογὴν ὑμῶν). Paul does not explain what he means by the term "election," indicating that it was already familiar to the Thessalonians.[5] While the meaning of the term is not entirely clear, Paul's use of it in Rom 9–11 is helpful. In Rom 11:5, for example, the term designates God's election of a remnant from Israel through the gospel: "So too at the present time there is a remnant chosen by grace." Significantly, then, the term is applied to Christian converts who have accepted the gospel and so have been divinely elected. Divine election of the Thessalonians is the result of God "calling" through the gospel (1 Thess 2:12; 4:7; 5:24).

In 1:5, Paul clarifies how the Thessalonians came to be divinely elected: "because (ὅτι) our gospel came to you not only in word, but also in power and the Holy Spirit (ἐν δυνάμει καὶ ἐν πνεύματι ἁγίῳ) with full conviction." The gospel comes to the Thessalonians "in power and the Spirit," suggesting that the Spirit's activity accompanied Paul's preaching and played a role in the conversion of the Thessalonians (cf. 1 Cor 2:4–5).[6] Later on, in 1 Thess 4:7, Paul reminds the Thessalonians that God is the one "who gives his Holy Spirit" and who called them to holiness. Conversion, then, is the result of God's elective activity manifested through the preaching of the gospel and the accompanying activity of the Spirit.

In 1 Thess 1:6–7, Paul recalls the Thessalonian acceptance of the gospel: "And you became imitators of us and of the Lord, for you received the word in much affliction, with joy inspired by the Holy Spirit; so that you became an example to all the believers in Macedonia and in Achaia." God's election of the Thessalonians is further evident from their acceptance of the word in affliction and with joy inspired by the Spirit.[7] In 1:8, Paul continues: "for not only has the word of the Lord sounded

---

5. The term ἐκλογή is absent from the LXX, but is found in Rom 9–11 four times: Rom 9:11; 11:5, 7, 28.

6. Malherbe, *Paul and the Thessalonians,* 29.

7. This Thessalonian reception of the word is again mentioned in 1 Thess 2:13: "And we also thank God constantly for this, that when you received the word of God which you received from us, you accepted it not as the word of men but as what it really is, the word of God, which is at work in you believers."

forth from you in Macedonia and Achaia, but your faith in God
has gone forth everywhere, so that we need not say anything."
Not only have the Thessalonians been exemplary in spreading
the "word," but their reputation as believers has spread everywhere (cf. Rom 1:8).[8] With the mention of "faith" (πίστις) in
1:8, the conversion theme is once again sounded. The expression "faith in God" (πρὸς τὸν θεόν) designates conversion as a
coming to faith in the one true God, that is, as a movement "toward" (πρός) the one God away from false gods. This movement
toward the one God is clarified in the next verse (1:9) where
conversion is described as a turning "toward" God from idols.[9]
Thessalonian "faith in God," then, is conversion faith founded
upon the acceptance of the one true God.[10]

In 1:9–10, Paul continues the thought of 1:8 by affirming the
good reputation of the Thessalonians. Paul and his coworkers
had heard from the people of Macedonia and Achaea about his
initial "welcome" among the Thessalonians:

> For the people of those regions [Macedonia and Achaea]
> report concerning us what kind of welcome we had among
> you, and how you turned to God from idols, to serve a
> living and true God (καὶ πῶς ἐπεστρέψατε πρὸς τὸν θεὸν
> ἀπὸ τῶν εἰδώλων δουλεύειν θεῷ ζῶντι καὶ ἀληθινῷ) and
> to wait for his son from heaven, whom he raised from the
> dead, Jesus, who rescues us from the wrath to come.

These two verses are widely viewed as a recollection of Paul's
missionary preaching in Thessalonika,[11] a claim which is supported by the parallels of Acts 14:15 and *Acts Paul* 7:2 to be

---

8. Paul further discusses the Thessalonian "faith" in chap. 3. For example in
3:2, Paul speaks of Timothy having been sent back to the Thessalonians to establish
them "in their faith" (cf. 3:5, 6, 7).

9. Paul-Émile Langevin, *Jésus Seigneur et l'eschatologie. Exégese de textes prépauliniens*
(Studia: travaux de recherche 21; Paris: Desclée de Brouwer, 1967), 47–48, observes
the coherence of 1:8–10 as a unit from the parallel statements of 1:8a, 1:8b, and
1:9a. See also Rigaux, *Saint Paul: Les épîtres aux Thessaloniciens*, 387.

10. Best, *Thessalonians*, 65.

11. R. Bultmann, *Theology of the New Testament* (trans. K. Grobel; New York: Scribner's, 1951, 1955), 1:67; Günther Bornkamm, *Early Christian Experience* (New York:
Harper & Row, 1966), 32; Weiss, *The History of Primitive Christianity*, 1:233; Malherbe, *Paul and the Thessalonians*, 30–31; Best, *Thessalonians*, 86; Langevin, *Jésus
Seigneur*, 60; Everding, "The Living God," 318; and Gerhard Schneider, "Urchrist-

examined below. From these verses it is also clear that the Thessalonian community consisted of former idol-worshipers who converted from idolatry.[12]

However, the lack of explicit reference to Christ's crucifixion in these verses is odd and needs clarification.[13] First, the language in these verses is likely an excerpt of what Paul had preached and not representative of his whole kerygma.[14] In these verses Paul is selective in stressing certain elements of his monotheistic kerygma, which served a specific epistolary purpose in 1 Thessalonians.[15] Second, the language of 1 Thess 1:9–10 has an "unpauline" character in the sense that it reflects traditional kerygma employed by other Christian missionaries that had roots in Jewish tradition. In these verses Paul apparently employs a traditional kerygma that he inherited from early Christian tradition, and so the excerpt of 1 Thess 1:9–10, as traditional kerygma, should not be expected to convey Paul's special interest in the crucified Christ (cf. Rom 1:3–4).

A closer look at the traditional character of the language in 1 Thess 1:9–10 furnishes some insight into the function and significance of the living God in the Pauline kerygma. Traditional character is evident from a number of points, beginning with a concentration of *hapax legomena*.[16] For example, the de-

---

liche Gottesverkündigung in hellenistischer Umwelt," *Biblische Zeitschrift* 13 (1969): 59–75.

12. It is possible that 1:9–10 refers to Gentile God-fearers formerly attached to the synagogue in Thessalonika (cf. Acts 17:4).

13. The statement in 1:10 about Jesus being "raised from the dead" implies his crucifixion. However, based on the lack of any reference to the cross, some do not accept these verses as a summary of Paul's preaching. On this see J. Munck, "1 Thessalonians 1:9–10 and the Missionary Preaching of Paul," *NTS* 9 (1962–63): 104–5. However, see Best, *Thessalonians*, 87, for a critique of Munck's position. G. Friedrich "Ein Tauflied hellenisticher Judenchristen: 1 Thess. 1,9 f.," *Theologische Zeitschrift* 2 (1965): 502–16, argues for the function of these verses in baptismal liturgy.

14. Best, *Thessalonians*, 87. Robert M. Grant, *Gods and the One God* (LEC; Philadelphia: Westminster, 1986), 46, observes of 1 Thess 1:9 that every item in this statement requires amplification and proof and presumably received it in the apostle's preaching."

15. Commentators generally acknowledge the significance of 1:9–10 in anticipating themes taken up later in 1 Thess 4–5, especially the eschatological themes in 4:13–5:11. Best, *Thessalonians*, 87; Earl J. Richard, *First and Second Thessalonians* (Sacra Pagina; Collegeville, Minn.: Liturgical Press, 1995), 74.

16. Richard, *First and Second Thessalonians*, 53, observes that "there are an unusual number of non-Pauline terms and idioms clustered in verses 9–10. . . . " See also

scription of God as "living and true" is found nowhere else in the New Testament and is a typically Jewish designation for God (Jer 10:10; *Jos. Asen.* 11:10).[17]

Further, in verse 9, there is the term "to turn" (ἐπιστρέφειν), which is found only three times in Paul's letters, occurring here and twice elsewhere in Gal 4:9 and 2 Cor 3:16. However, Paul prefers the use of other terminology in speaking about conversion, particularly, the terminology of faith, using the verb "to believe" (Rom 13:11; 1 Cor 3:5; 15:2; Gal 2:16).[18] 1 Thess 1:8 is a good example of Paul's preferred manner of expression, referring to the Thessalonian "faith in God." In biblical and Jewish tradition, the term "to turn" in biblical and Jewish tradition, was a term for repentance designating Israel's "return" to God from sinful ways.[19] However, in early Christianity the term acquired a technical sense for conversion from idols, as, for example, in Acts of the Apostles.[20] The term was useful in designating a movement from pagan unbelief to the convert's exclusive commitment to God (*Jos. Asen.* 11:10; Acts 14:15; 15:19; 26:18). In conversion, the convert "turns" from idols to an exclusive commitment to the one God, entailing a radical break with the past. Best observes that this technical use of the term "brings out the extent of the rupture with pagan ways."[21]

Moreover, the Jewish roots of 1 Thess 1:9 emerge in the an-

Collins, *Studies in the First Letter to the Thessalonians*, 254; Everding, "The Living God," 318; Langevin, *Jésus Seigneur et l'eschatologie*, 53–55; Rigaux, *Saint Paul*, 389; Best, *Thessalonians*, 82; and Bussmann, *Themen der paulinischen Missionspredigt*, 45–56.

17. Everding, "The Living God," 318; Best, *Thessalonians*, 82–83; Bussmann, *Themen der paulinischen Missionspredigt*, 45; Friedrich, "Ein Tauflied," 504–5; Rigaux, *Saint Paul*, 392–93; and Langevin, *Jésus Seigneur et l'eschatologie*, 67–68

18. A close relation between "believing" and "turning" to God is illustrated in Acts 11:21. Also, in 1 Thess 1:6; 2:13, conversion is expressed as a "receiving" of the word (Best, *Thessalonians*, 82; Richard, *First and Second Thessalonians*, 54).

19. The term goes back to the Hebrew term *teshubah*. In Israel's scriptures the term is found in the prophetic preaching of repentance, in which Israel is urged to "return" to covenantal loyalty, e.g., Jer 3:12; 4:1; 5:3; Hos 3:5, 5:4; 6:1; 7:10, etc. On the biblical and Jewish background of the term see Langevin, *Jesus Seigneur*, 59; Rigaux, *Les épîtres aux Thessaloniciens*, 389; Richard, *First and Second Thessalonians*, 53–54; and Bussmann, *Themen der paulinischen Missionspredigt*, 39.

20. Acts 3:19; 9:35; 11:21; 14:15; 15:19; 18:20; 28:27. See also 1 Pet 2:25 and James 5:20 for this technical use. See Beverly R. Gaventa, *From Darkness to Light* (Philadelphia: Fortress Press, 1986), 41–42.

21. Best, *Thessalonians*, 82. Along these lines, Richard, *First and Second Thessalonians*, 54.

tithesis between idols and God, a pattern of language that recalls Jewish formulations previously discussed, e.g., *Jos. Asen.* 8:5 and Bel 5 Th.[22] That 1 Thess 1:9b employs the living God antithetically is evident from the close relation of the two clauses in 1:9b: "and how you turned to God from idols, to serve a living and true God."[23] The antithesis between God and idols in the first clause extends to the living and true God of the second. The God to whom the Thessalonians "turned" in the first clause is the living and true God of the second.

Also reflecting a Jewish background in 1:9b is the expression of the convert "serving" God (δουλεύειν), a striking expression in light of Paul's penchant for using servant/Lord terminology in connection with Christ.[24] More commonly for Paul, however, "Jesus is the Lord" whom the believer "serves" (2 Cor 4:5; Rom 10:9; Phil 2:11). It is therefore unusual to find 1 Thess 1:9 expressing the result of conversion as the convert serving God.[25] Converts "serve" the God who is living and true, implying the lordship of the living God. Implied here is the notion that Gentile conversion entailed a change of lordships, moving from bondage to pagan gods to a new life rendered in service to the living God.[26] In Jewish tradition also, monotheism entails being a "servant" to the living God and "service" entailed both worship and adherence to the commandments.[27]

---

22. Rigaux, *Les épîtres aux Thessaloniciens*, 392; Best, *Thessalonians*, 86. Bussmann, *Themen der paulinischen Missionspredigt*, 54, observes that 1 Thess 1:9–10 has all the marks of a hellenistic-Jewish missionary formulation that had been modified in pre-Pauline Christian circles.

23. Everding, "The Living God," 315–16, observes that 1 Thess 1:9 forms a "precise antithesis" between the living God and idols. Cf. Richard, *First and Second Thessalonians*, 52.

24. The exceptions are Rom 6:22 and Gal 4:8–9 (Bussmann, *Themen der paulinischen Missionspredigt*, 43).

25. Richard, *First and Second Thessalonians*, 55, observes that the theme of serving God "emanates from non-Pauline Jewish thinking, a usage nonetheless with which Paul would have been sympathetic."

26. This "service" to the one God is reflected in Gal 4:8–9: "Formerly when you did not know God, you were in bondage (ἐδουλεύσατε) to beings that by nature are no gods; but now that you have come to know God, or rather, be known by God, how can you turn back again to the weak and beggarly elemental spirits, whose slaves you want to be once more?"

27. For example, Daniel is described as a "servant" of the living God (Dan 6:20 MT); and in Dan 6:27 LXX, the Gentile sympathizer promises to "adore and serve (προσκυνῶν καὶ δουλεύων) him [the living God]." Hellenistic Jews could refer to

Shifting attention to 1 Thess 1:10, the christological content
of this verse is also "uncharacteristic" of Paul, further suggesting
his indebtedness to traditional formulations. For example, God
raised Jesus, his "son," from the dead, a statement that links
Jesus' sonship to the eschatological event of the parousia.[28] As
interpreters frequently note, this use of "son" in an eschatological setting is unusual, since Paul prefers the titles of "Lord" or
"Christ" when referring to the parousia.[29] Further, the relative
clause in 1:10, "whom he raised from the dead," is a traditional
formulation used in early Christian preaching (e.g., Acts 3:14;
4:10; 1 Pet 1:21; Heb 11:19; Rom 4:24, etc.).[30] Finally, the last
clause of 1:10 asserts that the resurrected Jesus is he "who delivers us from the coming wrath." Again, traditional character is
evident in several elements, specifically, in the theme of "coming wrath" and in the verb "to deliver."[31] In this context, God's
wrath is likely directed against Gentile idolatry, something that
would have motivated potential converts to convert.

These observations on 1 Thess 1:9–10 thus suggest that Paul's
monotheistic kerygma reflects his inheritance and use of language from Jewish and early Christian tradition. Paul, in his
proclamation of the living God to Gentiles, stood in continuity with a preaching strategy developed in earlier Jewish and
Christian traditions.

---

their one God as the "living Lord" (2 Macc 7:33; 15:4). 2 Macc 7:33 is interesting
in that the "living Lord" is "angry" with the Jewish nation, which he rebukes and
disciplines; but "he will again be reconciled with his own servants."

28. Interpreters detect in 1:10 evidence of an early Christian Son of Man tradition
that has been modified and fused with a Son of God tradition (Richard, *First and
Second Thessalonians*, 56; Bussmann, *Themen der paulinischen Missionspredigt*, 46; and
Collins, *Studies in the First Letter to the Thessalonians*, 256). Also, the use of ἀναμένειν
is uncharacteristic in the eschatological context of 1:10.

29. 1 Cor 1:8; 2 Cor 1:14; Phil 1:6; 1 Thess 4:16; 5:23. Best, *Thessalonians*, 86,
observes that "the clauses about the resurrection and the Parousia may come from
an earlier period when the Church was exclusively Jewish Christian."

30. The clause ὅν ἤγειρεν ἐκ τῶν νεκρῶν employs the definite article τῶν, which
is not typical of Paul who prefers the expression ἐγήρεν ἐκ νεκρῶν (Collins, *Studies*,
254–55; Bultmann, *Theology of the New Testament*, 1:80–83; Bussmann, *Themen der
paulinischen Missionspredigt*, 51; and Langevin, *Jésus Seigneur*, 85–87).

31. In speaking of eschatological deliverance, ῥύεσθαι is unusual since Paul more
often employs the verb σῴζειν. Also, the preaching of impending wrath was traditional in early Christianity (e.g., Acts 17:31 and Hebrews 6:2). Bultmann, *Theology
of the New Testament*, 1:73–77.

Evidence of the Living God in Post-Pauline Sources

If 1 Thessalonians 1:9–10 were the only evidence of the living God in Paul's kerygma, this would be a flimsy foundation, indeed, for the claim that Paul customarily proclaimed the living God. One would expect more evidence if Paul did, in fact, regularly proclaim the living God to Gentiles. Fortunately, however, there are other texts that support this claim: the post-Pauline sources of Acts of the Apostles and the *Acts of Paul and Thecla.*[32] These post-Pauline sources confirm Paul's use of the living God in missionary preaching to Gentiles and serve to broaden the evidential base beyond that of 1 Thess 1:9–10.

In using these post-Pauline sources to supplement 1 Thess 1:9–10, however, caution must be exercised. On the one hand, these sources stand in some kind of continuity with and thus reflect genuine Pauline tradition of the living God; on the other hand, they may also represent the enrichments and developments of later post-Pauline tradition. In the following discussion, then, I will therefore be careful not to assume simply that Acts 14:15 and *Acts Paul* 7:2 represent genuine Pauline tradition; rather, these two sources will be explored in a critical manner to show that they do, in fact, contain a genuine reminiscence of Paul proclaiming the living God in antithesis to idols. 1 Thessalonians 1:9 will therefore be employed as a critical control on post-Pauline tradition, enabling the recognition of genuine living God tradition in post-Pauline sources.

Acts 14:15–17

Paul's preaching of the living God in Acts 14:15 is strikingly parallel to 1 Thess 1:9 and is often considered in discussions of the latter.[33] The language of Acts 14:15–17 comes as part of a

---

32. 1 Tim 4:10 could be added to the list of evidence, since it uses the living God in a kerygmatic context. However, it does not present the epithet in antithesis to idols and so will not be included. Mark J. Goodwin, "The Pauline Background of the Living God as Interpretive Context for 1 Timothy 4.10," *JSNT* 61 (1996): 65–85.

33. The significance of Acts 14:15 as a parallel to 1 Thess 1:9 is recognized by some interpreters. For example, Best, *Thessalonians,* 87; Richard, *First and Second Thessalonians,* 52; F. F. Bruce, *1 and 2 Thessalonians* (WBC; Waco, Tex.: Word Books, 1982), 17; and K. Lake and H. J. Cadbury, *The Beginnings of Christianity. Part 1: The Acts of the Apostles* (trans. and ed. K. Lake and F. J. F. Jackson; 5 vols.; repr., Grand Rapids: Baker, 1979), 4:166.

short missionary speech that is clearly marked by the hand of Luke, but also involves a reminiscence of Paul's actual preaching among the Gentiles. A number of observations support this claim. Luke has not relied on Paul's letters in composing his Acts speeches, and so literary borrowing cannot explain why Acts 14:15 is strikingly parallel to 1 Thess 1:9.[34] Either Acts 14:15–17 is grounded in actual Pauline tradition or it makes use of an early Christian kerygma commonly used in the first century.[35] These two options are not mutually exclusive and, either way, Luke remembers Paul as a preacher of the living God. Acts 14:15 can therefore be taken as reflecting the kind of kerygma employed by Paul and other early Christian missionaries.

Further, however inventive Luke was in crafting his episodes, he likely drew upon traditional sources that provided reminiscences of Paul's actual missionary work and preaching. Second Timothy 3:10–11 provides evidence supporting the existence of such a source in Luke's composition of Acts 14. Second Timothy 3:10–11 reflects a tradition of Paul's missionary work in Antioch, Iconium, and Lystra, similar to the setting in Acts 14: "Now you have observed my teaching, my conduct, my aim in life, my faith, my patience, my love, my steadfastness, my persecutions, my sufferings, what befell me at Antioch, at Iconium, and at Lystra . . . "[36] (2 Tim 3:10–11).

A final observation indicates the reliability of Acts 14:15 as a witness of the living God in Paul's kerygma. In the whole corpus of Luke-Acts the living God epithet is employed only once, in Acts 14:15. Of all the speeches in Acts, it is striking that the living God is found only in that speech where Paul addresses

---

34. The consensus is that Acts represents an independent witness in regard to Paul's letters. Raymond Brown, *An Introduction to the New Testament* (New York: Doubleday, 1997), 324; and David Wenham, "Acts and the Pauline Corpus II: The Evidence of Parallels," *The Book of Acts in Its First Century Setting* (Grand Rapids: Eerdmans, 1993), 215–58.

35. The work of Ulrich Wilckens, *Die Missionsreden der Apostelgeschichte: Form- und traditionsgeschichtliche Untersuchungen* (WMANT 5; Neukirchen-Vluyn: Neukirchener Verlag, 1961, 1963) should be mentioned here. Wilckens observed that Luke's sermons to Gentile audiences in Acts 14:15–17 and 17:22–31 were based upon traditional Christian kerygma represented in 1 Thess 1:9–10 and Heb 5:11–6:2.

36. Ernst Haenchen, *The Acts of the Apostles: A Commentary* (Philadelphia: Westminster, 1971), 433.

an idolatrous pagan audience. This singular usage of the living God thus attests to Luke's awareness of a special connection between Paul and the living God.

Luke's use of the epithet comes in Paul's speech at Lystra and occurs in the narrative unit of Acts 14:8–18, which has a characteristic Lucan style. Extensive similarities between it and the sermon in Acts 17:22–31 are evident.[37] The composition of the unit is masterful in evoking a pagan milieu: "every detail in this account contributes to this masterfully composed portrait of a rural pagan village."[38] At the beginning of the episode Paul and Barnabas flee from Iconium to Lystra to escape from hostile crowds (14:5–6). Upon their arrival in Lystra, the two missionaries encounter a cripple, whom they heal in the sight of the populace (14:8–10). This display of divine power at work in the apostles (14:14) creates an overwhelming impression, provoking the populace to deify the two apostles. Based upon the miracle, the Lystrans believe that Zeus and Hermes have appeared in mortal guise among them, taking Barnabas as Zeus and Paul as Hermes because "he was the chief speaker" (14:12). Further, "the priest of Zeus, whose temple was in front of the city, brought oxen and garlands to the gates and wanted to offer sacrifice with the people" (14:13).

In horrified response, Barnabas and Paul tear their garments and remonstrate with the people:

> Men, why are you doing this? We are also men, of like nature with you, and bring you good news, that you should turn from these vain things to a living God (εὐαγγελιζόμενοι ὑμᾶς ἀπὸ τούτων τῶν ματαίων ἐπιστρέφειν ἐπὶ θεὸν ζῶντα), who made the heaven and the earth and the sea and all that is in them.[39] In past generations he allowed all the nations to walk in their own ways; yet he did not

---

37. Martin Dibelius, *Studies in the Acts of the Apostles* (trans. M. Ling; ed. H. Greeven; London: SCM, 1956), 71–72. Eduard Schweizer, "Concerning the Speeches in Acts," in *Studies in Luke-Acts* (ed. Leander E. Keck and J. Louis Martyn; Philadelphia: Fortress Press, 1980), 208–16.

38. Carl Holladay, "Acts," *Harper's Bible Commentary* (ed. James L. Mays; San Francisco and New York: Harper & Row, 1988), 1097.

39. The participle εὐαγγελιζόμενοι has no direct object as one would expect; however, a variant witness, Codex D, does furnish one: ὑμῖν τὸν θεὸν ὅπως κτλ.

leave himself without witnesses, for he did good and gave
you from the heavens rains and fruitful seasons, satisfying
your hearts with food and gladness. (Acts 14:15–17)

This address to the Lystrans represents "the first sermon to Gentiles delivered without any connection with the synagogue and
the facilities it offered to Gentile sympathizers."[40] The content
and brevity of the speech are determined by the immediate
situation to which it responds: the speech aims at preventing
the Lystrans from deifying Paul and Barnabas. In this setting,
then, there was no need for articulating the kerygma in its en-
tirety, thus clarifying the absence of any reference to Jesus in
the speech.[41]

This speech gives us a sense of how Paul would have presented the monotheistic kerygma in a popular pagan setting,
and it illustrates the usefulness of the living God in counter-
ing pagan polytheism. After asserting that he and Barnabas
were "men" of like mortal nature with the Lystrans, Paul
then encouraged the Lystrans to abandon "vain things" (τῶν
ματαίων), a term for idolatry in the LXX and Jewish literature.[42] As in 1 Thess 1:9, idolatrous Gentiles are urged "to turn"
(ἐπιστρέφειν) from their idolatrous practices to a living God,
Who alone is worthy of Gentile reverence. Early Christians frequently employed the verb "to turn" in their kerygma, as, for
example, in Acts 2:38; 3:19, etc. A significant parallel to Acts
14:15 is found in Acts 15:19–20, where James, at the Jerusalem
council, advises that "we should not trouble those of the Gentiles who turn to God, but should write them to abstain from
the pollutions of idols...."[43]

---

40. Haenchen, *Acts of the Apostles*, 431.

41. Christology is implied in the mention of the good news (εὐαγγελιζόμενοι) in
14:15 and in 14:9, where the cripple is said to have "the faith to be made well"
(πίστιν του σωθῆναι). Haenchen, *Acts of the Apostles*, 431, observes that the latter
"presupposes that Paul had been speaking of Jesus as σωτήρ."

42. The expression designates idolatry in 2 Chr 11:5 LXX; Hos 5:1 LXX; Ezek
8:10 LXX; Jer 2:5, 10:3 LXX; Wis 13:1; *Let. Arist.* 134; etc. On this usage see Everding,
"The Living God," 321–22; Haenchen, *The Acts of the Apostles*, 428; and Gerhard
Schneider, *Die Apostelgeschichte* (HTKNT 5; 2 vols.; Freiburg: Herder, 1982), 2:160.

43. In Acts 15:19–20 the requirements for Gentile converts are likely derived
from the Mosaic Law, specifically Lev 17–18. If so, then the Gentile converts are

Next, the main subject of the address is announced with the mention of the living God.[44] Paul urges the Lystrans to turn "to a living God who made the heaven and the earth and the sea and all that is in them" (ὅς ἐποίησεν τὸν οὐρανὸν καὶ τὴν γῆν καὶ τὴν θάλασσαν καὶ πάντα τὰ ἐν αὐτοῖς).[45] Paul employs here a biblically styled relative clause that clarifies the identity of the living God as the biblical creator who made heaven and earth. The clause is a common biblical expression (e.g., Exod 20:11 LXX; Ps 145:6 LXX; Isa 42:5 LXX; Jer 10:11 MT; Acts 4:24; etc.). Paul's speech amounts to "a brief homily on the providence of the living Creator."[46] Later in the Areopagus speech, Paul speaks similarly about God as creator: "the God who made the world and everything in it, being Lord of heaven and earth, does not live in shrines made by hand, nor is he served by human hands, as though he needed anything, since he himself gives to all men life and breath and everything" (Acts 17:24–25). This identification of the living God as the biblical creator reflects a Jewish tradition, as in Bel 5 Th, where the living God is he "who has created heaven and earth and has dominion over all flesh." Acts 14:15, like Bel 5 Th, identifies the living God as the creator in a context of idol polemic, recalling how the living God is traditionally set in opposition to dead idols and thus defined as creator.[47]

Acts 14:15, with its identification of the living God as biblical creator, provides a basis for inferring the presence of the creator theme in 1 Thess 1:9–10. The latter is an excerpt of kerygma that does not represent the whole of Paul's preaching.

---

viewed as acquiring a status similar to that of resident aliens within the Jewish-Christian community.

44. Marion L. Soards, *The Speeches in Acts: Their Content, Context, and Concerns* (Louisville: Westminster/John Knox, 1994), 89.

45. Acts 4:24 offers a parallel use of the formula: "And when they heard it, they lifted their voices and said, "Sovereign Lord, who did make the heaven and the earth and the sea and everything in them, who by the mouth of our father David, your servant...."

46. Grant, *Gods and the One God*, 20–21.

47. Everding, "The Living God," 322–23; and Stenger, "Die gottesbezeichnung 'lebendiger Gott,'" 63–64. Jacques Dupont, O.S.B., *The Salvation of the Gentiles: Studies in the Acts of the Apostles* (trans. J. R. Keating; New York: Paulist, 1979), 70, observes of Acts 14:15 that "Christians merely take over the formula that the Jews used to describe the conversion of pagans to the one true God of Israel...."

Paul would have certainly clarified the fuller meaning of the living God for his Gentile audiences as the life-giving creator. That Paul taught the living God as creator is suggested not only from Acts 14:15, but also from Jewish background of the living God, e.g., Bel 5 Th. The living God's identity as creator is traditional and implicit in antithetical formulations of idol polemic. Further, the creator theme in 1 Thess 1:9–10 manifests itself in the living God's act of raising Jesus, an act of life-giving and new creation.[48] In raising Jesus, the living God had acted as creator in giving life.

Acts 14:15 thus confirms the portrait of Paul as proclaimer of the living God to Gentiles, serving to reinforce what was previously concluded from 1 Thess 1:9. While the formulations in 1 Thess 1:9 and Acts 14:15 are not exactly identical, they are still very similar in their basic structure. Both formulations employ antitheses that contrast the living God and idols; and both passages use the verb "to turn" in clarifying conversion as a radical break from idolatry. First Thessalonians 1:9–10 and Acts 14:15 thus indicate Paul's strategy in teaching monotheism to Gentile audiences, a strategy that promoted the one true living God in antithesis to other gods.

Further, Acts 14:15 helps in clarifying how Paul understood God's "living" character. In Acts 14:15, God was "living" not only in the sense of having created the world and sustaining it; God was also "living" in miraculous cures that were effected through apostles Paul and Barnabas. The apostles' healing of the cripple in 14:8–10 also serves to demonstrate the living God's life-giving activity.[49]

Acts of Paul and Thecla 7:2

The *Acts of Paul and Thecla* is generally dated to the late second century[50] and is viewed as an instance of early Christian

---

48. Best, *Thessalonians*, 82–83, observes of 1 Thess 1:9–10 that "the living God is not merely one who is alive but one who gives life, both the life of creation and the new life of redemption."

49. The speech in Acts 14:15–17 may serve to interpret the miraculous cure in 14:8–10.

50. Johannes Quasten, *Patrology* (3 vols.; repr., Westminster, Md.: Christian Classics, 1990), 1:130. Wilhelm Schneemelcher, *New Testament Apocrypha* (trans. R. McL.

popular literature written for purposes of edification and entertainment.[51] As a literary work, the *Acts of Paul* is episodic in character, consisting of a sequence of episodes loosely framed by narrative links that tell the story of Paul's missionary travels in Asia Minor. The Pauline speech is a primary literary device employed in the work, which gives expression to important aspects of Christian belief in the second century. Of note are a few speeches in which Paul uses the living God in his address to Gentile audiences.[52] Of these speeches, *Acts Paul* 7:2 is especially significant because it presents Paul speaking of the living God in antithesis to idols, furnishing a parallel to the previous formulations in 1 Thess 1:9 and Acts 14:15. Typically, scholarly discussion has neglected this and other occurrences of the living God in the *Acts of Paul* as possible sources of living God tradition.[53] The following discussion will thus attempt to redress this neglect by exploring *Acts Paul* 7:2 as a reminiscence of the living God in Paul's first century preaching.

Is it possible that the *Acts of Paul* reflects Paul's first century preaching of the living God? The issue of the work's historical reliability has been debated for about a century and involves complex literary questions that are bound up with determining the literary relationship of the *Acts of Paul* to New Testament sources, particularly canonical Acts, Paul's letters, and the Pas-

---

Wilson; 2 vols.; rev. ed.; Louisville: Westminster/John Knox, 1992), 2:234–35. Léon Vouaux, *Les Actes des Paul et ses lettres apocryphes* (Paris: Librairie Letouzey, 1913), 97–102; and Carl Schmidt, ΠΡΑΞΕΙΣ ΠΑΥΛΟΥ: *Acti Pauli* (Hamburg: J. J. Augustin, 1936), 127–30.

51. David E. Aune, *The New Testament in Its Literary Environment* (LEC; Philadelphia: Westminster, 1987), 141. Also, Schneemelcher, *New Testament Apocrypha*, 2:79. Dennis R. MacDonald, *The Legend and the Apostle: The Battle for Paul in Story and Canon* (Philadelphia: Westminster, 1983).

52. There are five occurrences of the living God in *Acts Paul*: (1) 3:37 in Thecla's Iconium speech before the authorities (Schneemelcher, 2:245); (2) 4:28 in a fragmentary speech given by Paul in Myra (Schneemelcher, 2:247); (3) 7:2 in Paul's address to two Gentile women in Ephesus (Schneemelcher, 2:252); (4) 11:4, and (5) 11:5 in Paul's martyrdom speech before Roman officials (Schneemelcher, 2:262).

53. For example, Everding, in his comprehensive examination of the living God, treated numerous second century sources but completely omitted any discussion of *Acts Paul*. He, however, did discuss occurrences in the *Shepherd of Herm. Vis* 2:3.2; 3:7.2; 6:2.2; *Ign. Phld.*, 1:2; *1 Clem.* 58:2; Clement of Alexandria, *Paed.* 2:83.1; and *Apology of Aristides* 16.

toral epistles.[54] Nobody denies that the author of the *Acts of Paul* was familiar with New Testament sources, but the crucial question is whether the author was dependent on these sources in composing individual episodes.[55] While it is likely that some elements in the *Acts of Paul* are drawn from New Testament sources,[56] it is also likely that the author used local traditions in composing individual episodes, traditions that circulated independently of New Testament writings. Recent scholarship on the *Acts of Paul* has called attention to its folkloric characteristics that retain "...some particularities of oral narrative."[57] More generally, the apocryphal acts "are not entirely fictional, but combine oral traditions (in some cases reaching back into the first century) with creative imagination."[58] Dennis MacDonald has argued that the material in the *Acts of Paul* is informed by "an old but still vital oral tradition."[59]

The task of determining whether a primitive oral tradition informs an episode can be decided only on the basis of individual narratives. However, a strong case can be made that *Acts Paul* 7:2 is grounded in the author's use of local traditions that go back to Paul's actual preaching of the living God in the first century. This claim is supported by two observations. First, the Ephesus episode, of which *Acts Paul* 7:2 is a part, bears the marks of oral traditions that have been reworked by the author. This narra-

---

54. Willy Rordorf, "Tradition and Composition in the Acts of Thecla: The State of the Question," *Semeia* 38 (1986): 46–49, furnishes a helpful survey of scholarship on this issue, discussing the seminal work of Carl Schlau, Theodore Zahn, William Ramsay, Adolf von Harnack, Carl Schmidt, and Wilhelm Schneemelcher.

55. There seems to be a complete lack of relation between the *Acts Paul* and canonical Acts. Schneemelcher, *New Testament Apocrypha,* 2:82, concludes that *Acts Paul* did not use canonical Acts as a literary model. For a recent discussion, see Richard Bauckham, "The Acts of Paul as a Sequel to Acts," in *The Books of Acts in Its First Century Setting* (ed. B. Winter and A. Clarke; Grand Rapids: Eerdmans, 1993), 1:105–52.

56. Schmidt, ΠΡΑΞΕΙΣ ΠΑΥΛΟΥ: *Acta Pauli,* 108–12.

57. Rordorf, "Tradition and Composition," 52. See also Schneemelcher, "Acts of Paul," 2:327–49; Helmut Koester, *Introduction to the New Testament: History and Literature of Early Christianity* (Philadelphia: Fortress Press, 1982), 2:324.

58. Aune, *The New Testament in Its Literary Environment,* 142. Schneemelcher offers seminal discussion in identifying traditional material in the *Acts Paul.* See Schneemelcher, *New Testament Apocrypha,* 2:79.

59. MacDonald, *The Legend and the Apostle,* 18–19, 21.

tive provides "an indication of the author's methods of working, making use in his composition of older traditions."[60] The second observation concerns the distinctive manner in which the living God is formulated in *Acts Paul* 7:2. The epithet's occurrence there is distinctive and unparalleled with respect to New Testament occurrences. There is nothing about the formulation that suggests it is the product of a literary dependence on 1 Thess 1:9 or Acts 14:15.

At the same time, however, the living God in *Acts Paul* 7:2 does have a genuine Pauline "ring" to it, evident in the way that it employs the epithet in antithetical contrast to idols. The antithetical style of the formulation in *Acts Paul* 7:2 recalls 1 Thess 1:9 and Acts 14:15. With respect to New Testament occurrences, then, *Acts Paul* 7:2 is simultaneously distinctive and similar, an unusual situation that is best explained, not by the writer's creative exegesis of New Testament sources, but rather by the use of traditional material.

The Ephesus story in the *Acts of Paul* begins with a report of Paul's arrival in Ephesus and his preaching there. This preaching attracts a following of women, which disrupts the social life of the city and leads to Paul's arrest and imprisonment. Paul is thus condemned to fight the beasts in the arena of Ephesus, awaiting his fate in jail. Into this narrative setting the author has introduced a story about the conversion of a Gentile woman named Artemilla.[61] The story depicts Paul giving a short address to Artemilla and her friend Eubula. Artemilla "put on dark clothes, and came to him [Paul] with Eubula. But when he saw her he groaned":

> Woman, ruler of this world, mistress of much gold, citizen of great luxury, splendid in thy raiment, sit down on the floor and forget your riches and your beauty and your finery. For these will profit you nothing if thou pray not

---

60. Schneemelcher, *New Testament Apocrypha*, 2:226; MacDonald, *The Legend and the Apostle*, 21–23.

61. Schneemelcher, *New Testament Apocrypha*, 2:226, observes that the story of Artemilla's conversion bears the marks of being originally independent from its present context, and this suggests that the unit has been secondarily inserted.

to God.... Beauty grows old, and great cities are changed, and the world will be destroyed in fire because of the lawlessness of men. God alone abides and the sonship that is given through him in whom men must be saved. And now Artemilla, hope in God and he will deliver you, hope in Christ and he will give you forgiveness of sins and will bestow upon you a crown of freedom, that you may no longer serve idols and the steam of sacrifice, but the living God and the father of Christ (ἵνα μηκέτι εἰδώλοις λατρεύῃς καὶ κνείσαις ἀλλὰ ζῶντι θεῷ καὶ πατρὶ Χριστοῦ), whose is the glory forever and ever." And when Artemilla heard this, she, with Eubula, besought Paul that he would forthwith baptize her in God.

Paul's speech in prison effects a desire for conversion and baptism in Artemilla. In a subsequent episode, the narrative describes the miraculous release of Paul from prison that enables him to baptize Artemilla.

More significant, however, is the speech itself, in which is Paul uses the living God to convert Artemilla. Paul speaks of the living God in contrast to idols, recalling the pattern of kerygma seen in 1 Thess 1:9 and Acts 14:15. Paul exhorts Artemilla to renounce her service to idolatry and to "no longer serve idols and the steam of sacrifice, but the living God and the Father of Christ...." The antithetical thrust of this statement is evident in the expression "that you may no longer serve idols... but the living God...." The "but" carries adversative force and creates an antithetical effect similar to that of 1 Thess 1:9 and Acts 14:15. In this way, then, *Acts Paul* 7:2 has a genuine Pauline ring to it.

However, the use of the living God in *Acts Paul* 7:2 also remains distinctive with respect to New Testament occurrences, representing a Pauline speech that is unique in its details and narrative setting. Significantly, the term "to turn" (ἐπιστρέφειν) is absent in *Acts of Paul* 7:2, which one would expect, if it were dependent on New Testament sources. Paul does not urge the convert to "turn" to the living God, as in 1 Thess 1:9 and Acts 14:15. Further, the motif of "the steam of sacrifice" designates pagan cult practice that has no parallel in the New Testament.[62] This distinctiveness, coupled with the observation of genuine Pauline character, points to the use of a Pauline tradition that is independent of the New Testament. *Acts of Paul* 7:2, then, furnishes additional evidence of Paul as the proclaimer of the living God.

Paul's Kerygma and Teaching of the Living God

I will now explore what Paul teaches his Gentile converts about the living God. In what way would Paul have clarified God's "living" character to his Gentile converts? Interpreters generally assume that Paul's teaching on the living God is a repetition of Old Testament teaching and that the living God functions simply as a polemical term in missionary preaching, serving to show that idols were "dead" and not worthy of worship. The living God is thus viewed as the God of Israel who is living and active in contrast to idols which are lifeless objects. While this view is certainly correct, more remains to be said. The fuller meaning of Paul's teaching on the living God has not been explored in any depth, nor has this teaching been clarified in relation to its Jewish background.

In exploring Paul's fuller teaching on the living God, 1 Thess 1:9–10; Acts 14:15–17; and *Acts Paul* 7:2 provide a useful starting point. These excerpts of kerygma represent basic monotheistic teaching that Paul himself would have amplified with additional teaching, clarifying for his converts the identity and character of the living God.[63] The question remains, then, as to how Paul would have amplified these excerpts in 1 Thess 1:9–10; Acts 14:15–17; and *Acts Paul* 7:2. Happily, some hints are found in the Jewish background of the living God (chaps. 3 and 4) and in Paul's monotheistic teaching found elsewhere in his letters. Paul's own God-talk (Rom 1:18–25; 1 Cor 8:4–6) and the Jewish

---

62. H. G. Liddell and R. Scott, *A Greek-English Lexicon* (Oxford: Clarendon, 1985), 965, defines ἡ κνίσα as a steam or odor which exhales from roasting meat. The term is associated with the smell from a burnt sacrifice.

63. Grant, *Gods and the One God*, 46.

background of the living God provide valuable clues on Paul's fuller teaching and enable some inferences beyond the kerygmatic excerpts. As will be seen, Paul's view of the living God is rooted in the notion of a life-giving creator who raised Jesus from the dead.

Paul expresses his kerygma of the living God as part of a wider strategy of introducing exclusive monotheism to Gentile converts. His kerygma of the living God serves to convey, in concise fashion, the requirements of an exclusive commitment to the one God. Paul taught the living God in antithesis to idols, as the one God and creator, who made the world and gave life. Rudolf Bultmann observed some years ago that "Christian missionary preaching in the Gentile world could not be simply the christological kerygma; rather, it had to begin with the proclamation of the one God . . . it was actually true that the Christian mission first reached those classes in which polytheism was still a living force."[64] First Thessalonians 1:9, Acts 14:15, and *Acts Paul* 7:2 thus illustrate the manner in which Paul preached monotheism to Gentiles, using the traditional Jewish pattern of language that set the living God in contrast to idols.

In 1 Thess 1:9 the antithesis appears in the two clauses of 1:9b: "and how you turned to God from idols, to serve a living and true God." The opposition between God and idols in the first clause is extended to the living and true God of the second.[65] This language is "traditional monotheistic terminology used to heighten the contrast with [idols]"; further, the location of "living" in the construction brings it closer to the idol motif, "suggesting a contrast of 'living'/'dead' . . . or/and 'potent'/'impotent.' "[66] A similar antithesis is also present in Acts 14:15: "We . . . bring you good news, that you should turn from these vain things to a living God. . . . " The living God here is contrasted with idolatry as "vain things." Gentiles turn from idolatry to a living God, designating the two simultaneous movements in conversion, one away from idolatry and the other toward the new life of faith. Both formulations in 1 Thess 1:9–10 and

---

64. Bultmann, *Theology of the New Testament,* 1:65.
65. Grant, *Gods and the One God,* 46.
66. Everding, "The Living God," 318–19.

Acts 14:15 thus indicate Paul's strategy in teaching monotheism to Gentile audiences, a strategy that involved antithetically opposing idolatry with the worship of the one true living God.

This antithetical pattern of Pauline kerygma has its roots in Jewish living God tradition, as is widely recognized.[67] Commentators generally acknowledge the Jewish character of this pattern of language, calling it "Jewish missionary terminology," "Graeco-Jewish propaganda," "Jewish preaching to the heathen," or "Hellenistic-Jewish mission formula."[68] More specifically, we have seen that this antithetical pattern in Pauline kerygma is rooted in a pattern of language common in Hellenistic Judaism in sources such as Dan 5:23 LXX; 6:27–28 LXX; *Jos. Asen.* 8:5; *Sib. Or.* 3:762–66; and Bel 5 Th. Paul, in other words, inherited Jewish traditions of the living God that he employed in preaching and teaching monotheism.

However, while interpreters recognize the Jewish roots of this antithetical language in 1 Thess 1:9 and Acts 14:15, they have done little to explore the implications of these roots for a fuller understanding of the Pauline living God. Apart from acknowledging Jewish roots and citing parallels from Jewish sources, little has been done to exploit what this Jewish background has to contribute to a deeper understanding of the Pauline living God. Primarily, the Jewish background of the living God reinforces and clarifies Paul's preaching of the living God as creator. The creator theme is implicit in the antithetical logic that contrasts the living God and idols. In contrast to idols, the living God was unique and superior as the God who made all things, giving life in the beginning and in the present. Bel and the Dragon 5 Theodotion expresses the axiom of Jewish living God theology that informs Paul's preaching: " . . . I do not revere manmade idols, but the living God who created heaven and the earth and has dominion over all flesh." This identity of the liv-

---

67. Everding, "The Living God," 318; Best, *Thessalonians*, 86; Bussmann, *Themen der paulinischen Missionspredigt*, 54; and Dupont, *The Salvation of the Gentiles*, 70.

68. Stenger, "Die Gottesbezeichnung 'lebendiger Gott' im Neuen Testament," 64–65; Everding, "The Living God," 318; Best, *The First and Second Epistles to the Thessalonians*, 86; and Bussmann, *Themen der paulinischen Missionspredigt*, 54–55; Bruce, *1 and 2 Thessalonians*, 18; and Collins, *Studies on the First Letter to the Thessalonians*, 234.

ing God as biblical creator is implicit wherever the living God is employed in antithesis to idols, as in 1 Thess 1:9. This claim is supported by Acts 14:15: "We are also men, of like nature with you, and bring you good news, that you should turn from these vain things to a living God, who made the heaven and the earth and the sea and all that is in them."

The antithetical logic that contrasts the living God and idols also conveys a polemic against other gods as "idols" that are dead and dumb; and so Paul's monotheistic kerygma also would have involved a polemic directed against the gods worshiped by potential converts. Idols were made by human hands and were perishable and unable to save. Idolatry was absurd because it was directed toward something "handmade" and created. The idolator worshiped a created object rather than the true invisible creator who had made all things (cf. Rom 1:20–25). The Jewish and Christian worship of the living God, however, was true worship because it was directed to the invisible heavenly creator. The living God made all things, and as such, was eternal creator, active in sustaining the world and in exercising universal sovereignty. Paul, therefore, in preaching the living God, would have appealed to the irrationality of worshiping idols and the true wisdom of acknowledging the living God as creator. Paul followed in the footsteps of Hellenistic Jews, proclaiming the eternal and heavenly living God, the creator and source of life.

Paul's monotheistic language in 1 Cor 8:4–6 and Rom 1:18–25 further confirms this claim. In the former Paul cites a credal confession of the one God as creator: "Hence, as to the eating of food offered to idols, 'we know that an idol has no real existence,' and that 'there is no God but one.' For although there are many so-called gods in heaven and on earth—as indeed there are many gods and many lords—yet for us there is one God, the Father from whom are all things and for whom we exist (ἀλλ᾽ ἡμῖν εἷς θεὸς ὁ πατὴρ ἐξ οὗ τὰ πάντα καὶ ἡμεῖς εἰς αὐτόν) ... " (1 Cor 8:4–6). This confession employs the missionary theme of the "one God" set in opposition to idols that have "no real existence" (8:4). Moreover, the creator theme appears in 8:6. This one God is also the "father" from whom all things come.[69] The term "father" clarifies God's role as the source and goal of all things, that is, as creator. The suggestion, then, is that Paul, in clarifying the living God to his Gentile converts, would have used the kind of language found in 1 Cor 8:6. The living God was the father from whom all things come.[70]

Paul's God-talk in Rom 1:18–25 also provides a glimpse into how Paul amplified his teaching on the living God.[71] In Rom 1:20, for example, Paul says, "ever since the creation of the world, his invisible nature, namely, his eternal power and deity, has been clearly perceived in the things that have been made." In 1:23 he asserts that idolators "exchanged the glory of the immortal God for images resembling mortal man or birds or animals or reptiles"; and finally, in 1:25, idolators "...exchanged the truth about God for a lie and worshiped and served the creature rather than the Creator who is blessed forever! Amen." This language clarifies how Paul would have expanded upon the living God to his Gentile audiences. Paul sets the living God's eternal power (1:20) and immortality (1:23) in opposition to the perishable images of mortal man (1:23); also he contrasts the truth about the one God with the lie of false worship (1:25); and he opposes the worship of the creator to the worship of the creature (1:23, 25).[72]

For Paul, then, God was "living" as the eternal and transcendent creator God. As creator, the living God made all things at the beginning of creation, but he also continues to sustain and govern the world. He is the divine "father" from whom all things

---

69. Paul employs a similar expression in Rom 11:36: "For from him and through him and to him are all things." The prepositions "from" and "to" define God as the origin and goal of all things. These expressions reflect Hellenistic philosophical and religious traditions, but have likely been mediated through Hellenistic Jewish tradition. Hans Conzelmann, *1 Corinthians* (Hermeneia; trans. J. Leitch; Philadelphia: Fortress Press, 1957), 144.

70. Grant, *Gods and the One God*, 47, comments that "the reality of the living God was inferred from his miraculous creation and governance of the existing world, as well as by his continuing revelation through his prophets."

71. Interpreters recognize that Rom 1–2 reflects Pauline kerygma. Albrecht Oepke, *Die Missionspredigt des Apostles Paulus* (Leipzig: Hinrichs, 1920), 82–83; Johannes Weiss, *The History of Primitive Christianity*, 239–41; Günther Bornkamm, "Faith and Reason in Paul," *Early Christian Experience* (New York: Harper & Row, 1966), 30–33; Bussmann, *Themen der paulinischen Missionspredigt*, 42–43; and Malherbe, *Paul and the Thessalonians*, 31–32.

72. Bussmann, *Themen der paulinischen Missionspredigt*, 42–43.

come. All people have their beginning in this one living God, who alone is worthy of worship from Jew and Gentile alike.

Paul also clarifies God's "living" character in connection with the resurrection of Jesus, mentioned in 1 Thess 1:10. In the latter, Paul proclaims the living God as raising Jesus from the dead, a point that serves to express the active and saving character of this God. The reference to resurrection in 1 Thess 1:10 is theocentric in its function, serving to elucidate the active and living character of the God mentioned in 1:9. The living God raised Jesus from the dead in a powerful act of life-giving, thus clarifying his identity as the creator and source of life. The living God's action in raising Jesus also manifests a saving action in which God delivers his "son," a deliverance which recalls his past interventions in the affairs of Israel, acting powerfully to deliver his people in times of need. The resurrection, then, represents the living God's newest act of deliverance in a long line of deliverances on behalf of the people of God.

First Thessalonians 1:10 mentions the resurrection in the short formula, "and to wait for his son from heaven, whom he raised from the dead" (ὅν ἤγειρεν ἐκ τῶν νεκρῶν). This formula is a traditional early Christian expression adopted by Paul (cf. 1 Cor 15:1–12).[73] The Greek wording, with its use of the definite article ("... from the dead") is not typical of Paul, indicating his use of traditional material.[74] In fact, there is evidence that the relative clause of 1:10 is a pre-Pauline formulation that was secondarily added to the monotheistic formulation of 1:9.[75] Interpreters observe that the sequence of content in 1 Thess 1:10 "... flows better if the relative clause, bearing the resurrection theme, is omitted."[76] Regardless of the pre-history of

---

73. Bultmann, *Theology*, 1:80–82. Langevin, *Jesus Seigneur et L'eschatologie*, 86–87, describes the resurrection formula of 1 Thess 1:10 as "wholly primitive formula," due to its frequent use and stereotypical character.

74. Collins, *Studies in the First Letter to the Thessalonians*, 254–55; Friedrich, "Ein Tauflied hellenisticher Judenchristen," 505–6; and Bussmann, *Themen der paulinischen Missionspredigt*, 51.

75. Bussmann, *Themen der paulinischen Missionspredigt*, 51.

76. Richard, *First and Second Thessalonians*, 57; Langevin, *Jésus Seigneur*, 101–2. Schneider, "Urchristliche Gottesverkündigung," 65–66, observes that the christological elements of 1:10 were secondarily inserted into and subordinated to the proclamation of God in 1:9.

1 Thess 1:10, its function is clear, serving to clarify the creative and life-giving character of the living God.[77] The resurrection clause thus has a theocentric aim in highlighting the life-giving power of the living and true God in Jesus' resurrection.

Further, interpreters tend to downplay or miss altogether the connection between the living God and Jesus' resurrection in 1 Thess 1:9–10.[78] The connection is not explicit, but it can be inferred from two observations. First, in Pauline tradition, God is generally the subject who is active in the raising of Jesus (e.g., Rom 4:24; 8:11; 10:9; Gal 1:1; and 2 Cor 13:4). Second, the syntax of 1 Thess 1:9–10 clearly identifies the living God of 1:9 as the subject "he" in the relative clause of 1:10, "whom he raised from the dead." The syntax of 1:9–10 thus links the living God with Jesus' sonship and resurrection. Jesus is "his" (=the living God's) son, suggesting an allusion to the Hosean expression "sons of the living God," an expression designating the future eschatological Israel. Applied to Jesus, the plural form "sons" is modified into the singular "son of the living God." Matthew 16:16 confirms the existence of an early Christian tradition which identifies Jesus as the Hosean "son of the living God."[79] Peter confesses Jesus as "the Christ, the Son of the living God." Therefore, both Matt 16:16 and 1 Thess 1:9–10 reflect an early Christian tradition in which Jesus is described as a son of the living God, recalling Hosea's prophecy about God restoring Israel as "sons of the living God."

Interpreted this way, 1 Thess 1:9–10 suggests an early Christian tradition which identified Jesus as a "son of the living God." God's raising of Jesus fulfills the Hosean promise of the living God to restore Israel as "sons of the living God" and also manifests Jesus' representative role as the new Israel, the "son of the living God." In raising Jesus, the living God signals his intention of bringing Hosea's prophecy of restoring Israel to fulfillment.

---

77. Collins, *Studies in the First Letter to the Thessalonians,* 255.

78. Everding, "The Living God," 319.

79. Matt 16:16 reflects a traditional confession of Jesus in the early church: "He said to them, 'But who do you say I am?' Simon Peter replied, 'You are the Christ, the Son of the living God'" (Matt 16:15–16). Everding, "The Living God," 319, however, sees no "percipient connection" between the epithet and the reference to resurrection.

Jesus' resurrection is the means by which the living God inaugurates the fulfillment of the Hosean prophecy and is bound up with God's formation of a new covenant people. Through the resurrection, Jesus has become the representative "son" who is "restored"[80] to life and through whom the eschatological sons (=believers) will be restored. Viewed in this way, Jesus' identity as "son of the living God" in 1 Thess 1:9–10 is thus a sign of the eschatological sonship that will characterize Gentile converts, and the resurrection of Jesus is inextricably bound up with the restoration of Israel and the foundation of new communities of faith. The resurrection leads to the restoration of future Israel as the "sons of the living God," who, in Rom 9:26, are called from among Jews and Gentiles.

For Paul and other early Christians, the living God's raising of Jesus has its roots in biblical tradition.[81] The resurrection fulfills scriptural prophecy (Hos 2:1 LXX) and is an extension of the biblical and Jewish theme of the living God as giver of life. Jesus' resurrection is the means by which the living God is active in rescuing his people from death and destruction. The resurrection recalls the living God's role in history as the deliverer of his people (e.g., Josh 3:10–11 LXX; 2 Kgs 19:4, 16 LXX/MT; Dan 6:26–27 LXX; Bel 23–42 Th; and 3 Macc 6:28). It also recalls the living God's role as the source of life, like life-giving water is to a thirsty deer (Ps 41:2 LXX). The living God will create "sons of the living God," who will number as the sands of the sea, and this dramatic increase in "sons" reflects the life-giving power of the living God (cf. *Jub* 1:24–25).

However, Paul, in preaching that the living God raised Jesus from the dead, also preaches something fundamentally new and distinctive with respect to earlier biblical and Jewish tradition. Jesus' resurrection brings about a profound change in the way

---

80. This association of Jesus' resurrection and the sonship theme is also found in Rom 1:3–4. Martin Hengel, *The Son of God: The Origin of Christology and the History of Jewish-Hellenistic Religion* (Philadelphia: Fortress Press, 1976), 64.

81. Everding, "The Living God," 320. Joseph Fitzmyer, *To Advance the Gospel* (New York: Crossroad, 1981), 206, observes that the resurrection "represents the personal power of Yahweh, the creator, who fashioned for himself a people; it is his life-giving power which manifested itself on various occasions in Israel's behalf, particularly at the Exodus from Egypt and the passage of the Red Sea. . . . "

that Paul and other early Christians come to view the living God of Israel. The living God was no longer simply the covenantal God of Israel or even the universal creator of Hellenistic Jewish tradition. For Paul and other early Christians, the living God, "who makes the dead alive" (Rom 4:17; 2 Cor 1:9) comes to be defined as the creator God who manifested himself in a definitive act of eschatological life-giving on Easter Sunday.[82] The resurrection of Jesus represents a new and decisive step in Israel's history and involves a profound transformation of Jewish monotheism.[83]

The resurrection of Jesus is closely linked to a new understanding of the living God among Paul and other early Christians. Jesus' resurrection, for Paul, was an eschatological event in which the living God was creating and reconstituting the people of God.[84] Jesus' resurrection inaugurates the eschatological creation of communities of faith, churches of the living God (cf. 1 Tim 3:15). Paul thus proclaims Jesus' resurrection as an eschatological act of new creation, which holds implications for the establishment of new communities of faith.

Paul's teaching of the living God in 1 Thess 1:9–10 also consists of eschatological motifs: the approaching eschatological wrath of the living God and Jesus' role in delivering believers from this wrath.[85] For Paul, God also "lives" in terms of being active against idolators and manifesting "wrath" against them (1:10). Paul's preaching of divine wrath is an extension of monotheism, since "Christian preaching of the one true God is at the same time eschatological proclamation, preaching of the impending judgment of the world."[86] This preaching of divine wrath serves to convict the hearers of their sinfulness and thus motivate conversion.

One wonders, however, about the function of "coming wrath"

---

82. Collins, *Studies on the First Letter to the Thessalonians,* 240.
83. Moxnes, *Theology in Conflict,* 270, observes that the resurrection "was the truly *new* act which the Christians ascribed to him [God]...."
84. Ibid., 271.
85. Acts 17:30–31 offers an example of the judgment theme in Paul's preaching. For a discussion see Bultmann, *Theology,* 1:73–77; Weiss, *The History of Primitive Christianity,* 233–34; and Bussmann, *Themen der paulinischen Missionspredigt,* 56.
86. Bultmann, *Theology of the New Testament,* 73–75; Pak, *Paul as Missionary,* 10.

in its relation to Paul's teaching on the living God. Some clues
as to what Paul taught about this coming wrath are present in
both the Jewish tradition of the living God and other Pauline
allusions to divine wrath in 1 Thessalonians and Romans. Jewish
and Pauline sources indicate a close link between idolatry and
the living God's wrath. In particular, the Jewish background of
the living God draws a close connection between Gentile idolatry and divine wrath. In *Jos. Asen.* 11:7–10, for example, the
living God is a "jealous and terrible God toward those who worship strange gods"; and in *Sib. Or.* 3:762–66, the immortal living
One "is angry at whoever commits these sins" (=idolatry and
sexual immorality).[87] Jeremiah 10:10 also expresses this link between idolatry and the anger of the living God: " ... At his wrath
the earth quakes and the nations cannot endure his indignation." The living God, then, has an active fearsome character in
expressing "wrath" against idolators.

This close link between idolatry and God's wrath continues in
the New Testament, especially in Rom 1–2 where divine wrath
is "revealed from heaven against all ungodliness and wickedness of men who by their wickedness suppress the truth" (1:18).
Divine wrath is a present reality in response to human ungodliness, which, at root, is the human refusal to honor God as
creator (Rom 1:21–23). Here the link between idolatry and the
living God's wrath is clear: divine wrath is directed against idolators because it is an explicit rejection of God as creator. The
practice of idolatry implies a refusal to reverence and honor the
God who created all things.

Paul's preaching of God's "coming wrath" was therefore a
logical concomitant of a powerful and active living God who
expects acknowledgment from all people. As universal lord and
creator, the living God expects Gentiles to acknowledge his lordship and is active in judging those who refuse to do so. In
1 Thess 1:9, then, the exhortation to "turn" from idols is closely
linked to the warning about the living God's coming wrath in
1:10. The two motifs fit together very closely in Paul's preach-

---

87. *Sib. Or.* 3 speaks frequently of God's wrath, e.g., 3:307–9; 3:556–57; 3:632–
34. In Dan 5:23, 26–28 LXX the living God was active in deposing Belshazzar who
rejected worshiping him and desecrated temple vessels in idolatrous rites.

ing—God's living wrath would come upon those who refused
to renounce idolatry in favor of the one true God.[88] The threat
of coming wrath serves to convict Gentiles of their need for repentance and conversion.[89] Hebrews 10:31 may well summarize
how Paul's message would have convicted the hearts of Gentile
converts: "it is a fearful thing to fall into the hands of the living
God."[90]

Paul's preaching of divine wrath, however, is always accompanied by the more hopeful note of eschatological salvation. This
preaching of God's wrath is closely linked with eschatological
salvation, as in 1 Thess 1:10.[91] Jesus's resurrection makes him
the glorified son in heaven, who will return to deliver the Thessalonians from "coming wrath." God's resurrection of Jesus thus
assures his future role as eschatological deliverer at the Parousia, a role which is more fully portrayed in 1 Thess 4:14, 16:
"For since we believe that Jesus died and rose again, even so,
through Jesus, God will bring with him those who have fallen
asleep.... For the Lord himself will descend from heaven with a
cry of command, with the archangel's call, and with the sound
of the trumpet of God." The living God, it seems, raises Jesus
from the dead, to serve an eschatological salvific role.[92] The living God, in raising Jesus from the dead, thus provides hope of
eschatological deliverance.

Alongside the wrathful divine judge in 1 Thess 1:10, there is
always the merciful living God who provides the means of deliverance from the coming wrath. In 1 Thess 5:9 Paul could thus

---

88. In Rom 2 the day of wrath is a day of future eschatological judgment on
which God's righteous judgment will be revealed (2:2, 5, 8; Pak, *Paul as Missionary*,
82).

89. Cf. Acts 17:31 and 1 Cor 3:13–15. Malherbe, *Paul and the Thessalonians*, 32,
notes that the aim of preaching wrath and deliverance themes was "to create conflict
in his readers and convict them of their sinful condition."

90. Everding, "The Living God," 296–307, classifies five early Christian uses of
the living God under the rubric of "The Dreadful Divine Judge," Heb 10:31; 3:12;
9:14; 12:22; and the *Testament of Jacob*. On Heb 10:31, Everding notes that the living
God epithet is used "to designate the dreadful divine judge and to strengthen the
warning to those who 'sin deliberately after receiving the knowledge of truth.'"

91. The expression "coming wrath" is also used in Col 3:6 and found in a context
where idolatry is denounced.

92. Langevin, *Jésus Seigneur*, 88. Langevin also notes that the unusual use of the
name of "Jesus" reflects primitive Christian tradition and indicates the soteriological
function of *Yeshua* as eschatological savior.

assure his Thessalonian converts that God "has not destined us
for wrath, but to obtain salvation through our Lord Jesus Christ"
(cf. Rom 5:9). First Timothy 4:10 summarizes well this hopeful
note in Paul's preaching of the living God: "For to this end we
toil and strive, because we have our hope set on the living God,
who is the Savior of all men, especially of those who believe." As
the living God had raised Jesus, so too would he impart life to all
believers in a general resurrection at the end of the world. On
this basis, then, Paul himself, as a prisoner in Rome, could stand
confidently before his Roman executioners and, according to
tradition, tell his executioners: "believe in the living God, who
raises up from the dead both me and all who believe in him."[93]

Conclusions

Paul does, indeed, proclaim the living God in his monotheistic kerygma to Gentiles (1 Thess 1:9–10; Acts 14:15; and *Acts
Paul* 7:2) and, in doing so, employs a Jewish strategy that formulates the living God in antithesis to idols. This antithetical
strategy was useful in highlighting the superior character of the
living God in contrast to other gods and thus served to motivate
Gentile conversion to the living God. Gentiles should convert
to this living God because he alone is the creator who made
them. In contrast to idols, the living God is the invisible creator characterized by eternal power and deity (Rom 1:18–25).
It is folly to worship other gods, which are nothing more than
"idols," handmade, lifeless and unable to save. For Paul, then,
and his churches, the epithet "living God" carries fundamental
kerygmatic significance that serves to evoke the associations of
his missionary preaching and Gentile conversion, as in 2 Cor
3:3 and 6:16.

To a large extent, Paul's teaching about the living God follows the main tenets of Jewish monotheism. The living God is
active as the biblical creator who had made the world and all
that is in it. As the father "from whom are all things" (1 Cor

---

93. *Mart. Paul* 5. The text is quoted from Schneemelcher, *New Testament Apocrypha*, 2:262.

8:6), the living God is active in sustaining the world and is the universal lord active in exercising dominion over it (Acts 14:15; cf. Bel 5 Th). Gentiles should devote themselves to the exclusive worship of the living God not only because he alone is deserving of such worship, but also because he is active in punishing idolators who reject his lordship. God is thus "living" in the sense of manifesting divine wrath against idolators (1 Thess 1:9–10; Rom 1:18–25; cf. Acts 17:30–31). Paul's message was: "It is a fearful thing to fall into the hands of the living God" (Heb 10:31).

Paul's teaching on the living God, however, was more than a simple continuation of Jewish monotheism. The living God is no longer simply the covenantal God of Israel or even simply the universal creator of Jewish tradition. For Paul, the living God is also the God who raised Jesus from the dead, entailing a distinctive Christian redefinition of earlier Jewish traditions. For Paul and other early Christians, the living God is, fundamentally, the God who gave life to Jesus in the resurrection. This means that, for Paul, the resurrection is theocentrically conceived since it is the living God who is the active subject behind the raising of Jesus. Paul therefore taught the living God in connection with Jesus' resurrection because the resurrection demonstrates the creative life-giving power that characterizes this God.

Further, this living God who raised Jesus from the dead continues to give life in the post-resurrectional era in the ministry of Paul. For example, in Acts 14:8–18, the living God is active in the healing ministry of Paul and Barnabas. Healing power is manifested in Paul's cure of the cripple in Lystra, reflecting the superior character of the living God in contrast to other gods. Finally, in raising Jesus, the living God provides assurance of future eschatological life for all believers in a general resurrection of the dead (1 Thess 1:9–10; 4:13–18). For this reason, the living God, indeed, is the object of hope and the Savior of all who believe (1 Tim 4:10).

Chapter Six

Conversion to the Living God in Paul's Letters

卐卐卐卐卐卐卐卐卐卐

The living God, for Paul, carries not only the association of his kerygma, but also the corresponding association of Gentile conversion. Paul's proclamation of the living God is closely linked to Gentile conversion. He preaches the living God to Gentile audiences and the result is conversion to the living God. Paul's use of the epithet in his letters thus functions as part of Pauline conversion language and serves an epistolary strategy in which Paul recalls his readers to the foundational experience of conversion. One wonders, however, how Paul understands Gentile conversion to the living God. How does Paul view conversion to the living God and in what does conversion consist?

These questions presuppose some understanding of conversion language in Paul's letters, that is, how to identify it and where it is found. There is, however, some difficulty in identifying Pauline conversion language that stems from the nature of Paul's letters. They are not missionary tracts, nor do they give explicit descriptions of the conversion process. They are directed to those already converted to Christian faith and are often pastoral in character. Still, conversion language is recognizable in a number of passages where Paul draws upon terms and themes of his missionary kerygma, which he then recasts for use in his epistolary discourse.[1] For example, in 1 Thess 1:4–10

---

1. C. H. Dodd, *The Apostolic Preaching and Its Developments* (repr., Grand Rapids: Baker, 1980), 9, observed some years ago that, "the epistles are, of course, not of the nature of kerygma. They are all addressed to readers already Christian, and they deal with theological and ethical problems arising out of the attempt to follow the

Paul constructs his thanksgiving period out of terms and themes that recall his missionary preaching and the foundational experience of conversion. Terms such as election (1:4), the Spirit (1:5), faith in God (1:8), and serving a living God (1:9) form a network of language that alludes to the conversion of the Thessalonians.

The following discussion, then, explores the network of conversion language surrounding the living God in 1 Thessalonians and other Pauline letters, taking a very specific approach to the topic of conversion. My approach gives exclusive focus to the literary-theological expressions of conversion in Paul's letters, paying close attention to Paul's rhetoric and theology of conversion.[2] What is conversion in Paul's view? Conversion, for Paul, can be defined as "a radical change in which past affiliations are rejected for some new commitment and identity. . . ."[3] Gentile converts turn from the worship of other gods, rejecting past affiliations, and commit themselves to a new life of service rendered to the living God. Gentile converts are said to move from darkness to light or from death to life. Further, Paul understands conversion theologically, that is, as something that results from a divine initiative expressed through the gospel and the activity of the Spirit. God "calls" converts through the gospel, and in response converts turn to the living God.

Moreover, Gentile conversion for Paul is a divine initiative of life-giving in which the living God recreates converts and brings Gentile communities to life as part of a new creation. Through the gospel and the Spirit, the living God creates communities

---

Christian way of life. . . . They have the character of what the early Church called 'teaching' or 'exhortation'. They presuppose the preaching."

2. Gaventa, *From Darkness to Light,* represents the literary-theological approach to conversion taken in this book. Other treatments referred to are Arthur Darby Nock, *Conversion: The Old and New in Religion from Alexander the Great to Augustine of Hippo* (repr., Lanham, Md.: University Press of America, 1988); idem, *Essays on Religion and the Ancient World* (ed. Zeph Stewart; Cambridge, Mass.: Harvard University Press, 1972), 63–68; Malherbe, *Paul and the Thessalonians,* 21–33; Wayne Meeks, *The First Urban Christians: The Social Word of the Apostle Paul* (New Haven: Yale University Press, 1983), 51–73.

3. Gaventa, *From Darkness to Light,* 12. Gaventa distinguishes conversion from two other types of personal change. "Alternations" are changes that do not involve a rejection of the past; and "transformation" is a radical change of perspective that is similar to Kuhn's paradigm shift.

called churches of the living God (1 Tim 3:15). Romans 9:25–26 offers an illustration of Gentile conversion as the result of the life-giving activity of the living God. In Rom 9:25–26, Paul thinks about Gentile conversion in analogy with God's work of creating *ex nihilo*. Further, through conversion, the living God calls Gentiles into existence and gives them new life as covenantal "sons of the living God." Conversion expresses God's eschatological initiative of bringing new covenant promises to fulfillment. Gentile conversion is thus a fulfillment of new covenant prophecy and this is the thought behind 2 Cor 3:3 and 6:16.

The Living God in Paul's Conversion Theology

In Paul's view, conversion to the living God is fundamentally a divine initiative and the result of divine activity. In 1 Thess 1:4–10 Paul employs three distinctive motifs that express this divine initiative of conversion: (1) the convert's response of "faith in God" (1:8), to which Paul refers using the conventional language of "turning"; (2) conversion as a divine "election" (1:4) and "call" (2:12; 4:7; 5:24); and (3) the activity of the Spirit, who makes Gentile hearts receptive to the gospel (1:5–6). Beginning with the first motif, 1 Thess 1:8 indicates Paul's penchant for speaking about conversion "faith" rather than employing the conventional language of repentance (μετανοεῖν) and turning to God (ἐπιστρέφειν).[4] Paul does make occasional use of these terms in his letters, e.g., 1 Thess 1:9; 2 Cor 3:16; Gal 4:9; Rom 2:4.

However, faith language is more fundamental to Paul's view of conversion, and he more frequently refers to conversion by using the vocabulary of faith, often employing the verb "to believe" in the aorist tense.[5] In 1 Thessalonians 1:8 Paul alludes

---

4. Gaventa, *From Darkness to Light*, 44. Paul employs conventional language of "repentance" in 2 Cor 7:9–10; 12:21; and Rom 2:4. The term ἐπιστρέφειν in 1 Thess 1:9 may carry covenantal associations from prophetic notions of repentance and exilic return, e.g., Hos 3:5; Isa 45:22; Deut 4:30. See Paul Aubin, S.J., *Le problème de la conversion: Étude sur une terme commun a l'hellenisme et au christianisme des trois premiers siècles* (Paris: Beauchesne, 1963).

5. Bultmann, "πιστεύω," *TDNT* 6:218–19 lists numerous examples of faith language designating conversion, e.g., Rom 10:14–17; 1 Cor 1:21; 2:4–5; 3:5, 15:2; Gal 2:16; 1 Thess 1:7; 2:13.

to conversion as "faith in God."[6] Here conversion faith is a response to God's initiative in the gospel and entails the acceptance of exclusive monotheism in which the convert rejects idols and turns to the living God (1:9). The rhetorical question of 2 Cor 6:15 also reflects the Pauline view of conversion faith: "what has the believer in common with an unbeliever?" Paul's faith language thus reflects his theology of conversion in which conversion is a response to the divine initiative.[7]

Another way in which Paul expresses the divine initiative of conversion is through the motif of divine "call." Conversion is the result of God calling Gentiles through the gospel (1 Thess 2:12; 4:7; 5:24). Second Thessalonians 2:13–14a expresses the thought in this way: "But we are bound to give thanks to God always for you, brethren beloved by the Lord, because God chose you from the beginning to be saved, through sanctification by the Spirit and belief in the truth. To this he called you through our gospel...." Also, in 1 Corinthians, the Corinthians are "called to be saints..." (1:2), and Paul later reminds them of this call by speaking of divine election: "For consider your call brethren; not many of you were wise according to worldly standards, not many were powerful, not many were of noble birth; but God chose what is foolish in the world to shame the wise, God chose what is weak in the world to shame the strong..." (1 Cor 1:26–28; cf. 7:17–22).

Further, God's call through the gospel is an expression of God electing Gentile converts. In 1 Thess 1:4–5, for example, the Thessalonians show themselves to be God's elect in the way that they received the gospel: "for we know brethren beloved by God (ἠγαπημένοι ὑπὸ θεοῦ) that he has chosen you (τὴν ἐκλογὴν ὑμῶν). For our gospel came to you not only in word

---

6. Cf. Heb 6:1.

7. Gaventa, *From Darkness to Light,* 44, notes that "indeed, the very structure of [Paul's] conversion theology militates against the use of conventional conversion language. *Epistrephein* and *metanoun* most often connote the action of one who changes his or her convictions and thus turns to God....But in Paul's letters it is made clear over and over again that God is the one who acts to include believers....Thus when Paul has reason to speak about the beginning of faith, he does so by reference to God's action rather than to human action...."

but also in power and the holy Spirit and with full conviction."[8]
This divine election-call results in converts becoming God's
"beloved," as in Rom 9:25. This term "beloved" has biblical background, designating Israel as the object of divine covenantal
love, and it is also frequently applied to the Jewish people in
their special covenantal relation to God (e.g., Deut 7:6–8; Isa
43:4; 3 Macc 6:11; Wis 16:26; *Jub.* 1:25, etc.).[9] Implicit here is
the idea that Israel is a covenantal "son" and the object of God's
affection (cf. Exod 4:22–23; Hos 11:1).

The application of this covenantal term "beloved" to the
Thessalonians in 1 Thess 1:4 indicates some kind of covenantal status resulting from conversion. As Gentile converts, the
Thessalonians have become God's "beloved" covenantal elect.
The implication is that the Thessalonians have some kind of
covenantal identity, which Paul, unfortunately, does not clarify.[10]
Also, the Thessalonians' status of God's beloved elect implies
their identity as God's sons or children, something which is
also implied in 1:3 where Paul refers to God as "our father"
(cf. 3:11). By implication, then, the Thessalonian converts have
become covenantal children in relation to their divine father,
although again, Paul is not explicit in stating this view.

Finally, the Spirit motif in Paul's letters and Acts also serves
to express the initiative of the living God in converting Gentiles. Acts frequently presents the missionary role of the Spirit,
motivating the apostles to bold proclamation and being poured
out on Gentile converts (e.g., 4:32; 10:44–47). In Paul's letters,
the Spirit plays a similar missionary role (e.g., 1 Thess 1:5–6).
That Paul's missionary preaching is accompanied by the Spirit
is attested in Gal 3:2–5; Rom 15:18–19; and 1 Cor 2:4–5. In the
latter passage, Paul's "speech and message were not in plausi-
ble words of wisdom, but in demonstration of the Spirit and of
power, that your faith might not rest on the wisdom of men but

---

8. The syntactical links of these two verses establish v. 5 as the ground for Paul's
assertion of divine election in v. 4.

9. Edwin Freed, *The Apostle Paul, Christian Jew: Faithfulness and Law* (Lanham,
Md.: University Press of America, 1994), 68.

10. It is possible to explain the Thessalonian election in terms of the new
covenant, given the activity of the divine Spirit in Thessalonika (cf. Ezek 36–37).

in the power of God" (1 Cor 2:4–5). Paul's reference to "the demonstration of the Spirit" assumes that the Corinthians are familiar with the Spirit's activity as a datum of their conversion experience.[11] For Paul the Spirit motif carries the association of Gentiles converting and being baptized. Paul's mention of the Spirit, then, serves as an allusion to the foundation of Gentile communities, as in 2 Cor 3:3, where the Spirit of the living God was active in "writing" the Corinthian "letter."

Paul's rhetoric of conversion also involves language that describes the transformative effect that conversion has on Gentile converts. Again, my interest is primarily in Paul's theological view of conversion in contrast to the social reality of conversion in the Pauline communities. For Paul, the root idea of conversion is that it effects "a radical change in which past affiliations are rejected for some new commitment and identity."[12] This radical change is expressed in 1 Thess 1:9 where converts turn from idols to a new life rendered in service to the living God. Implied here is the rejection of past affiliations and a new monotheistic identity bolstered by the social reality of the Pauline communities. Paul utilizes a variety of metaphors and expressions for describing the radical change brought about by conversion. For example, conversion effects a movement from darkness to light.[13] In 1 Thess 5:4–5, for example, Paul describes his converts as "sons of light" because "we are not of the night or of darkness." In 2 Cor 4:4, unbelievers are in darkness because they cannot see "the light of the gospel of the glory of Christ" (cf. Rom 1:21), and in 4:6, Paul alludes to conversion when he speaks of God shining "into our hearts to give the light of the knowledge of the glory of God in the face of Christ" (cf. Rom 2:19; Acts 26:17–18). Further in 2 Cor 6:14b the rhetorical question, "what fellowship has light with darkness," presupposes an understanding of conversion as a movement from darkness to light.

---

11. David Lull, *The Spirit in Galatia: Paul's Interpretation of Pneuma as Divine Power* (SBLDS 49; Chico, Calif.: Scholars, 1980), 57–59.

12. Gaventa, *From Darkness To Light*, 12; Malherbe, *Paul and the Thessalonians*, 30.

13. The light/darkness antithesis has Jewish background. For example, *Jos. Asen.* 8:9 and Philo, *Virtues*, 179.

The metaphor of converts coming to light from darkness carries the associations of an intellectual awakening. Before conversion, converts were in ignorance, error, and darkness, but through conversion they come to the knowledge of truth and illumination.[14] Converts are enlightened by the apprehension of monotheistic truth which changes for them the whole picture of reality. Further, this metaphor of conversion as a movement from darkness to light recalls God's act of creating light out of darkness (e.g., *Jos. Asen.* 8:9 and 2 Cor 4:6). Conversion is viewed on analogy with God's creation of light and reflects the life-giving initiative of a new creation.

Conversion for Paul is also a liberation from enslaving powers that formerly held converts in bondage.[15] In converting, converts reject other so-called "gods," viewing them as "idols" (1 Thess 1:9) or demons that are unworthy of worship. Conversion entails a reorientation away from those spiritual powers and entities to which the converts were formerly enslaved. This is presupposed in the rhetorical question of 2 Cor 6:15, "what accord has Christ with Belial?" Also, in Galatians 4:9–10, Paul asserts: "Formerly, when you did not know God, you were in bondage (ἐδουλεύσατε) to beings that by nature are no gods; but now that you have come to know God...." Similarly, Acts 26:17–18 describes the effect of Paul's missionary work as liberating Gentiles "from the power of Satan to God...."

The converts' acceptance of monotheistic truth therefore changes the whole picture of reality, bringing about an intellectual awakening to monotheistic truth. In 1 Cor 8:4, for example, converts know "that an idol has no real existence," and "that there is no God but one." In 1 Thess 4:5 Paul contrasts the monotheistic knowledge of the Thessalonians with the "heathen who do not know God." The Thessalonian converts, liberated from their former ignorance, have come to "know" the one God. In Galatians 4:8–9, where converts formerly "did not know

---

14. Bultmann, *Theology*, 1:66–67.

15. Pak, *Paul as Missionary*, 8, observes that the service rendered to the living God by converts "... is manifested in recognition of the unique lordship of God, to the exclusion of all other beings."

God," now "they have come to know God, or rather to be known by God" (cf. 2 Cor 2:14 and 4:2).

Conversion thus also entails a change of lordships. Liberated from enslaving spiritual powers, Gentile converts enter into the service of the God who is true and living. The new life of service holds practical implications for the convert's life and behavior. Conversion to the living God entails a new life of holiness in which converts abandon former pagan practices and associations. Paul can thus allude to conversion by speaking of holiness, purity, and sanctification.[16] In 1 Cor 1:2, for example, he reminds the Corinthians that they were "called to be saints" and "sanctified in Jesus Christ" (cf. 2 Cor 1:1). First Thessalonians 4:3–8 is an exhortation based upon the holiness requirements of Gentile conversion.[17] In it, the theme of "holiness" (ἁγιασμός) stands opposed to "impurity" (ἀκαθαρσία). In 4:3–5, God's will for the converts is their "sanctification" (ἁγιασμός), that they "know how to take a wife...in holiness (ἐν ἁγιασμῷ) and honor, not in the passion of lust like the heathen who do not know God"[18] (4:4–5). This exhortation to holiness is grounded in God's call and the giving of the Spirit. In 4:7, "God has not called us for uncleanness, but in holiness" (ἐν ἁγιασμῷ); and in 4:8, "whoever disregards this, disregards not man but God, who gives his Holy Spirit to you." This type of conversion language also appears in 2 Cor 7:1, which speaks of the need for "cleansing" (καθαρίσωμεν) and "holiness" (ἁγιωσύνην) in the Christian life.

The holiness requirements that come with conversion are also expressed in Paul's use of the temple motif in 1 Cor 3:16–

---

16. Elpidius Pax, "Beobachtungen zur Konvertitensprache im ersten Thessalonicher brief," *Studii Biblici Franciscani Analecta* 21 (1971): 226–27, observes that new converts tend to remain rooted in past practices and thus the need for exhortation. Paul's ethical exhortation stems from the concern that new converts not relapse into pagan ways.

17. 1 Thess 4:1–8 is the first explicitly paraenetic material in 1 Thess, serving to develop the implications of "serving God" in 1:9. The aim of "pleasing God" in 4:1 recalls the motif of "serving" God in 1:9 (Malherbe, *Paul and the Thessalonians*, 51, 76); Brian S. Rosner, ed., *Understanding Paul's Ethics: Twentieth-Century Approaches* (Grand Rapids: Eerdmans, 1995), 351–60.

18. A significant parallel to 1 Thess 4:3–8 is also found in Rom 6:22: "for just as you once yielded your members to impurity and greater and greater iniquity, so now yield your members to righteousness for sanctification."

17; 6:19; and 2 Cor 6:16. Through conversion, the Corinthians have become a community of saints or God's holy temple, indicating the community as a sphere of holiness and a locus of the Spirit's indwelling. The community that is God's "temple" is, by definition, a holy people. In 1 Cor 3:16–17, Paul reminds the Corinthians that they are a "temple of God" because God's Spirit is present among them. Conversion to the living God thus entails adherence to standards of holiness that are expressed in Paul's ethical exhortations throughout his letters. For example, conversion entailed the renunciation of idols and sexual immorality (cf. Acts 15:20; 1 Cor 6:9–10; 1 Thess 4:1–8).[19] Such requirements recall the ethical monotheism required of Jewish proselytes (e.g., *Sib. Or.* 3:762–66).

Finally, conversion, in Paul's view, expresses the creative and life-giving activity of the living God. The living God gives life in conversion, the life-giving effects of which are expressed in numerous ways. For example, the Spirit is the agent of divine life in conversion, as Paul makes clear in 2 Cor 3:6 (cf. Rom 1:3–4; 8:10–11). Also, divine life-giving is implicit in the transformation of Gentiles into God's beloved elect (1 Thess 1:4), implying new life as adopted sons of God. As a result of conversion, converts are recreated and placed in a new relationship to God as sons and daughters who can address God as "father" (Rom 8:14–17; 9:25–26; 2 Cor 6:18). However, conversion for Paul is more fundamentally a corporate and eschatological act of new creation (2 Cor 5:17). It is primarily an eschatological new creation that is cosmic in character and aimed, not only at transforming individuals, but at recreating the world.

This corporate character of conversion is expressed in the creation of faith communities, that is, in church communities. For example, in 1 Thess 1:1, Paul says: "To the church of the Thessalonians in God the father (ἐν θεῷ πατρὶ) and the Lord Jesus Christ." The use of the expression "in God" can be taken instrumentally, "as indicating that the assembly was called into

---

19. Jewish and early Christian tradition commonly assumed that idolatry was at the root of pagan immorality, e.g., Wis 14:12: "For the idea of making idols was the beginning of fornication, and the invention of them was the corruption of life." Cf. Rom 1:18–32.

existence by God the creator, who made them his family."[20] The church (ἐκκλησία) of the Thessalonians is therefore a church established through the living God's creative power, electing converts to new life in the family of God. A similar point is expressed in 1 Tim 3:15 through the use of the expression "church of the living God." The post-Pauline author writes to instruct his readers on "how one ought to behave in the house of God":

> I hope to come to you soon, but I am writing these instructions to you so that, if I am delayed, you may know how one ought to behave in the house of God, which is the church of the living God (ἥτις ἐστὶν ἐκκλησία θεοῦ ζῶντος), the pillar and bulwark of truth.[21]

The expression is clearly ecclesial in character, standing in apposition to "the house of God" (ἐν οἴκῳ θεοῦ), which is a description of the church, going back to 3:5.

What interpreters fail to realize, however, is the significance of the genitive expression "of the living God," as a subjective genitive which conveys a genitive of origin. The church of the living God is that community that is the living God's because it has it origins in the living God. The expression, in other words, suggests a community that has divine origins and is established by the activity of the living God.[22] These divine origins likely refer to the preaching of the gospel and conversion as the means by which the living God founded the church community. The expression "church of the living God" thus suggests a community whose identity is rooted in conversion to the living God. In 1 Tim 3:15 "God is 'living' as the father who gives life to this family, which his love has called into existence and which he sus-

---

20. Malherbe, *Paul and the Thessalonians,* 79.

21. The expression "church of the living God" is a *hapax legomenon* that remains largely neglected among the commentators (Everding, "The Living God," 311–13). See Kraus "Der lebendige Gott," 198, and Stenger, "Die Gottesbezeichnung 'lebendiger Gott,'" 68–69.

22. Hans Windisch, *Der zweite Korintherbrief* (MeyerK 6; Göttingen: Vandenhoeck & Ruprecht, 1924), 106, is on the right track when he explains 2 Cor 3:3 in connection with 1 Tim 3:15 and the expression "church of the living God." His suggestion is that the church of the living God is a community created through the life-giving power of the Spirit of the living God.

tains."[23] A similar thought informs 2 Cor 6:16 and the "temple of the living God."

Conversion Theology in Rom 9:25–26

Rom 9:24–26 offers an encapsulation of Paul's conversion theology and illustrates how Paul thought about conversion to the living God. In these verses Paul uses prophetic texts to speak about conversion as initiated by the living God and expressed as a gospel "call." This divine call brings about new life for Gentile converts, who were formerly "not my people," but are transformed into "sons of the living God." Conversion here is a life-giving act which recreates Gentiles out of their non-existent state into children of the living God. Further, Rom 9:25–26 also introduces an aspect of Gentile conversion not previously discussed in this chapter. It links conversion to new covenant prophecy. Romans 9:25–26 shows that, for Paul, Gentile conversion is closely linked to God's initiative of establishing a new covenant people. Conversion is directed to the formation of the future Israel envisioned by the prophets Hosea, Jeremiah, and Ezekiel. Romans 9:25–26 thus illustrates that, in Paul's view, Gentile conversion is inextricably bound up with the living God's activity of reconstituting Israel and fulfilling new covenant promises. The same pattern of association linking Gentile conversion and new covenant prophecy also appears in 2 Cor 3:3 and 6:16, and so Rom 9:25–26 provides crucial background for interpreting the living God in 2 Corinthians.

Interpreters widely acknowledge that Rom 9:24–26 alludes to Gentile conversion based upon its use of the recurring call motif. However, there is little or no discussion of how other elements in these verses serve the allusion. The living God epithet, in particular, suffers from this neglect and is typically treated as incidental in the passage since it occurs in a scriptural citation from Hos 2:1 LXX.[24] To be sure, the epithet in Rom 9:26

---

23. Quinn, *The Letter to Titus*, 303. Cf. George Knight, *Commentary on the Pastoral Epistles*, (NIGTC; Grand Rapids: Eerdmans, 1992), 180.

24. The use of the living God in Rom 9:25–26 is often dismissed as incidental. For example, Everding, "The Living God," 283–85. Other commentators are silent

is quoted as part of a scriptural citation. However, what interpreters fail to realize is that Paul uses the scriptural text to speak about conversion, and the living God plays an integral role in this strategy of alluding to Gentile conversion. This is clear when one considers the rich background of living God tradition, including the epithet's function in the Pauline kerygma (1 Thess 1:9; Acts 14:15; *Acts Paul* 7:2). Further, the Hosean expression "sons of the living God" also occurs in Jewish texts which either associate the expression with Gentile sympathizers or use it to designate Gentile proselytes (*Jos. Asen.* 19:8; 3 Macc 6:28; Esth 8:12q LXX). Therefore, before Paul uses the expression "sons of the living God" in Rom 9:26, it already has some connection with Gentile conversion.

In its literary context Rom 9:25–26 occurs as part of the wider unit of Rom 9:6–29 that addresses the issue of God's faithfulness to Israel. Paul attempts here to show that his gospel of justification is consistent with God's elective action in Israel's history. God is not arbitrary in electing some as instruments of salvation and rejecting others. There is no injustice in divine election, since its ultimate aim is the salvation of both Jews and Gentiles. In 9:20–23, Paul introduces the imagery of the divine potter as a metaphor for expressing God's creative activity and salvific purpose.[25] The divine potter has endured with much patience vessels of wrath "... in order to make known the riches of his glory for the vessels of mercy, which he has prepared beforehand for glory, even us whom he has called, not from the Jews only but also from the Gentiles..." (9:23–24).

Significantly, Rom 9:24 identifies the vessels of mercy with Jewish and Gentile converts to Christian faith: "even us whom he has called, not from the Jews only, but also from the Gentiles." God's call, through the gospel, is directed both to Jews and Gentiles, something which Paul documents by the use of a

---

on the epithet in Rom 9:26. For example, Ernst Käsemann, *Commentary on Romans* (trans. G. Bromiley; Grand Rapids: Eerdmans, 1980), 273–74; Joseph A. Fitzmyer, *Romans* (AB 33; New York: Doubleday, 1993), 573; and Ulrich Wilckens, *Der Brief an die Römer* (EKK NT VI.2; 3 vols.; Neukirchener: Benziger, 1987), 2:206.

25. Cf. Isa 29:16; 45:9; Jer 18:1–6; Wis 15:7–9; and Sir 33:10–13.

catena of scriptural texts in 9:25–29. The texts come from Hos 2:25, 2:1 LXX (9:25–26) and Isa 10:22–23, 1:9 LXX (9:27–29):[26]

> [25]As indeed he says in Hosea, "Those who were not my people I will call 'my people,' and her who was not beloved I will call 'my beloved.' [26]And in the very place where it was said to them, 'You are not my people,' they will be called 'sons of the living God'" (ἐκεῖ κληθήσονται υἱοὶ θεοῦ ζῶντος). [27]And Isaiah cries out concerning Israel: "though the number of the sons of Israel be as the sand of the sea, only a remnant of them will be saved; [28]for the Lord will execute his sentence upon the earth with rigor and dispatch." [29]And as Isaiah predicted, "If the Lord of Hosts had not left us any children, we would have fared like Sodom and been made like Gomorrah" (9:25–29).

The majority of interpreters view Rom 9:25–26 as documenting the call of Gentile converts in 9:24.[27] Käsemann, for example, concludes that "in chiastic contrast to the order in v. 24 the Gentiles are the recipients of the promise, which lifts them out of chaos and makes them beloved children and the eschatological people of God."[28] In contrast, the Isaian quotes of 9:27–29 would seem to have specific reference to the remnant of Jews called by God.[29]

An inspection of specific motifs in Rom 9:25–26 reinforces the conclusion that, through them, Paul intentionally alludes

---

26. The conflation of scriptural texts from Hos is likely Paul's own handiwork (Dietrich Alex Koch, *Die Schrift als Zeuge des Evangeliums* [Tübingen: J. C. B. Mohr, 1986] 167). James D. G. Dunn, *Romans 9–16* (WBC 38B; Dallas: Word Books, 1988), 2:570, observes that 9:25–26 is too closely integrated into its context "for it to have been a preformed piece." Käsemann, *Commentary on Romans,* 274, also agrees that Paul is responsible for the arrangement of Rom 9:25–26.

27. C. E. B. Cranfield, *A Critical and Exegetical Commentary on the Epistle to the Romans* (ICC; 2 vols.; Edinburgh: T. & T. Clark, 1979) 2:499, 501; Käsemann, *Commentary on Romans* 274; and Wilckens, *Der Brief an die Römer,* 2:206. Joseph A. Fitzmyer, *Romans,* 573, concludes that the words in Romans 9:26 "...are now transferred by Paul to the call of the Gentiles..." and that the verse "echoes Paul's own designation of the Christian as the 'children of God' (8:21) now applied to Gentile Christians." Some, however, take "not my people" in Rom 9:25–26 to refer to both Israel and the Gentiles. Dahl, *Studies in Paul,* 146.

28. Käsemann, *Commentary on Romans,* 274.

29. The citation in Rom 9:27 is an abbreviated form of Isa 10:22–23 LXX that has been assimilated to the beginning of Hos 2:1 LXX.

to Gentile conversion. For example, I have already mentioned how the expression "sons of the living God" in 9:26 alludes to Pauline and early Christian preaching of the living God (1 Thess 1:9; Acts 14:15; and *Acts Paul* 7:2).[30] For Paul and his readers the mention of the living God in a context mentioning the divine "call" would have evoked the associations of early Christian kerygma and Gentile conversion. Further, by Paul's day Jewish tradition already used the epithet in its missionary language, as attested by its use in antithetical formulations of idol polemic (Dan 5:23 LXX; 6:27–28 LXX; Bel 5 Th; *Jos. Asen.* 8:5) and in texts portraying Gentiles acknowledging the reality and power of the living God (Dan 6:27–28 LXX; Bel 23–42 Th; 3 Macc 6:28; Esth 8:12q LXX).[31] Further, the Hosean expression "sons of the living God" served to designate Gentile proselytes in *Jos. Asen.* 19:8. The Jewish and early Christian evidence thus suggests that "sons of the living God" was a text already linked to Gentiles and Gentile conversion.

Paul, then, in Rom 9:26 can apply Hos 2:1 LXX to Gentile converts with no explanation or clarification because the application was already familiar. Paul operates with a precedent that links Hos 2:1 LXX with Gentile converts and can thus assume his readers' familiarity with this association. To say this, however, does not detract from Paul's innovativeness in using the text of Hos 2:1 LXX in Rom 9:26. He employs the Hosean text in a scriptural catena of his own making that serves his own particular epistolary needs.

The most visible and agreed upon allusion to conversion in Rom 9:24–26 is in the motif of divine call, which occurs three

---

30. Dunn, *Romans 9–16*, 572, comments on the epithet living God in Rom 9:26 by noting its function in Jewish idol polemic, a function that was taken over by the first Christians. He cites 1 Thess 1:9 and 2 Cor 6:16 as parallels. Strathmann, "λαός," *TDNT* 4:54 notes that in Rom 9:25, Paul sees "a prophecy of the conversion of Gentiles which he promotes and experiences in his missionary work." Also, Irenaeus, *Against Heresies*, 3:9.1, is relevant. Irenaeus interprets Rom 9:25 in terms of God "calling us to the knowledge of Himself, from the worship of stones, so that those who were not a people were made a people, and she beloved who was not beloved."

31. In 3 Macc 6:28 and Esth 8:12q LXX the Hosean expression "sons of the living God," while referring to the Jewish community delivered by God, still stands closely associated with Gentiles recognizing the reality of the Jewish living God. See the earlier discussion in chap. 2.

times. This motif reflects Paul's conversion theology, stressing God's initiative of calling Gentiles through the preaching of the gospel.[32] As noted previously, the divine call comes through the gospel and serves to initiate the conversion of Gentiles.[33] In 1 Thess 4:7, for example, God has "called" the Thessalonians through the gospel, leading to their election (1.4) and "faith in God" (1:8). Also, in Rom 8:28–30 God's call is linked with justification, suggesting this kerygmatic nuance of the call. God, then, in Rom 9:25–26 calls Gentile converts through the preaching of the gospel to become "sons of the living God."

Romans 9:25 indicates the importance of the call motif since Paul has added it to the original text of Hos 2:25 LXX [2:23 MT]. Paul, in other words, modifies Hos 2:25 LXX to speak about Gentile conversion by adding the call motif to the original LXX wording.[34] In its original form, Hos 2:25 LXX makes no mention of God's call: "And I will have mercy on those without mercy, and I will say to those not my people, you are my people...." Romans 9:25 reads: "I will call (καλέσω) those who were not my people 'my people' and her who was not beloved, 'my beloved.'" Paul modifies the original Hosean verse in two ways. He inverts the order of the two Hosean clauses and he adds the call motif. The expression "I will call (καλέσω)" now stands in place of the original "I will say," governing both clauses in the verse.[35] This Pauline modification results in the placement of "I will call" at the beginning of 9:25, putting it in the prominent initial position, which serves to link it with the preceding "he has called" of 9:24.

Further, the call motif occurs in Rom 9:26, but in this case

---

32. Wilckens, *Der Brief an die Römer,* 2:205.

33. 1 Thess 4:7; 2 Thess 2:14; 1 Cor 1:2; 7:18, 20, 24; Gal 1:6; Eph 4:4; Col 3:15; cf. 1 Pet 2:9–10.

34. Käsemann, *Commentary on Romans,* 274, attributes the combination of the two Hosean texts to Paul. Dunn, *Romans 9–16,* 571–72, observes that καλέσω is "almost certainly Paul's insertion"; also Paul has replaced ἐρῶ with καλέσω "so that the key idea of 'calling' appears in both members of the quotations." See also Fitzmyer, *Romans,* 573.

35. Cranfield, *Romans* 2:499, n. 4, comments that "as a result of this inversion, the reference to 'not my people,' which is particularly suitable to the Gentiles, comes first."

Paul works with the original Hosean text almost verbatim,[36] suggesting that Hos 2:1 LXX was already well suited to speak about Gentile conversion: "and in the very place where it was said to them, 'you are not my people,' they will be called, 'sons of the living God.'" In this verse the call motif occurs in a passive verb: "they will be called" (κληθήσονται)[37] signifying a "divine passive" that implies God as subject.[38] In Rom 9:26, then, God calls Gentile converts who, as a result, experience a reversal of status, passing from "not my people" to covenantal sonship.[39] This reversal of status described in Rom 9:25–26 constitutes another allusion to Gentile conversion. The reversal pattern in Rom 9:25–26 reflects the dynamics of Gentile conversion and its transformative effects. The references to those who are "not my people" designate Gentiles who historically have no claim to being called God's people (cf. 1 Pet 2:9–10). Conversion, then, reverses this status of non-peoplehood and transforms Gentiles into "my people" and "sons of the living God."

Moreover, Rom. 9:25b expresses this transformation in terms of "her who was not beloved" (καὶ τὴν οὐκ ἠγαπημένην) becoming "beloved" (ἠγαπημένην).[40] The use of "beloved" in this context recalls the same term used in 1 Thess 1:4 to describe the Thessalonian converts (cf. 2 Thess 2:13). Conversion makes the Thessalonians "brethren beloved by God" (ἠγαπημένοι ὑπὸ θεοῦ), indicating that the term "beloved" functions as Pauline conversion language (cf. 2 Cor 7:1). Against this background, it becomes clearer that Paul inserted the term "beloved" into the

---

36. There is some question about whether the term ἐκεῖ was added by Paul or is found in some version of Hos 2:1 LXX (Fitzmyer, *Romans,* 573 and Cranfield, *The Epistle to the Romans,* 1:500).

37. This verb recalls the passive form in 9:7, which cites Gen 21:21 LXX.

38. Wilckens, *Der Brief an die Römer,* 192.

39. The sonship motif in 9:26 can be interpreted in connection with Rom 8:14–17. In 8:14, for example, those led by the Spirit are "sons of God" (υἱοί); in 8:15, the baptized cry out "Abba Father," having received the spirit of "sonship" (υἱοθεσίας); and in 8:16, "it is the Spirit himself bearing witness with out spirit that we are children of God" (Fitzmyer, *Romans,* 573, and Wilcken, *Der Brief an die Römer,* 2:206).

40. The manuscripts B and V both attest the verb ἀγαπᾶν, but this is probably the result of later Christian editorial work prompted by Rom 9:25. 1 Pet 2:10 also cites Hos 2:25 LXX, but uses ἠλεημένοι, which is closer to the original Hosean text (Dunn, *Romans 9–16,* 571, and Käsemann, *Commentary on Romans,* 274).

Hosean text to reinforce the allusion to Gentile conversion.[41] In this and other ways, then, the Hosean texts in Rom 9:25–26 are made to speak about Gentile conversion and serve Paul's aim of scripturally documenting the assertion about the call of Gentiles.

Finally, the language in Rom 9:24–26 expresses the deeper theological significance of Gentile conversion as God's act of life-giving, a point which is borne out by several observations. Through the image of the divine potter, the creator theme is already implicit in the immediate literary context of Rom 9:20–23 (cf. Jer 18:1–11; Isa 45:9–10). God, as creator, refashions the old vessel into a new one. Also, the creation theme is expressed in the call motif of 9:24–26 that designates the creator's life-giving call.[42] Romans 4:17 illustrates the link between the divine call and divine life-giving: "as it is written, 'I have made you the father of many nations,'" in the presence of God in whom he believed, who gives life to the dead and calls into existence the things that do not exist" (καὶ καλοῦντος τὰ μὴ ὄντα ὡς ὄντα). God's call here is a creation *ex nihilo* which "calls into existence the things that do not exist"; and this creation from nothing is analogous to God raising the dead. This divine action of creating from nothing and giving life to the dead finds its immediate referent in God's bestowal of a son upon Abraham and Sarah. The God who raises the dead reverses the barrenness of Sarah's womb by giving her a son and this son means life for "many nations." In the birth of Isaac, God shows his power to create life out of deathlike barrenness.

The pattern of language in Rom 9:25–26 reflects the reversal scheme expressed in 4:17, where God reverses the deathlike sit-

---

41. Rom 9:25–26 and 1 Thess 1:4–10 are linked through their use of parallel language and themes. They employ the living God epithet in contexts that refer to Gentile conversion; both passages describe Gentile conversion as God's work, the result of divine elective action (1 Thess 1:4 speaks of "election," whereas Rom 9:24–26 speaks of God's "call"); and both passages refer to Gentile converts as God's "beloved" (1 Thess 1:4; Rom 9:25). Also note the elective language in Rom 9:13: "Jacob I loved, but Esau I hated."

42. Käsemann, *Commentary on Romans,* 274; Wilckens, *Der Brief an die Römer,* 2:206. This view of the divine call as giving life goes back to biblical and Jewish notions of the creator calling things into existence, e.g., Wis 11:25; *2 Bar.* 21:4, 48.8; Philo, *Spec. Laws* 4.187; *Jos. Asen.* 12:1–2.

uation of Abraham and Sarah. More specifically, the expression "things that do not exist" (τὰ μὴ ὄντα) in Rom 4:17 corresponds to "not my people" (τὸν οὐ λαόν μου) in Rom 9:25–26.[43] In the latter, the living God calls those who were not my people to become "my people." Through conversion, God reverses the status of non-existence which characterizes the pre-conversion life of Gentiles; and he does so by giving new life to Gentile converts, a life that transforms Gentiles into "sons of the living God."[44] Romans 4:17 thus furnishes a significant hint for interpreting the call motif in Rom 9:24–26. In the latter, the divine call expresses a divine action that seeks to recreate Gentile converts on analogy with resurrection from the dead. The living God's call in Rom 9:24–26 reverses a deathlike situation of Gentiles who come to new life through conversion. In Rom 9:26, then, "the living God has shown his life-giving power because he has made those who were 'not my people,' 'my people' and 'sons of the living God,' and so has manifested and confirmed his power as creator by calling those who did not exist into existence."[45]

In Rom 9:25–26, then, Paul views Gentile conversion on analogy with God creating the world and raising the dead to life. Through the divine call and conversion, the living God raises "dead" Gentile converts to new life, calling them into existence as "sons of the living God." The living God imparts new life to Gentile converts who become "sons" situated in a filial relation with their divine father. Converts are adopted as "sons" who cry out to God as their father, "Abba" (Rom 8:14–17). This sonship status attained by Gentile converts also indicates the fulfillment of new covenant prophecy. The reversal of status that transforms Gentiles into "sons of the living God" indicates their new identity as covenantal children. Gentile converts, in other words, become new covenantal sons in fulfillment of Hos 2:1, 25 LXX. The implication here is that God's initiative in converting Gentiles is, at the same time, a divine means for inaugurating

---

43. Moxnes, *Theology in Conflict,* 252–53.

44. This idea of conversion as expressing divine life-giving is found in *Jos. Asen.,* in which conversion is the result of a life-giving call (8:9; 15:5) that transforms converts into "sons of the living God" (19:8).

45. Stenger, "Die Gottesbezeichnung 'lebendiger Gott' im Neuen Testament," 65.

the establishment of a new covenant people. 1 Pet 2:9–10 uses Hos 2:25 LXX to express this point: "But you are a chosen race, a royal priesthood, a holy nation, God's own people that you may declare the wonderful deeds of him who called you out of darkness into his marvelous light. Once you were no people, but now are God's people; once you had not received mercy but now you have received mercy."

Conclusions

Paul uses the epithet living God as a way of alluding to the foundational event of Gentile conversion in 1 Thess 1:9–10 and Rom 9:25–26. In Paul's use, the epithet alludes to three aspects of the conversion experience: (1) the kerygmatic roots of conversion—Gentiles hear the kerygma of the living God proclaimed in the mission field; (2) the faith response—Gentiles respond by turning from their former idolatry to faith in the living God; and (3) the foundation of a Gentile community—conversion to the living God is constitutive of Gentile communities, whose origins go back to the activity of the living God. For Paul, then, the epithet living God functions as conversion language, alluding to key aspects in the foundation of Gentile communities.

A primary aspect of Gentile conversion, in Paul's view, is that it reflects God's work and initiative of transforming the hearts of Gentile believers. Paul, in other words, views conversion theologically and employs a variety of terms that express the divine initiative of conversion. For example, the living God operates through the gospel, "calling" Gentiles to faith. This call evokes a faith-response that is constitutive of conversion and consists in the convert's recognition and acceptance of the one true God. In converting to the living God, Gentiles renounce their former gods as nothing more than idols or demons. The resulting transformation is an intellectual enlightenment in which the convert moves from pagan darkness to the light of monotheistic truth. Conversion thus results in a new life defined by an exclusive service rendered to the living God who alone is worthy of worship. This new life of service also entails a holy life on the part of Gentile converts, empowered by the Holy Spirit.

Further, the Spirit in Paul's letters also functions as conversion language, evoking the experience of divine power that accompanied Paul's preaching and brought about the experience of conversion (1 Thess 1:5–6; Gal 3:2–5; 1 Cor 2:4–5; Rom 15:18–19). The divine power of the Spirit plays an important role in Gentiles converting to the living God, and Paul can use the Spirit motif in alluding to the missionary origins of a community. The expression "Spirit of the living God" in 2 Cor 3:3 functions in this way, alluding to the foundational events of conversion in Corinth. Further, the bestowal of the Spirit in conversion and baptism marks a Gentile community as God's temple and the locus of the Spirit's indwelling (1 Cor 3:16–17; 6:19; 2 Cor 6:16). The presence of the Holy Spirit motivates the community to a life of holiness.

Paul also alludes to conversion as an event associated with God's life-giving action. God's eschatological life is made available in the mission field through the preaching of the gospel and the activity of the Spirit. Conversion to the living God is viewed on analogy with a movement from death to life. Through conversion, Gentiles receive new life as God's children and beloved elect (1 Thess 1:3–4; Rom 8:14–17). Through conversion, the living God calls converts from darkness to light, recalling the Genesis creation of light and expressing the life-giving initiative of a new creation (1 Thess 5:4–5; 2 Cor 4:4; 6:15; Acts 26:18). Further, Romans 9:25–26 is explicit in describing this procreational aspect of conversion. On analogy with God raising the dead (Rom 4:17), Gentile converts, who were "not my people," are recreated through conversion as "my people" and "sons of the living God."

Ultimately, conversion to the living God for Paul is directed to the broader goal of bringing about an eschatological new creation (2 Cor 5:17). Through Gentile conversion, the living God establishes Gentile communities of faith as new families of God and these communities have their origins in conversion to the living God. They are "in God the Father ..." (1 Thess 1:2), indicating their divine origins in the God "from whom are all things" (1 Cor 8:6). They are "church(es) of the living God" whose roots are missionary in character (1 Tim 3:15; cf. 2 Cor

6:16). Moreover, the living God establishes these communities as part of a wider divine initiative of fulfilling new covenant prophecy and restoring the future Israel envisioned by the prophets. In Rom 9:25–26 Hosea's prophecy of a future Israel restored by divine action becomes a prophecy of Gentile conversion. Through conversion, Gentiles become "sons of the living God," an expression that indicates the new covenantal identity of the converts. God's call is thus a creative life-giving call that brings new life to Gentiles as new covenantal sons and daughters in fulfillment of Hosea's new covenant prophecy. This link between Gentile conversion and new covenant prophecy holds important ramifications for understanding 2 Cor 3:3 and 6:16.

Chapter Seven

2 Corinthians 3:3 and the Spirit of the Living God

⛶⛶⛶⛶⛶⛶⛶⛶⛶⛶⛶⛶

I turn now to Paul's use of the living God in 2 Cor 3:3 and 6:16 to interpret these two verses against the background of living God traditions examined in the previous chapters: biblical traditions associating the living God with covenantal themes; Hellenistic-Jewish traditions that promote the living God as creator in antithesis to idols; and Pauline kerygmatic traditions in which the living God raises Jesus from the dead. In this chapter, however, the focus will be on 2 Cor 3:3 with its rich and multivalent expression "the Spirit of the living God." The Pauline significance of this expression involves a complex melding of different backgrounds and represents Paul's innovative use of these backgrounds. I will argue that Paul, in coining the expression "Spirit of the living God," makes creative use of two traditional motifs, "Spirit" and "living God," that he combines into a single expression, creating a *hapax legomenon* in the Bible. The expression carries multiple associations that serve Paul's specific epistolary aims in 2 Cor 3:3.

The Spirit of the Living God: Recent History of Interpretation

In 2 Cor 3:3, Paul tells the Corinthians that he has no need of recommendation letters because they themselves perform this commendatory function: "(3a) and you show that you are a letter from Christ ministered by us, (3b) written not with ink, but with the Spirit of the living God, (3c) not on tablets of stone but on tablets of fleshy hearts." Although interpreters generally acknowledge the extraordinary character of the content in this verse, basic questions about it remain unexplored. For example, what does the expression "Spirit of the living God" mean and what are its origins as a *hapax legomenon* in the Bible? Little has been done to address such questions and explore the function of the expression within the overall structure of the verse.[1] I will therefore attempt to show that the expression "Spirit of the living God" functions as a compact allusion to the conversion of the Corinthians, and that the epithet living God plays a crucial role in this allusion.

The following discussion thus begins with a recent history of interpretation that investigates standard trends and approaches to the expression "Spirit of the living God." There are several advantages to beginning the discussion in this way. A recent history of interpretation serves to highlight the prevailing scholarly neglect of the expression as an allusion to Paul's preaching ministry in Corinth and the resulting conversion. Also, while most interpreters miss the kerygmatic significance of the expression, a few have recognized this significance and provide illuminating comments that are worth reviewing. A final advantage to doing a history of interpretation is that it serves to contextualize the expression in its literary context. The expression "Spirit of the living God" remains enigmatic because it occurs in a literary context that is notoriously dense, employing a rapid sequence of complex motifs and shifting imagery. A review of scholarly interpretation will thus contextualize the expression "Spirit of the living God" within the framework of 2 Cor 3:3 and highlight specific exegetical issues to which an interpretation of the expression is linked.

In turning to the "Spirit of the living God" and its recent history of interpretation, I begin with the widespread trend

---

1. Commentators generally acknowledge the uniqueness of the expression "Spirit of the living God." For example, Everding, "The Living God," 330, observes that the expression "is unique in biblical and extra-biblical literature"; Hans Windisch, *Der zweite Korintherbrief* (MeyerK 6; Göttingen: Vandenhoeck & Ruprecht, 1924), 106, notes that the expression is unparalleled in the Bible; and Ralph Martin, *2 Corinthians* (WBC; Waco, Tex.: Word Books, 1986), 52, observes that the expression is "an exceptional title—found only here in the Bible."

that ignores the presence of the epithet in 2 Cor 3:3 and so avoids the issue of the living God altogether. In this approach, commentators tend to remain silent on Paul's use of the epithet, assuming that it is an equivalent term for "God."[2] There is nothing unusual or special in Paul's use of the epithet. The expression "Spirit of the living God" is assumed to be synonymous with the more common expression "Spirit of God." The problem with this approach is that it ignores the rich biblical, Jewish, and early Christian significance of the epithet examined in previous chapters. Another popular approach to "Spirit of the living God" explains the expression as Paul's creative transformation of biblical language, specifically, Exod 31:18 LXX, which is identified as the generative source: "And he gave to Moses, when he had made an end to speaking with him upon Mount Sinai, the two tables (πλάκας λιθίνας) of the testimony, tables of stone, written with the finger of God"[3] (Exod 31:18 LXX). In this approach "Spirit of the living God" is the result of "...a transformation of the Exodus text 'written by the finger of God,' since even the instrumental dative of the source is retained."[4] This explanation has in its favor linguistic parallels found in 2 Cor 3:2–3 and Exod 31:18 LXX. For example, both texts refer to God "writing" on stone tablets.

There are, however, several drawbacks to this approach. For example, it does not explain the presence of the living God epithet in 2 Cor 3:3, nor is the Spirit motif attributable to Exodus.[5] In fact, no textual version of Exodus, either Hebrew or Greek,

---

2. J. F. Collange, *Énigmes de la deuxième épître de Paul aux Corinthiens: Étude exegetique de 2 Cor. 2:14–7:4* (SNTSMS 18; Cambridge: Cambridge University Press, 1986), 52–53, renders the expression as 'Spirit of God." C. K. Barrett, *The Second Epistle to the Corinthians* (HNTC; Peabody, Mass.: Hendrickson, 1973), 108–9, makes no comment about the living God, limiting his discussion to the spirit motif alone. See also P. E. B. Allo, *Saint Paul. Seconde épître aux Corinthians* (Paris: Librairie Lecoffre, 1956), 81, who cites parallel usages but does not comment on the meaning of the epithet.

3. Earl Richard, "Polemics, Old Testament, and Theology. A Study of II Cor. III,1–IV,6," *RB* 88 (1981): 340–67. Also, R. Martin, *2 Corinthians*, 52; J. F. Collange, *Énigmes*, 51; and Richard Hays, *Echoes of Scripture in the Letters of Paul* (New Haven: Yale University Press, 1989), 128–29.

4. Earl Richard, 'Polemics, Old Testament, and Theology," 348.

5. Furnish, *II Corinthians*, 195. Richardson, *Paul's Language about God*, 152, recognizes that "this phrase...does not occur in any of the verses in the Old Testament which may be the basis of Paul's thought and language."

contains any mention of the living God. The transformation of Exod 31:18 into "Spirit of the living God" would have to create the epithet out of thin air, so to speak. It is therefore unlikely that Exod 31:18 by itself serves to explain the origins of the expression "Spirit of the living God," and one wonders if there are not better scriptural parallels for clarifying the origins of the expression.[6]

Another approach to "Spirit of the living God" focuses on the rhetorical function of the expression within the overall context of the verse. In this approach interpreters explain "Spirit of the living God" as highlighting the divine means by which God, metaphorically, "writes" the Corinthian "letter." Paul sets "Spirit of the living God" in contrast to "ink," signifying human instrumentality.[7] Alfred Plummer, for example, concludes that "the epithet accentuates the contrast between the abiding illumination of the Spirit and the perishable blackness of inanimate ink."[8] Similarly, Henry Everding says that the expression "is used as a rhetorical device which accents the superiority and correctness of the Spirit as that which is in keeping with the nature of God more than a code 'written in ink.' "[9] These assessments are certainly correct, but they are incomplete and leave fundamental questions about the expression unaddressed, such as the meaning of the living God in the verse.

A further approach to "Spirit of the living God" also neglects the epithet "living God" in 2 Cor 3:3, but it is valuable in focusing on the Spirit motif. This approach is valuable for interpreting "Spirit of the living God" since it sheds light on the Spirit motif, which is directly linked to the epithet and thus has some relevance to understanding the epithet.[10] It takes its

---

6. Windisch, *Der zweite Korintherbrief,* 106, has cited other possible scriptural parallels, e.g., Ezek 37:5; Deut 4:33 LXX; Dan 4:19 LXX; and Hos 2:1 LXX.

7. For example, Scott J. Hafemann, *Suffering and Ministry in the Spirit: Paul's Defense of His Ministry in II Corinthians 2:14–3:3* (Grand Rapids: Eerdmans, 1988), 206; and Windisch, *Der zweite Korintherbrief,* 106.

8. Alfred Plummer, *A Critical and Exegetical Commentary on the Second Epistle of St. Paul to the Corinthians* (ICC; Edinburgh: T. & T. Clark, 1985), 82.

9. Everding, "The Living God," 331. See also Hafemann, *Suffering and Ministry in the Spirit,* 206, who stresses the Spirit of the living God as "the means by which this letter belonging to Christ has been written."

10. For example, Ingo Hermann, *Kyrios und Pneuma: Studien zur Christologie der*

cue from 2 Cor 3:6 where Paul describes the Spirit as an agent of divine life-giving. In 3:6 Paul asserts that he is a competent minister of the new covenant, not in a written code but in the Spirit, "for the letter kills, but the Spirit gives life" (τὸ γὰρ γράμμα ἀποκτέννει, τὸ δὲ πνεῦμα ζῳοποιεῖ).[11] The Spirit is the life-giving power (present tense) associated with the new covenant, in contrast to the "letter" which kills.[12] The life-giving Spirit of 2 Cor 3:6 is thus decisive in influencing the interpretation of the "Spirit of the living God" in 3:3 as the agent of divine life-giving in Corinth. Paul's assertions about the Spirit in 2 Cor 3:6 are read back into 3:3 and applied to the Spirit of the living God.

Further, while interpreters agree that the "Spirit of the living God" gives life in 2 Cor 3:3, there is little or no discussion of the precise nature of this life-giving, nor is much attention given to the role of the living God in this context. The few attempts that are made to specify the nature of this life-giving are, again, largely indebted to the influence 2 Cor 3:6. Interpreters assume the life-giving capacity of the Spirit in 2 Cor 3:3 under the influence of the verb "to make alive" in 3:6, which, in turn, is paralleled by Rom 8:10–11.[13] The latter associates the Spirit's life-giving with both Jesus' resurrection and the future resurrection of the dead (cf. Rom 1:3–4). The Spirit's life-giving is thus associated with the eschatological reality of resurrection, both past and future (cf. 2 Cor 5:5). While these observations are cer-

---

paulinischen Hauptbrief (Munich: Kösel, 1961), 28; Kraus, "Der lebendige Gott," 197. Richardson, *Paul's Language about God*, 152, observes that "Paul no doubt felt it necessary to amplify the single word πνεύματι, making clear its theological significance."

11. There is a vast literature and history of interpretation on this verse. For recent discussions see Furnish, *II Corinthians*, 198–200; Richardson, *Paul's Language about God*, 152–55; Thomas E. Provence, " 'Who Is Sufficient for These Things?' An Exegesis of 2 Corinthians ii 15–iii 18," *NovT* 24 (1982): 62–68; and Heikki Räisänen, *Paul and the Law* (Philadelphia: Fortress Press, 1986), 243–45.

12. The closest Pauline parallels are Rom 2:29 and 7:6. Furnish, *II Corinthians*, 200, notes that the letter motif "is not fully synonymous with 'the law.' " What Paul rejects here is that way of using the law "which presumes that its 'letter' provides a sure way to righteousness and life."

13. Furnish, *II Corinthians*, 185, calls Rom 8:11 "the closest parallel to this thought elsewhere in Paul's letters." Rom 8:11: "If the Spirit of him who raised Jesus from the dead dwells in you, he who raised Christ Jesus from the dead will give life (ζῳοποιήσει) to your mortal bodies also through his Spirit which dwells in you."

tainly valuable, they do not get at the exact nuance of the Spirit's
life-giving in 2 Cor 3:3. This nuance has to do with life-giving in
the present as is suggested from the present tense "makes alive"
in 3:6 (cf. 2 Cor 2:15–16a). In 2 Cor 3:3, the "Spirit of the living
God" is the source of a present manifestation of eschatological
life that comes through Paul's preaching ministry (cf. 2 Cor 3:8;
3:16–18; and 6:6).[14]

Finally, some interpreters attempt to explain the expression
"Spirit of the living God" in connection with the scriptural background of the new covenant, especially that of Ezekiel and
Jeremiah. The Spirit in 2 Cor 3:3 is "the power of the eschatological new covenant."[15] Allusions to the new covenant are
already present in 2 Cor 3:2 in the expression "written on your/
our hearts" (Jer 38:33 LXX); and in 3:3c in the reference to the
Spirit of the living God "writing...on tablets of fleshy hearts."
In the latter Paul undeniably alludes to Ezek 11:19 and 36:26,
both of which speak of God giving a "new spirit" to Israel as
part of the future covenant. The expression "Spirit of the living God" is thus closely linked to Ezekiel's "new spirit," a divine
spirit that in Ezek 37:1–14 restores dead Israel to new life.[16]

In this approach, however, there are problems with interpreters overstating the influence of Ezekiel and singling out
Ezekiel as the sole generative source of motifs in 2 Cor 3:3.
Such an approach does not fully account for the Pauline significance of the Spirit, which is a rich and polyvalent term that
cannot be reduced to a single meaning. While the "Spirit of
the living God" certainly does recall Ezekiel's spirit, the Pauline
view of the Spirit has other referents, including a kerygmatic
referent designating the Spirit as an active power in the mission field. Second, the background of Ezekiel's new covenant
language does not account for the presence of the epithet "living God" in 2 Cor 3:3. The expression "Spirit of the living God"
is a *hapax legomenon* in the Bible and cannot be traced to any

---

14. Barrett, *The Second Epistle to the Corinthians*, 108–9; and Furnish, *II Corinthians*, 189.

15. Kraus, "Der lebendige Gott," 197.

16. Some interpreters view the Spirit motif in terms of its prophetic background (Collange, *Énigmes*, 52; Provence, "Who Is Sufficient for These Things?" 66–67).

biblical source, including the prophet Ezekiel. Finally, Ezekiel's new covenant language does not account for the antithetical phrasing of 2 Cor 3:3c, "not on tablets of stone, but on tablets of fleshy hearts" (οὐκ ἐν πλαξὶν λιθίναις ἀλλ᾿ ἐν πλαξὶν καρδίαις σαρκίναις). It remains unclear what motivated Paul to introduce the motif of "not on tablets of stone" at the beginning of 3:3c.[17]

In terms of literary function the expression "Spirit of the living God" stands at a pivotal point in 2 Cor 3:3b, introducing a new line of thought in 3:3c. This new line of thought represents an odd jump in Paul's thought that must be accounted for. The reader expects the use of paper or parchment in continuation of the letter theme. However, Paul introduces scriptural-covenantal motifs in 3:3c, and so the metaphor of the letter seems to break down. The difficulty here is accentuated by the direct sequence of the living God at the end of 3:3b and tablets of stone at the beginning of 3:3c. The transition of 3:3b and 3:3c juxtaposes "Spirit of the living God" with the Pentateuchal motif "not on tablets of stone."[18] The question of transition therefore remains: how does 3:3c serve to develop the thought of 3:3b? In particular, what motivated the transition from "Spirit of the living God" to "not on tablets of stone?"

There are numerous attempts to explain this "jump" in Paul's logic. One approach appeals to extrinsic factors, such as the language of Paul's opponents and their Mosaic traditions.[19] J. Murphy-O'Connor, for example, observes that Paul introduces the tablets of stone "because Paul associated the bearers of the letters of recommendation with the Mosaic law."[20] The same explanation could be given to the expression "Spirit of the

---

17. Provence, "Who Is Sufficient for These Things?" 60, observes that "by the end of v. 3 the metaphor has shifted so completely as hardly to be relevant to the image of the ἐπιστολή at all." See also Plummer, *Second Epistle of St. Paul to the Corinthians*, 82; and Hafemann, *Suffering in Ministry and the Spirit*, 204.

18. Hafemann, *Suffering in Ministry and Spirit*, 206–7, observes that this transition is not "a mere repetition of thought" since "the second contrast functions to amplify the first."

19. Dieter Georgi, *The Opponents of Paul in Second Corinthians* (Philadelphia: Fortress Press, 1986), 242–50, explains Paul's "jerky argumentation" in this section as reflecting a critical engagement with opponents.

20. Jerome Murphy-O'Connor, *2 Corinthians* (Cambridge: Cambridge University Press, 1991), 32; cf. Räisänen, *Paul and the Law*, 244.

living God." The epithet "living God" is part of the opponents' vocabulary which Paul takes up and engages in his response. While this is certainly possible, the problem here is that both the epithet "living God" and the Spirit are part of Paul's own theological vocabulary, as discussed in the previous chapters. Paul and the Corinthians are already familiar with the living God from Paul's earlier missionary teaching in Corinth. Why, therefore, appeal to extrinsic factors, when a simpler explanation lies closer at hand?

Another attempt at resolution focuses on the scriptural background of the Spirit motif and then appeals to Paul's "theological innovation" or "daring interpretive act."[21] Paul is creative in innovating with scriptural motifs of the new covenant, the most important of which derives from Ezekiel. At the end of 3:3b, Paul mentions the "Spirit of the living God," triggering a complex network of associations that starts with Ezekiel's new covenant "spirit." The motif of Ezekiel's "spirit" in 3:3b then triggers the broader associations of Ezekiel's new covenant; in particular, the idea of God writing upon "tablets of fleshy hearts" at the end of 3:3c. Further, the reference to Ezekiel's "tablets of fleshy hearts" carries the antithetical associations of Ezekiel's "heart of stone" in Ezek 11:19 and 36:26. The prophet's new covenantal "tablets of fleshy hearts" are contrasted with Israel's "heart of stone."[22] With the pejorative "heart of stone" in mind, Paul then jumps imaginatively to the Pentateuchal motif of "tablets of stone" in 3:3c. The antithesis of 3:3c thus pivots on Ezekiel's contrast but has been creatively transformed into a contrast of stone tablets and tablets of fleshy hearts.[23] Paul thus gives the language of Ezekiel "a new turn.... His thought flies from the stone heart to its opposite number, the heart of flesh;

---

21. Richard B. Hays, *Echoes of Scripture in the Letters of Paul* (New Haven: Yale University Press, 1988), 129; Collange, *Énigmes*, 53; and Plummer, *Second Epistle of St. Paul to the Corinthians*, 82.

22. Martin, *2 Corinthians*, 52, observes that "Paul has innovated in a remarkable way: he has assimilated 'heart of stone' to 'tablets of stone.' " Cf. Barrett, *The Second Epistle to the Corinthians*, 109; Bultmann, *The Second Letter to the Corinthians*, 72–73; and Provence, "Who Is Sufficient for These Things?" 60–61.

23. Hays, *Echoes of Scripture*, 129.

this he mentions as a contrast to the stone tablets, omitting to mention the heart of stone altogether."[24]

This approach has some value in perceiving the complexity and subtlety with which Paul handles scriptural language. However, it remains unconvincing on two points. First, the conditions of Ezekiel's "stony heart" are not actually expressed in 2 Cor 3:3, nor does Ezekiel ever contrast tablets of fleshy hearts with the Mosaic law.[25] Such an explanation requires considerable imagination to leap from Ezekiel's "stoney hearts" to the Pentateuchal "tablets of stone" in 3:3c, and it goes beyond what the evidence will bear.[26] Second, this approach suffers from the same weakness as other approaches previously examined. It does not adequately account for the presence of the living God epithet in 2 Cor 3:3. Neither Ezekiel nor Exodus offer the generative source for the living God epithet in this verse. From what source, then, did Paul derive his use of the epithet, and why did he choose to employ it exactly at the point of transition to 3:3c?

What interpreters fail to consider in explaining the transition of 2 Cor 3:3b and 3:3c is the traditional background of the living God as a factor. In biblical and Jewish tradition, the living God was portrayed as the giver of the Decalogue who inscribed the commandments on two stone tablets. For Jews and Jewish-Christians in the first century, mention of the living God would have triggered the association of the "stone tablets" inscribed on Sinai/Horeb. There is, then, a fundamental congruence of the living God and the stone tablets of the law. Further, in biblical tradition the living God is also closely linked to new covenant prophecy, particularly that of Hos 2:1 LXX [1:10 MT]. Romans 9:25–26 reinforces this link, showing that, for Paul, conversion to the living God, understood in its deeper theological significance, comes in fulfillment of the new covenant. Could it not be, then, that "not on tablets of stone but on tablets of fleshy

---

24. Räisänen, *Paul and the Law,* 244.
25. Hafemann, *Suffering and Ministry in the Spirit,* 214–15.
26. Also, caution ought to be exercised in relying too much on late rabbinic parallels by themselves.

hearts" in 2 Cor 3:3c is generated as an association of the epithet living God in 3:3b?

The Spirit of the Living God
and Paul's Allusion to Conversion

The expression, "Spirit of the living God," represents a novel combination of motifs which have no parallel in biblical and Jewish literature, and so it has remained an enigma among interpreters. What interpreters fail to realize is that the expression is a Pauline creation that carries a fundamental kerygmatic significance in alluding to the foundations of the Corinthian community and Paul's apostolic role in those foundations. The expression "Spirit of the living God" is a rich and polyvalent term that serves Paul's epistolary aims of recalling the Corinthians to the event of their communal origins. Through the expression, Paul recalls the Corinthians to several important events in the foundations of the community: (1) Paul's missionary preaching of the living God in Corinth; (2) the activity of the Spirit which accompanied his preaching; and (3) the resulting experience of conversion to the living God that led to the foundation of the Corinthian community. The beauty of the expression, "Spirit of the living God," then, is its richness and compactness, encapsulating several different aspects of community origins, particularly Paul's role in those origins.

Three types of evidence support this view of the "Spirit of the living God" as an allusion to the foundational event of conversion in Corinth. The first type of evidence concerns the manner in which Paul utilizes the expression in 2 Cor 3:3. Nowhere in 2 Corinthians does Paul explain the meaning of the expression to his Corinthian readers, suggesting that an explanation was not necessary. Paul, in other words, employs the expression with no explanation because it is an allusion to something already familiar to his readers. However, one wonders, then, how the Corinthians would have been familiar with this *hapax legomenon*. It is possible, of course, that the expression was known in Corinth from Paul's opponents, who introduced it into the vocabulary of the Corinthians. However, this approach overlooks a more obvious explanation: the expression represents two traditional terms already familiar to the Corinthians from Paul's missionary preaching in Corinth. The "Spirit of the living God" consists of terms known to the Corinthians from Paul's initial missionary visit to Corinth. Paul simply combines these two familiar terms into the novel expression "Spirit of the living God." Interpreted this way, the expression would be comprehensible to the Corinthians as Paul's own encapsulation of his missionary role in Corinth. Further, it is likely that Paul coined the expression specifically for use in his composition of 2 Corinthians. The expression "Spirit of the living God" serves well his epistolary aims of self-commendation and functions as the key point in shifting his train of thought in 2 Cor 3:3.

A second type of evidence supports the "Spirit of the living God" as an allusion to Paul's ministry in Corinth: the epistolary context within which the expression occurs. Second Corinthians 2:14–7:4 represents a major literary unit within the letter, addressing the issue of Paul's apostolic credentials and the need for the Corinthians to reconcile with him. This unit is introduced by 2 Cor 2:14–4:6, in which Paul seeks to clarify his apostolic credentials by recalling the results of his ministry in Corinth. Paul's focus is on his role as proclaimer of the gospel and the power of this gospel in establishing the Corinthian community.[27] He commends himself as a genuine preacher of the gospel in contrast to "the many peddlers of God's word" (2:17). This epistolary strategy also characterizes 2 Cor 3:1–3, the passage which constitutes the immediate literary context for the expression "Spirit of the living God," and this context offers clues as to the significance of the expression.

The epistolary setting of 2 Cor 3:1–3 furnishes what can be described as a "missionary-conversion setting," which indicates a missionary-conversion significance of the expression "Spirit of the living God."[28] An inspection of the language and motifs in 2 Cor 3:1–3 serves to clarify individual components in

---

27. Erich Dinkler, "Die Verkündigung als eschatologisch-sakramentales Geschehen. Auslegung von 2 Kor 5,14–6,2," *Die Zeit Jesus: Festschrift für Heinrich Schleier* (ed. G. Bornkamm and K. Rahner; Freiburg: Herder, 1970), 169–70.
28. Everding, "The Living God," 330, n. 2.

this missionary-conversion setting. Two Corinthians 3:1–3 is an integral literary unit placed between the sub-units of 2 Cor 2:14–17 and 3:4–6. The latter are directly related in content, each unit addressing the theme of apostolic sufficiency. 3:4–6 explicitly resumes the line of thought begun in 2:16b–17. With 2 Cor 3:1–3, however, Paul's discourse seemingly shifts to another topic, that of recommendation letters brought to Corinth by certain individuals. In 3:1, Paul abruptly introduces the letter motif: "are we beginning to commend ourselves again? Or do we need as some do letters of recommendation to you or from you?" (3:1)[29] The second question indicates Paul's awareness of "some" who have come into Corinth with recommendation letters offered as proof of apostolic credentials. Paul has thus "come in for some criticism, from some quarter, for seeking to recommend himself in an inappropriate way."[30] 3:1–3 would therefore seem to have little relation to what precedes in 2:14–17 or what follows in 3:4–6.

However, 2 Cor 3:1–3 upon closer inspection, is integral to the surrounding discourse, standing in close relation to the theme of apostolic sufficiency. It functions as "a sort of parenthesis...although it is by no means beside the point."[31] In 3:2 Paul presents his apostolic credentials to the Corinthians: "You yourselves are our letter of recommendation, written on our hearts, to be known and read by all men."[32] The tangible existence of the Corinthian community provides Paul with the needed "commendation." Oddly enough, though, Paul in 3:2 asserts that the Corinthians are in "our hearts," while at the same time they are a letter "known and read by all." The turn

---

29. Hafemann, *Suffering in Ministry and the Spirit,* 182.
30. Furnish, *II Corinthians,* 192. Jerry L. Sumney, *Identifying Paul's Opponents: The Question of Method in 2 Corinthians* (JSNTSup 40; Sheffield: JSOT Press, 1990), 128–29, infers from 2 Cor 3:1b that "some preachers have come to Corinth with letters of recommendation which they use as evidence of apostolic status." See also Georgi, *The Opponents of Paul in Second Corinthians,* 242–46.
31. Furnish, *II Corinthians,* 192.
32. The reading "our hearts" is preferred to a reading of "your heart," the latter followed in the RSV and NAB. See Bruce Metzger, *A Textual Commentary on the Greek New Testament,* 3d ed. (London and New York: United Bible Societies, 1975), 577; Baird, "Letters of Recommendation," 166–72; Hafemann, *Suffering in Ministry and the Spirit,* 198–96; and Furnish, *II Corinthians,* 181.

of phrase in 3:2 is "...a little confusing because it makes two points at once: it emphasizes Paul's love for the Corinthians and the fact that they themselves are proof of Paul's legitimacy."[33] The phrase "in our heart" designates the great affection which Paul has for the Corinthians; he often speaks of bearing the congregation in his heart (e.g., Phil 1:7; 1 Thess 2:17–20).[34] At the same time, however, the phrase "known and read by all" refers to the tangible existence of the Corinthian community which attests Paul's work as an apostle. In 2 Cor 3:2, then, the Corinthian community is both the community that Paul affectionately bears in his heart and the community whose tangible existence bears witness to his success as an apostle.

In 2 Cor 3:3, Paul continues the letter imagery from the previous verses: "(3:3a) showing that you are a letter from Christ ministered by us (διακονηθεῖσα ὑφ᾽ ἡμῶν),[35] (3:3b) written not with ink but with the Spirit of the living God, (3:3c) not with stone tablets but with tablets of fleshy hearts." The Corinthians show that they are a "letter of Christ" (ἐπιστοὴ Χριστοῦ), meaning that, as a community, their origins are in Christ.[36] The allusion here is, in all likelihood, to the missionary origins of the community through the gospel. The preaching of Christ has led to the foundation of the Corinthian church. Further, this letter of Christ is "ministered by us," Paul indicating his own role as courier of the letter and "minister" of the community.[37] The verb "ministered" in 3:3a points to Paul's role as minister of the

---

33. Hays, *Echoes of Scripture in the Letters of Paul*, 127. Linda Belleville, "Paul's Polemic and Theology of the Spirit in 2 Corinthians," *CBQ* 58 (1996): 291, observes that "while it may be stretching the analogy to speak of a letter written on the gospel minister's heart, it aptly fits Paul's argument in chapters 1–7 that the true apostolic credentials are of an internal spiritual nature and not of an external material sort."

34. Furnish, *II Corinthians*, 194. Hafemann, *Suffering in Ministry and the Spirit*, 196, argues that the letter known and read by all could refer to Paul's suffering as an apostle, "for the suffering which Paul undergoes as an apostle, precisely because he was the one who was called to establish the church in Corinth, can be readily seen by all."

35. The subject of φανερούμενοι is "you yourselves" from the preceding clause in 3:2.

36. "Letter of Christ" is a subjective or authorial genitive (Furnish, *II Corinthians*, 182, 195; Martin, *2 Corinthians*, 51; and Barrett, *The Second Epistle to the Corinthians*, 108).

37. William Baird, "Letters of Recommendation: A Study of 2 Cor 3:1–3," *JBL* 80 (1961): 169. Hays, *Echoes of Scripture in the Letters of Paul*, 127, observes that v. 3

new covenant in 3:6, and its use in the past tense (aorist) likely indicates Paul's initial missionary work in Corinth.[38] Paul's act of "ministering" in Corinth makes him one of the "ministers" (διάκονοι) through whom the Corinthians "believed" (1 Cor 3:5; cf. 4:1). Paul also has a "ministry of the Spirit" (2 Cor 3:8), and later Paul speaks of his preaching as a "ministry of reconciliation" entrusted to him by God (2 Cor 5:18–20). In 2 Cor 3:3, then, the reference to Paul having "ministered" in Corinth expresses Paul's role in the formulation of the Corinthian letter: "the Corinthians owe their existence as Christians to Paul's ministry in Corinth."[39]

Second Corinthians 3:3b continues by stressing the divine authorship of the Corinthian letter: "... you are a letter ministered by us, written not with ink, but with the Spirit of the living God." The Corinthian letter, "ministered" by Paul and his coworkers, is written by the Spirit of the living God and is thus divinely authored. Paul's ministry in founding the Corinthian community is thus bound up with the activity of the Spirit that accompanied his preaching. As noted previously, most interpreters take "Spirit of the living God" as a functional concept, stressing the divine means by which God, metaphorically, "writes" the Corinthian "letter." The "Spirit of the living God" is set in contrast to human instrumentality (=ink) as the divine means of God writing.[40] With the expression "Spirit of the living God" Paul thus alludes to the foundation of the Corinthian community through conversion. Commenting on the expression, C. K. Barrett observes that "it was the Spirit who was the agent of the Corinthian conversion ... "; Victor Furnish observes that: "When Paul attributes to the Spirit the writing of the 'letter' from Christ, this is in full accord with his conviction

---

"images the courier's careful handling of the letter and, at the same time, reminds the Corinthians of Paul's ministry among them."

38. The verb "ministered" renders the aorist participle διακονηθεῖσα. Furnish, *II Corinthians*, 182, observes that "the aorist tense points back to the founding of the Corinthian congregation." See also Hafemann, *Suffering and Ministry in the Spirit*, 204; and Windisch, *Der zweite Korintherbrief*, 105.

39. Hafemann, *Suffering and Ministry in the Spirit*, 205.

40. Ibid., 206. See also Windisch, *Der zweite Korintherbrief*, 106.

that his gospel has been able to take root in places like Corinth because of the powerful working of the Spirit. . . . "[41]

Moving to the last clause of the verse in 3:3c, Paul describes the material on which the Spirit writes, "not on tablets of stone, but on tablets of fleshy hearts," alluding to the Pentateuch and Ezekiel. At this point in the verse, however, Paul's logic seems to take a new direction, abruptly shifting to covenantal themes. I will therefore leave off discussing 3:3c until the next section and here summarize the main points of the preceding discussion. The epistolary context of 2 Cor 3:1–3 offers significant clues for interpreting the expression "Spirit of the living God," since it is a missionary-conversion setting permeated by motifs of Paul's preaching and conversion. In 3:2–3 Paul shifts attention "from his own qualifications to the Corinthian community itself as the visible fruit of apostolic labor."[42] This apostolic labor is evident in the fact that he was "co-author" of the Corinthian community, having "ministered" there by preaching the gospel and by bringing the Corinthians to faith. While Paul asserts his role as "co-author" of the Corinthian community, he also subordinates his role to the activity of the living God's Spirit, stressing the divine grounding of his ministry. Paul reminds the Corinthians that "it is the very existence of the Spirit in the Corinthian church which supports Paul's claim to apostolic authority in Corinth, since he was the one through whom the Spirit came."[43]

A third and final type of evidence is decisive in showing that the "Spirit of the living God" alludes to Paul's ministry in Corinth: the epithet "living God." For Paul, the epithet carries the associations of his preaching to Gentiles and the conversion that resulted from it. Chapter 5 has shown that the living God was a regular component in Paul's monotheistic kerygma and carries the association of Gentiles converting. First Thessalonians 1:9; Acts 14:15; and *Acts Paul* 7:2 indicate that Paul proclaimed

---

41. Barrett, *The Second Epistle to the Corinthians,* 108; Furnish, *II Corinthians,* 195. Plummer, *Second Epistle of St. Paul to the Corinthians,* 82, observes that "the Spirit is an efficient force and the letter that it produces consists of living persons."

42. Hay, *Echoes of Scripture,* 127. Also, Hafemann, *Suffering in Ministry and Spirit,* 98.

43. Hafemann, *Suffering and Ministry in the Spirit,* 207.

the living God as a regular part of his monotheistic kerygma and Corinth would have been no exception to this practice. In Corinth, as in Thessalonika, Paul exhorted Gentiles to "turn" to the living God from "dumb idols" (2 Cor 3:16; 1 Cor 12:2) that "have no real existence" (1 Cor 8:4). In accepting Paul's gospel, the Corinthians put their faith in the living God who was "one God, the Father, from whom are all things..." (1 Cor 8:6); and they therefore came to the "knowledge" of monotheistic truth (2 Cor 2:14, 4:2). Further, the living God proclaimed in Corinth was the God "who raised the Lord Jesus" and who "will raise us also" (2 Cor 4:14; cf. 2 Cor 1:9). Paul could therefore use the epithet "living God" in 2 Cor 3:3 as a term already familiar to the Corinthians from his missionary work in Corinth.

Further, the use of the Spirit motif, in combination with the epithet, serves to reinforce the missionary-conversion significance of the expression. The Spirit in Corinth was an "agent of conversion."[44] It was the living God, acting through the Spirit, who brought about conversion in Corinth. As discussed above, the Spirit motif in Paul's vocabulary is a term for conversion, designating a divine power that accompanies and confirms Paul's preaching (1 Thess 1:4–6; 1 Cor 2:4–5; Gal 3:2–5; and Rom 15:18–19). This experience of the Spirit constituted a "primary datum" in the missionary foundation of Paul's communities.[45] First Corinthians 2:4–5 is particularly significant in showing that the Corinthian community had its origins "in demonstration of spirit and power." In fact, the expression "Spirit of the living God" can be interpreted as "a summary of Paul's prior description of his apostolic ministry of the Spirit in 1 Cor. 2:1–5, where the contrast between human instrumentality (2:1) and the power of the Spirit (2:4) is said to have determined both the method and the content of Paul's missionary preaching in Corinth."[46] Taken together, then, the epithet

---

44. Barrett, *The Second Epistle to the Corinthians,* 108. See also Furnish, *II Corinthians,* 182.

45. Lull, *The Spirit in Galatia,* 54–59. Hafemann, *Suffering and Ministry in the Spirit,* 206, describes 2 Cor 3:3 as "a summary of Paul's prior description of his apostolic ministry of the Spirit in I Cor. 2:1–5."

46. Hafemann, *Suffering and Ministry of the Spirit,* 206.

"living God" and the Spirit motif in 2 Cor 3:3 serve to evoke Paul's missionary preaching and the Corinthian experience of conversion.

This missionary-conversion significance of the expression "Spirit of the living God" also helps in clarifying the origins and function of the expression "Spirit of the living God" as a Pauline innovation. The expression consists of two terms already familiar to Paul and his readers from his ministry in Corinth. While the combination of the two terms is unique, the two terms themselves were familiar, thus making the resultant expression accessible to the readers. However, what factors led Paul to create this novel combination of terms? Both terms in the expression were already cognate through their common function in Paul's missionary preaching. Paul's proclamation of the living God was empowered by correlate manifestations of the Spirit, and so Paul merely completes a process of "rapport" begun in the mission field by bringing the two terms together into a single expression. The link between the two terms was also suggested from their common reference to divine life-giving. The living God was the life-giving creator, while the Spirit was God's animating "breath," as the biblical witness already suggests, e.g., Gen 2:7 and Ps 104:30.

Further, the expression "Spirit of the living God" is perfectly suited to Paul's epistolary aims in 2 Cor 3:3, suggesting that the epistolary setting was a factor influencing Paul in creating the expression. In continuing the motif of the recommendation letter, Paul needed an expression that would convey the extraordinary means by which the Corinthian "letter" was written, contrasted with the ordinary means of writing in ink. This expression also had to be dense and polyvalent enough to function as a nodal point for a complex melding of kerygmatic and scriptural motifs. The expression "Spirit of the living God" was suited to such a role because it encapsulated a whole host of kerygmatic associations into a single expression, evoking Paul's missionary preaching of the living God in Corinth and the resultant experience of the Spirit and conversion among the Corinthians. It also triggered recollections of Paul's role in these foundational events and linked him to the divine working of the Spirit.[47] The expression "Spirit the living God" thus serves to gather up and summarize Paul's preceding assertions about his apostolic credentials. However, the richness of the expression does not end with allusions to kerygma and conversion. The "Spirit of the living God" carries important biblical associations, thereby facilitating a shift from a kerygmatic line of thought in 3:3a–b to a scriptural line in 3:3c.

The expression "Spirit of the living God" thus reveals something of Paul's ingenuity in creating an expression that would further his epistolary aims. With its dense use of imagery and its rapid succession of ideas, 2 Cor 3:3 required an expression that could concisely express Paul's credentials as an apostle by recalling his kerygma, his preaching ministry, and his role in converting the Corinthians. At the same time, the expression had to allow for a shift to scriptural-covenantal themes in 3:3c that would bring out the deeper salvation-historical significance of Paul's work in Corinth. The "Spirit of the living God" was a perfect expression for the setting in which it is used.

2 Cor 3:3c: Biblical Background of the Living God

The expression "Spirit of the living God" facilitates a shift to a new line of thought in 2 Cor 3:3c, although one not entirely unrelated to the previous kerygmatic line. The abrupt introduction of a new line of thought in 3:3c has perennially perplexed interpreters. For example, one interpreter notes that "by the end of v. 3 the metaphor has shifted so completely as hardly to be relevant to the image of the [letter] at all."[48] What interpreters fail to realize is that biblical living God tradition is the generative source for the shift in 2 Cor 3:3c. For Paul "Spirit of the living God" triggers a host of biblical associations that come to expression in 2 Cor 3:3. The mention of the living God triggers thoughts of the Sinai covenant, the Decalogue, as well as the new covenant, another traditional biblical association of the

---

47. Relevant here is the observation that Paul employed kerygmatic summaries of his proclamation, brief excerpts of what he had preached, that were pertinent to his hortatory purposes, e.g., 1 Thess 1:9–10 and 2 Cor 4:5.

48. Provence, "Who Is Sufficient for These Things? 60.

epithet. The significance of "Spirit of the living God" is thus not restricted to its function of alluding to conversion in Corinth. Its significance extends also to the biblical motifs in 2 Cor 3:3c.

After Paul asserts that the Corinthians are a letter from Christ, written by the Spirit of the living God, he describes in 3:3c the material on which the Spirit writes, "not on tablets of stone, but on tablets of fleshy hearts." Interpreters are in agreement that these motifs stem from the Pentateuch (stone tablets) and from Ezekiel (tablets of fleshy hearts). "Not on stone tablets..." reflects Pentateuchal background and interpreters often cite Exod 31:18 LXX as its generative source. However, and as previously noted, the problem of singling out Exod 31:18 LXX as generative source is that it supplies neither the Spirit motif nor the living God epithet in 3:3b. A better choice for a generative source in the Pentateuch would be Deut 4:13 LXX, since it mentions God writing upon two tablets of stone in the same context where the living God speaks to Moses (4:33 LXX). The same could be said of Deut 5:22 LXX/MT since it also mentions God writing upon two tables of stone in the very same context where the living God speaks to Moses (5:26 LXX/MT).

However, another factor mitigates against singling out any single Pentateuchal text as generative source of "not on tablets of stone." That God writes the Decalogue on stone tablets is a general Pentateuchal allusion attested in numerous Pentateuchal texts.[49] Interpreters should therefore avoid limiting the allusion to any specific text. Further, Jews of the Hellenistic Diaspora had come to identify the living God as the giver of the Decalogue (e.g., Deut 4:33 LXX; 5:26 LXX/MT; Philo, *Decalogue* 67; 2 Macc 15:4; and *Sib. Or.* 3:762–66). The allusion, then, in 2 Cor 3:3c is also attributable to this association of the living God and the Decalogue in Jewish tradition, an association which is the source for "not on tablets of stone."

Second Corinthians 3:3c also brings the living God into as-

---

49. Furnish, *II Corinthians*, 195, notes that while Exod 31:18 LXX is important, the notion of God writing in 2 Cor 3:3 "is also in accord with several scriptural passages he [Paul] seems to have in mind as he continues to embellish his metaphor." Cf. Hafemann, *Suffering and Ministry in the Spirit*, 213.

sociation with the new covenant through the reference to the Spirit of the living God writing upon "tablets of fleshy hearts."[50] The motif of the Spirit writing on "tablets of fleshy hearts" constitutes an undeniable reference to Ezek 11:19 LXX: "And I will give them one heart and put a new spirit within them; I will take their stony heart (τὴν καρδίαν τὴν λιθίνην) out of their flesh and give them a heart of flesh" (καρδίαν σαρκίνην); and 36:26 LXX: "And a new heart I will give you, and a new spirit I will put within you; and I will take out of your flesh the heart of stone (τὴν καρδίαν τὴν λιθίνην) and give you a heart of flesh" (καρδίαν σαρκίνην). These two verses reflect the future reality of the new covenant in which God will give Israel a "heart of flesh," replacing its "heart of stone." According to Ezekiel, this "heart of flesh" will enable obedience to God's law and Israel's loyalty to God will be single-minded. Having a "new heart" and a "new spirit" also means a restoration of Israel as God's covenantal "people."[51] Moreover, in Ezek 37:1–14 the divine life-giving spirit of God will revivify a dead Israel. In Ezekiel's new covenant God's life-giving spirit reanimates the people and establishes them in an "everlasting covenant" (Ezek 37:26).

An allusion to Jeremiah's new covenant is also present in the mention of God writing upon "tablets of fleshy hearts." This motif of God writing upon the heart recalls Jer 38:33 LXX [31:33]: "but this is the covenant which I will make with the house of Israel after those days says the Lord: I will put my law within them, and I will write it upon their hearts; and I will be their God and they shall be my people." That Paul in 2 Cor 3:3c has Jeremiah's new covenant in view is also supported from the literary context. In 2 Cor 3:6 the allusion to Jeremiah's "new covenant" is explicit ("God, who has made us to be competent ministers of a new covenant..."), while 3:2 offers a covert allusion through the mention of the letter "written on our hearts."[52]

---

50. The variant reading πλαξὶν καρδίας σαρκίναις (F Ψ) is likely an attempt to improve the awkward original reading which is better attested. Metzger, *A Textual Commentary on the Greek New Testament*, 577.

51. This restoration to new covenantal status is expressed in the covenantal formulas found in Ezek 11:20 and 36:28: "...and they shall be my people and I shall be their God" (11:20); "and you shall be my people and I shall be your God" (36:28).

52. Furnish, *II Corinthians*, 181, 196. Richard, "Polemic, Old Testament, and The-

It is possible, then, that an allusion to Jeremiah hovers around the phrase "tablets of fleshy hearts" in 2 Cor 3:3c. However, even if the phrase does carry allusions to Jeremiah, it is Ezekiel's new covenant language that predominates. The work of the Spirit in Corinth is thus "evidence that the new age has arrived, i.e., the age of the 'fleshly heart' prophesied by Ezekiel."[53]

Paul's primary aim in 2 Cor 3:3c, then, is to highlight the life-giving effects of his ministry in Corinth. Through the preaching of the gospel and the activity of the Spirit, Paul's ministry has changed the hearts of the Corinthians and transformed them into God's new covenant people.[54] This new identity of the Corinthians as a covenantal people is later confirmed in 2 Cor 6:16 where Paul describes them as "the temple of the living God," which fulfills God's promise, "...and I will be their God and they shall be my people."[55] Second Corinthians 3:3c thus serves to show that Paul's ministry is a ministry of the new covenant in which the life-giving power of the Spirit has "written" upon the hearts of the Corinthians.[56] Paul's work in Corinth serves to bring about God's new covenant initiative and the fulfillment of biblical prophecy.

There is, however, a secondary aim in 2 Cor 3:3c that is made in the negative assertion that the Spirit of the living God writes "not on tablets of stone. . . ." Paul formulates 2 Cor 3:3c antithetically, seeking to clarify that the activity of the Spirit in founding the Corinthian community does not occur in connection with the Mosaic law. Paul's introduction of this motif is unexpected,

---

ology," 345–49. Hays, *Echoes of Scripture,* 128, observes that the echo of Jeremiah in this verse "might be dismissed as peripheral, were it not for the fact that the motif of the new covenant, a motif distinctive to Jeremiah, appears explicitly in the next sentence (v. 6)."

53. Hafemann, *Suffering and Ministry in the Spirit,* 222.

54. That the "tablets of fleshy hearts" refers to the Corinthian hearts is the common position among interpreters. See Windisch, *Der zweite Korintherbrief,* 107; Provence, "Who Is Sufficient for These Things?" 61; and Jan Lambrecht, *Second Corinthians* (Sacra Pagina 8; Collegeville, Minn.: Liturgical Press, 1999), 42.

55. Through contextual association, the prophecies of Ezek 11:19 and 36:26 are related to the new covenant formula "I will be their God and they will be my people" found in 11:20 and 36:28.

56. Hays, *Echoes of Scripture,* 131, observes that "as Paul's earlier allusion to Ezek 36 and 37 indicates, the life-giving power of the Spirit is shown forth precisely in the creation of an enfleshed eschatological community." Cf. Jan Lambrecht, *Second Corinthians* (Sacra Pagina 8; Collegeville, Minn.: Liturgical Press, 1999), 42.

since it breaks off from the letter motif. It is at this point that interpreters speak of Paul's logic breaking down into a confused mix of metaphors. Why, then, does Paul introduce the Pentateuchal motif "not on tablets of stone" at the beginning of 3:3c? I previously suggested an answer to this question. The transition at the end of 3:3b and the beginning of 3:3c makes perfect sense when it is remembered that the living God was the covenantal God of Israel who was associated with the Sinai covenant in Deut 4:33 LXX and 5:26 LXX/MT. Hellenistic Jewish tradition retains this association of the living God and the Decalogue (cf. Philo, *Decalogue* 67; 2 Macc 15:4; *Sib. Or.* 3:763). To Hellenistic Jews the living God was the God who gave the Mosaic law in establishing them as a covenantal people and this meant that the living God was central to Jewish identity. Jews distinguished themselves as a people of the living God who existed in a close covenantal relationship with him. The transition, then, between "Spirit of the living God" in 2 Cor 3:3b and "not on tablets of stone" in 3:3c presupposes this traditional Jewish view of the living God as giver of the Decalogue.

Paul, however, in 2 Cor 3:3c, does not want the Corinthians to take the Jewish view of the living God and confuse their new covenantal identity with that of the Sinai covenant, characterized as it was by "stone tablets." The question is why Paul needed to make such a clarification at all to his Corinthian readers. Perhaps he is responding in 3:3c to opponents who promoted the living God as giver of the Mosaic law and insisted on the practice of the law. Another possible explanation is that Paul himself proclaimed the living God to the Corinthians and spoke of the living God as the God of Israel and giver of the law. Taken this way, Paul seeks to clarify a misunderstanding based on his own earlier teaching of the living God. Whatever the reasons behind his need to assert "not on tablets of stone," Paul is unequivocal in presenting his ministry as a ministry of the new covenant distinct from that of the Sinai law-giving. The Corinthian conversion to the living God is therefore not a divine "election" that leads to membership in the Sinai covenant; rather it is an election associated with Ezekiel's vision of a new covenant. By using the expression "not on tablets of stone," Paul is able to specify that the living God, the traditional covenantal God of Israel, was now at work in a new way establishing the new covenant "on tablets of fleshy hearts."

Is Paul's assertion of "not on tablets of stone" in 2 Cor 3:3c therefore tantamount to a rejection of the Mosaic law? In addressing this question, one needs to exercise caution. To be sure, a pejorative function of the law is expressed in 2 Cor 3:6: "the letter kills" in contrast to the Spirit who gives life. Such a statement recalls the death-dealing function of the law in Rom 7:6. However, the law is not primarily at issue in 2 Cor 3:3 and, as Hafemann observes, "it is crucial . . . that we do not read the tablets of stone/tablet of fleshy heart contrast in 3:3 in terms of the letter/Spirit contrast in 3:6. Although closely related, Paul's point in these two contrasts is nevertheless not identical."[57] At issue in 2 Cor 3:3 are Paul's apostolic credentials shown in the creation of the Corinthian community. Paul brought the Spirit to Corinth, which led to the conversion of the Corinthians and their creation as a people of the new covenant. In 2 Cor 3:3c, then, Paul is concerned with people-formation and not with criticizing the law per se. His primary aim is to differentiate the past activity of the living God on Sinai/Horeb from his present activity in giving the Spirit and converting Gentiles. The tablets of stone in 3:3c are not completely pejorative in the sense commonly taken by interpreters. Rather, they designate a past mode of divine initiative in which the living God formed a covenantal people.

The antithetical language of 3:3c is thus characterized by a complex dialectic in which the living God is the initiator of both covenants. In this dialectic the motif of God writing upon stone tablets represents Paul's way of distinguishing Sinai/Horeb as an earlier mode of divine initiative and serves as a counterpoint to the new mode of divine life-giving in Paul's day. The living God's formation of the Corinthians as a new covenant people is not identical with his formation of Israel at Horeb/Sinai. In this light, then, the so-called abrupt "jump" in 2 Cor 3:3c becomes comprehensible as part of an unfolding logic of living

---

57. Hafemann, *Suffering and Ministry in the Spirit*, 213.

God tradition. The use of the expression "Spirit of the living God" at the end of 3:3b enables Paul to move in a broader salvation-historical direction by clarifying the deeper theological (=scriptural) significance of his ministry. The richness and polyvalence of the expression "Spirit of the living God" offers Paul a nodal point for subtly shifting his line of thought from earlier kerygmatic themes to biblical-covenantal thinking.

Paul as Mediator of Divine Life: Implications for 2 Cor 2:14–3:6

Second Corinthians 3:3 asserts that Paul is a mediator of eschatological life, which is both present and future, and his mediatorial role has its origins in his call and commission as an apostle of the living God. Paul's ministry is grounded in a call and commission from the living God, a point given explicit expression in the *Acts Paul* 3:17. The latter, while being a post-Pauline text, provides valuable evidence that Paul's apostolic identity goes back to a call from the living God. Addressing the procounsul, Paul says: "If I today am examined as to what I teach, then listen, Procounsul. The living God, the God of vengeance, the jealous God, the God who has need of nothing, has sent me since he desires the salvation of men.... "[58] Paul's identity as an apostle is grounded in the awareness of being "sent" by the living God, an idea that underlies his self-description in 2 Cor 2:14–3:6. For example, Paul's ministry is a victory parade in which he himself is the captive led about by the divine conqueror (2:14). Being led captive in God's triumphal procession suggests that Paul's ministry has its origins in a powerful initiative of the living God.[59]

The divine origins of Paul's ministry are also expressed in 2:17: "For we are not, like so many, peddlars of God's word but

---

58. The translation is taken from Schneemelcher, *New Testament Apocrypha*, 2:242.

59. Hafemann, *Suffering and Ministry in the Spirit*, 32–33. For similar views see John T. Fitzgerald, *Cracks in an Earthen Vessel: An Examination of the Catalogues of Hardships in the Corinthian Correspondence* (SBLDS 99; Atlanta: Scholars Press, 1988), 161–63. Lambrecht, *Second Corinthians*, 38–39, concludes that "through Paul's conversion on the way to Damascus God won in Christ a victory over Paul."

as men of sincerity, as commissioned by God (ὡς ἐκ θεοῦ), in the sight of God (κατέναντι θεοῦ) we speak in Christ"[60] (cf. 4:2). Paul preaches the gospel word "in the sight of God" and "as one commissioned by God."[61] In 3:5–6 Paul again asserts the divine basis for his apostolic confidence: "not that we are competent of ourselves to claim anything as coming from us; our competence is from God (ἐκ θεοῦ), who has made us competent to be ministers of a new covenant." Paul is sent "from God" and his mediatorial role is grounded in a self-awareness that everything he does is accountable before the living God. Second Corinthians 2:14–3:6 can thus be viewed as operating from the underlying presupposition that Paul is an apostle of the living God, a vehicle of divine life-giving in Corinth.

The validity of this claim is bolstered by the central placement of 2 Cor 3:1–3 within the framework of 2 Cor 2:14–3:6. As previously noted, 3:1–3 is a focal point of 2:14–3:6, standing at the center of 2:14–3:6.[62] Viewed in this way, 3:1–3 provides the interpretive clue to the whole, which 3:3 encapsulates in the phrase "Spirit of the living God." This expression serves as a compact allusion to the divine life-giving that comes through Paul's preaching ministry and thus supplies the presupposition that extends to the whole of 2:14–3:6. At this point, then, I will conclude by showing the importance of this presupposition for interpreting 2 Cor 2:14–3:6. Paul takes great pains in 2:14–3:6 to remind the Corinthians of his ministry's life-giving effects, employing three distinct and yet closely interrelated motifs that express these effects: (1) Paul's preaching of the gospel; (2) the activity of the Spirit accompanying Paul's preaching;

---

60. Sumney, *Identifying Paul's Opponents,* 127–28, observes that with 2:17, a specific situation in Corinth is in view involving a group of opponents, "hucksters," who peddle God's word.

61. Richardson, *Paul's Language about God,* 149–50 observes that "the emphasis falls on upon God as the source of the apostle's authority, and the one to whom he is responsible." See also Furnish, *II Corinthians,* 179.

62. Lambrecht, *Second Corinthians,* 43–45, also considers 2 Cor 2:14–3:6 as an independent unit divided into three parts: 2:14–17; 3:1–3; and 3:4–6. See also Lambrecht, "Structure and Line of Thought in 2 Cor. 2,14–4,6," *Biblica* 64 (1983): 344–50. Furnish, *II Corinthians,* 185, observes that 2:14–3:6 can be regarded as "introductory to the discussion proper, which takes place in 3:7–5:19."

and (3) God's new covenant initiative expressed through Paul's ministry.

The first of these motifs, Paul's gospel proclamation, runs like an unbroken thread through much of 2 Cor 2:14–7:4, but it is especially prominent in 2:14–3:6. In the latter, Paul repeatedly alludes to the life-giving effects of his gospel. For example, 2 Cor 2:14–16 offers references to Paul's preaching ministry in Corinth, a ministry that brings the knowledge of God and eschatological life. In 2:14 Paul moves in triumphal procession so that through him, God could "spread the fragrance of the knowledge of him everywhere." Here "the scent of the gospel is disseminated throughout the world"[63] and this dissemination spreads "the knowledge of him," which is a knowledge of God (cf. 2 Cor 4:6).[64] Paul's preaching in Corinth thus brings the knowledge of monotheistic truth (1 Thess 4:5; Gal 4:9; cf. 2 Cor 4:2), which is a source of life to the converts and illuminates the darkness of their pagan lives. Through conversion the Corinthians are recreated in the knowledge of truth about the living God who created them and from whom all life comes.

Paul's missionary role in mediating divine life is also expressed in 2:15–16a: "for we are the aroma of Christ to God among those being saved and those who are perishing, to one a fragrance from death to death, to the other a fragrance from life to life (οἷς δὲ ὀσμὴ ἐκ ζωῆς εἰς ζωήν)."[65] Here, as in 2:14, Paul's focus is on his role as proclaimer of the gospel. Second Corinthians 2:15–16a alludes to the mixed response that is evoked by the gospel, describing its double effect. Hearing the gospel leads to " ... a sorting among men, some having for their destiny life eternal ... , the others having eternal death. ... "[66] Acceptance of Paul and his proclamation of the living God was

---

63. Furnish, *II Corinthians*, 188. Lambrecht, *Second Corinthians*, 39, observes that "the verb *phaneroō* determines the function of the fragrance motif: it is a spreading and manifesting odor."

64. 2 Cor 4:6: "For it is God who said, 'let light shine out of the darkness,' who has shone in our hearts to give the light of the knowledge of the glory of God."

65. The expressions ἐκ θανάτου εἰς θάνατον and ἐκ ζωῆς εἰς ζωήν have parallels in the LXX and may indicate a Semitic idiom that expresses the superlative. There is some debate on the meaning of these olfactory motifs in 2 Cor 2:15–16 (Furnish, *II Corinthians*, 176–77; and Hafemann, *Suffering and Ministry in the Spirit*, 36–45).

66. Collange, *Énigmes*, 35. The same two effects are also distinguished in 1 Cor

of such significance that it determined the eschatological fate of the recipient. In 2:16a Paul asserts that his ministry is a vehicle for eschatological life. Acceptance of the gospel brings eschatological life, including "deliverance" from God's coming wrath at the Parousia of Jesus (1 Thess 1:9–10; cf. 5:9). The thought of 2 Cor 2:15–16a is also echoed in 1 Tim 4:10, where Paul sets his hope on the living God because he is the eschatological "Savior of all people, but especially of those who believe." Future eschatological "life" and salvation, then, originate in the living God, who makes "life" available through Paul's preaching ministry.

The life-giving effects of Paul's ministry are also expressed in the activity of the Spirit that accompanies his gospel preaching. Paul's ministry is bound up with the Spirit's activity of creating Gentile communities through conversion (cf. 1 Cor 2:4–5; 1 Thess 1:4–6). In 2 Cor 3:3 Paul is "co-author" of the Corinthian "letter" along with the Spirit of the living God. Paul identifies his preaching ministry so closely with the activity of the Spirit that he describes it as a "ministry of the Spirit" in 2 Cor 3:8. As an apostle of the living God, it is no surprise to find the living God's Spirit accompanying Paul's ministry. In 2 Cor 3:3 the Spirit functions as the life-giving agent of the living God. The life-giving activity of the Spirit is implicit in the expression "Spirit of the living God." The genitive phrase "of the living God" characterizes the living God as the originating power behind the Spirit.[67]

The expression "Spirit of the living God" in 2 Cor 3:3b serves to call attention to the life-giving effects that Paul's ministry has had on the Corinthians. This life-giving activity of the Spirit results in eschatological life experienced by the Corinthians here and now. For example, in 2 Cor 3:6, Paul says that God makes him competent to be a minister of a new covenant through the Spirit who "gives life" (present tense!). The implication here is that divine eschatological life is presently realized, a point that

---

1:18. Those who accept the word "are being saved," while those who reject it "are perishing." Cf. 2 Cor 4:3–4.

67. Hermann, *Kyrios und Pneuma,* 28. Lambrecht, *Second Corinthians,* 42, notes that in this phrase "God works 'with' (=by means of) the Spirit."

recalls the earlier assertion of 2:15–16a that Paul's ministry is "an aroma among those who are being saved" and a "fragrance from life to life." The Spirit "gives life" (present tense) as part of Paul's new covenant ministry.[68] Eschatological life and salvation in 2:16a and the Spirit's life-giving activity in 3:6b have their common point of reference in Paul's ministry of the Spirit.

Further, through Paul's proclamation of the living God and the activity of the living God's Spirit, the Corinthians have experienced new life as God's elect (1 Cor 1:26–28) and God's holy temple (1 Cor 3:16–17). The founding of the church in Corinth "is God's life-giving work, a new creation."[69] The activity and presence of the Spirit in Corinth shows that the Corinthians are God's "elect." Just as in Thessalonika, where divine election was assured by the gospel coming "in power and the Holy Spirit," so too in Corinth God "chose what is foolish in the world to shame the wise . . . " (1 Cor 1:27). Further, the life-giving effects of Paul's ministry in Corinth are expressions of a new covenant event. In 2 Cor 3:2–3 and 3:6 the founding of the Corinthian community is described in terms of the inauguration of the new covenant. The "Spirit of the living God" has written the Corinthian letter "on tablets of fleshy hearts," recalling the new covenant prophecy of Jer 38:33 LXX and Ezek 11:19, 36:26. Through conversion, the Corinthians have been given "life" as a new covenant community, with Ezekiel's "new spirit" in their midst; and this entails that the Corinthians represent the future Israel restored to new life through the revivifying power of the Spirit (Ezek 37:1–14). Romans 9:25–26 makes a similar point. Gentile converts, who were formerly "not my people," are transformed into "sons of the living God."

Paul's epistolary strategy in 2 Cor 2:14–3:6, then, operates from the presupposition that he is an apostle of the living God who has mediated, and still mediates, divine life to the Corinthians. As apostle of the living God, Paul ministers in tandem with the living God's Spirit and is himself a vehicle for eschatological

---

68. Stenger, "Die Gottesbezeichnung 'lebendiger Gott,'" 66. Furnish, *II Corinthians*, 189, notes that "3:6b may be seen as establishing the point of 2:16a.

69. Lambrecht, *Second Corinthians*, 41–42.

life which comes from the living God.[70] Gentile converts do not benefit from the life-giving effects of the gospel apart from the apostle who delivers it and so the reception of eschatological life in Corinth is bound up with acceptance of the apostle. As Paul puts it in 2:14–16a, the fragrance of the knowledge of God is spread "through us...for we are the aroma of Christ to God among those who are being saved and among those who are perishing." Therefore, relationship to Paul himself, as apostle, remains essential in the ongoing salvation of the Corinthians.

---

70. Furnish, *II Corinthians,* 188, observes that "so closely does Paul identify the gospel with the apostolate that he can proceed (in v. 15) to speak of the apostles themselves as the aroma of Christ...."

Chapter Eight

2 Corinthians 6:16b and the Temple of the Living God

༄༅༅༅༅༅༅༅༅༅

Second Corinthians 6:16b furnishes a second occurrence of the living God in the expression "for we are the temple of the living God." This expression identifies the Corinthian community as God's temple, the locus of the divine indwelling. A glance through the commentaries, however, shows that the "temple of the living God" remains an enigma and in need of further exploration. As with "Spirit of the living God" in 2 Cor 3:3, the expression in 6:16 is a *hapax legomenon* in biblical and Jewish tradition, making it difficult to interpret. Interpreters thus tend to focus on the more familiar temple motif in the expression, ignoring the epithet and taking it as equivalent to "God." Also, the expression remains an enigma because it occurs in a literary unit (6:14–7:1) that is a *crux interpretum* in New Testament scholarship, and it is considered by many to be a non-Pauline interpolation. Non-Pauline character emerges in a number of features, including the passage's placement that seems to disrupt the sequence of material in 6:11–13 and 7:2–4. Further, the passage uses language considered to be non-Pauline in character and expresses a separatist outlook that stands in tension with Paul's views (cf. 1 Cor 5:9–11).[1] Given these problems with the passage, it is no surprise, then, that the issues of Pauline author-

---

1. Furnish, *II Corinthians,* 374–83, and Martin, *2 Corinthians,* 190–95; and Linda L. Belleville, *Reflections of Glory: Paul's Polemical Use of the Moses-Doxa Tradition in 2 Corinthians 3.1–18* (JSNTSup 52; Sheffield: JSOT Press, 1991), 94–103. Also William J. Webb, *Returning Home: New Covenant and Second Exodus as the Context for 2 Corinthians 6:14–7:1* (JSOTSup 85; Sheffield: JSOT Press, 1993), 16–30, gives a useful history of research on the passage.

ship and contextual compatibility have dominated scholarly discussion, relegating other issues to marginal status.

One such marginalized issue concerns the content and character of material in the outer shell (6:14–16a, 7:1), including the expression "temple of the living God." The purpose of this chapter, then, is to explore this expression and show that a better understanding of it serves to illuminate the whole of 2 Cor 6:14–7:1. Important clues to understanding the expression lie in the living God's biblical, Jewish, and early Christian background, a background that has been neglected in treatments of 2 Cor 6:16b. In particular, the Pauline kerygmatic background of the living God (1 Thess 1:9; Acts 14:14) is useful in understanding 2 Cor 6:16b. While there is some minimal scholarly discussion of this background, it has not been translated into a full-fledged investigation of the "temple of the living God" and the outer shell. Commentators have not capitalized on what 1 Thess 1:9 has to teach about 2 Cor 6:16b. Finally, interpreters also fail to take advantage of 2 Cor 3:3 as a significant parallel of 6:16b. The former provides clues on the function and meaning of the "temple of the living God," but the neglect of 2 Cor 3:3 has hampered attempts to integrate the latter into the discussion.

The following discussion intends to advance the discussion of 2 Cor 6:16 in several ways. First, it will show that the expression "temple of the living God" draws upon and reflects early Christian and Pauline kerygmatic use of the epithet as in 1 Thess 1:9–10 and Acts 14:15. Set in opposition to idols, the expression designates Gentile communities that had their roots in conversion to the living God (cf. 1 Tim 3:15). The expression appealed to Paul as a reminder to the Corinthians about their newfound identity through conversion—they were Gentile converts transformed by Paul's proclamation of the living God.

Second, the kerygmatic significance of the expression "temple of the living God" holds implications for interpreting the whole of 2 Cor 6:14–7:1. I will show that 2 Cor 6:16b is a pivotal expression in the whole passage, providing an interpretive key and serving to integrate the thematic content of the outer shell (6:14–16a, 7:1) with that of the scriptural catena (6:16–18). By alluding to Paul's missionary kerygma and conversion, 6:16b provides a point of thematic coherence for the whole passage. The rhetorical questions in the outer shell (6:14–16a) reflect an underlying substratum of conversion language recalling the readers to their conversion roots. Further, the scriptural catena (6:16c–18) can be read as alluding to Gentile conversion, much in the same manner that Rom 9:25–26 uses scriptural texts to speak about Gentile conversion. These texts in 6:16c–18, promising the new covenant and exilic return, are used to draw out the deeper significance of Gentile conversion.

Third, the "temple of the living God" in 2 Cor 6:16b offers a significant formal parallel to the "Spirit of the living God" in 3:3. Second Corinthians 3:3 and 6:16 present similar uses of the living God in expressions that are ecclesial in character and that are closely related to new covenant prophecy. Paul's discourse in 2 Cor 2:14–7:4 is thus framed by two uses of the epithet and "rounded off," so to speak, by the second reference to the living God in 2 Cor 6:16b. The latter use of the epithet thus indicates Paul's compositional intent to frame the discourse of 2 Cor 2:14–7:4 with two references to the living God.

The following discussion is arranged into four sections. The first section is preliminary and serves to identify the working presuppositions that inform the examination of 2 Cor 6:16. My discussion here seeks to establish both the non-Pauline origins of 2 Cor 6:14–7:1, as well as its contextual compatibility within the wider framework of 2:14–7:4. Also I will review recent scholarly treatments of the 2 Cor 6:14–7:1 as a way of focusing on questions concerning the internal thematic coherence of 2 Cor 6:14–7:1, questions which this chapter aims to resolve. The second section has two aims. First, it considers the formal role of 2 Cor 6:16b within the framework of 2 Cor 6:14–7:1, demonstrating its pivotal function in that framework. I hope to show that the affirmation of 2 Cor 6:16b offers an interpretive key for grasping the thematic coherence of the whole passage. Second, this section will also demonstrate the missionary-conversion significance of the expression "temple of the living God" based upon Jewish and Pauline backgrounds.

Section three extends the implications of the preceding section to an interpretation of the outer shell (6:14b–16a, 7:1) and the scriptural catena (6:16c–18). In this section I will show that both the outer shell and the scriptural catena allude to the language and themes of Gentile conversion. The outer shell is informed by a substratum of conversion language that has been recast for paraenesis and the scriptural catena uses a particular selection of scriptural texts to allude to Gentile conversion, much in the manner of Rom 9:25–26. The fourth and final section will explore 2 Cor 6:16b as a formal correspondence to 2 Cor 3:3.

Working Presuppositions: Contextual Compatibility

Before investigating the "temple of the living God" in 2 Cor 6:16b, I will begin by clarifying the working presuppositions that inform my approach to the topic. Following the insights of Nils Dahl, David Rensberger, and others, I will approach 2 Cor 6:14–7:1 as a passage of non-Pauline origins but one that plays an integral role within the argument of 2 Corinthians. More specifically, 2 Cor 6:14–7:1 is an early Christian exhortation that was adopted by Paul or a close disciple for use in the wider argument of 2 Cor 2:14–7:4. These presuppositions represent a "middle ground" between the positions of Paulinists,[2] who maintain that 2 Cor 6:14–7:1 was written by Paul, and Qumranists,[3] who stress the Jewish origins of the passage and view it as having little

---

2. M. Thrall, "The Problem of II Cor. VI. 14–VII. 1 in Some Recent Discussion," *NTS* 24 (1977): 132–48. Barrett, *Second Epistle to the Corinthians*, 192–95; Gordon D. Fee, "II Corinthians VI.14–VII.1 and Food Offered to Idols," *NTS* 23 (1977): 140–61; Plummer, *Second Epistle of St. Paul to the Corinthians*, 204–6; and Jerome Murphy-O'Connor, "Philo and 2 Cor 6:14–7:1," *Revue Biblique* 95 (1988): 55–79.

3. The "Qumranists" stress the striking affinities between 2 Cor 6:14–7:1 and Qumran literature and suggests the Jewish origins for the passage. Joseph A. Fitzmyer, "Qumran and the Interpolated Paragraph in 2 Cor. 6.14–7.1," *CBQ* 23 (1961): 271–80; repr. in Joseph A. Fitzmyer, *Essays on the Semitic Background of the New Testament* (SBLSBS 5; Missoula: Scholars Press, 1974), 205–17; and Joachim Gnilka, "2 Cor 6:14–7:1 in the Light of the Qumran Texts and the Testaments of the Twelve Patriarchs," in *Paul and the Dead Sea Scrolls*, ed. J. Murphy O'Connor and J. H. Charlesworth (New York: Crossroad, 1990), 48–68.

or no compatibility in its present epistolary setting.[4] My discussion, then, accepts the non-Pauline origins of 2 Cor 6:14–7:1, but it also presupposes the passage's contextual compatibility in its present epistolary context. This middle ground thus posits "... Paul's modification of either an Essene document or a Christian document influenced by Essene tradition."[5]

It was Nils Dahl who gave classic expression to this mediating position by proposing an interpretation of 2 Cor 6:14–7:1 that answered "the pressing need for contextual integration, coherence in Pauline theology, and contact with Qumran."[6] Dahl accepts 2 Cor 6:14–7:1 as "a slightly christianized piece of Qumran theology" that was not originally written for the function that it now serves in 2 Corinthians.[7] Despite the non-Pauline origins of the passage, it makes good sense in its present context, and it should be given more attention as an integral passage in 2 Cor 2:14–7:4. Dahl observes that the passage's "... present location cannot be due to an accident; whoever inserted the fragment must have known what he was doing."[8] More specifically, the fragment functions to support the previous exhortations in 6:1–13 in which Paul urges the Corinthians to be reconciled to him as an apostle of God.[9] Second Corinthians 6:14–7:1, then, must have been inserted into its present context by Paul himself or somebody close to him.

A disputed point in Dahl's proposal is that the "unbelievers" of 6:14 should be identified with false apostles, thus giving an unexpected metaphorical twist to the term.[10] The term "unbelievers" typically refers to pagan non-believers in Paul's usage,

---

4. The views of the Qumranists have been influential in convincing New Testament scholars of the passage's non-Pauline character and of its Jewish origins. See Fitzmyer, "Qumran and the Interpolated Paragraph," 217; and Gnilka, "2 Cor 6:14–7:1," 60–61.

5. Webb, *Returning Home,* 29.

6. This is the assessment of Webb, *Returning Home,* 24. Dahl's proposal is found in "A Fragment in its Context: 2 Corinthians 6:14–7:1," *Studies in Paul: Theology for Early Christian Mission* (Minneapolis: Augsburg, 1977), 62–69.

7. Dahl, "A Fragment In Its Context," 63.

8. Ibid., 68.

9. Ibid., 65.

10. Ibid., 69. Webb, *Returning Home,* 193–97, takes issue with this interpretation, arguing that "Paul's normal referent to the use of ἄπιστοι runs counter to the false-apostles view."

but Dahl argues that the term in 6:14 refers to false apostles and he supports this claim by appealing to the polemical descriptions of Paul's opponents in 11:2–4; 11:14; and 12:21. For Dahl, then, "what is merely suggested by the insertion of the fragment (in 6:14–7:1) is here [11:2–4] stated in plain words: to join the false apostles in their opposition to Paul would mean to side with Satan/Belial in his opposition to Christ."[11] In its favor, Dahl's interpretation helps to integrate 6:14–7:1 in its immediate literary context, offering a smoother transition between 6:11–13 and 6:14. To take "unbelievers" in its usual Pauline sense in 6:14 entails an abrupt and jarring transition to the topic of pagan unbelievers. However, Dahl's interpretation does require a view that goes against Paul's normal usage of the term.[12] Therefore, this issue of the "unbelievers" in 2 Cor 6:14 remains difficult to resolve and my discussion will not be primarily concerned with this issue.

Dahl's arguments on the contextual compatibility of the passage have been advanced by a number of interpreters who seek to establish contextual compatibility with their own arguments. Even if Paul himself did not compose the passage, it still has certain affinities with the surrounding context and plays an integral role within the argument. David Rensberger, for example, concludes that the passage's "odd mixture of Pauline and non-Pauline features can best be explained by positing an exhortation composed by a Christian of sectarian or 'Essene' background, 'Paulinized' and used by the apostle to urge his readers to avoid his opponents just as they would avoid anything having to do with the side of evil."[13] Victor Furnish observes that "what evidence there is would seem to be best satisfied by the hypothesis that the passage is of non-Pauline composition, but

---

11. Dahl, "A Fragment In Its Context," 69.

12. Webb, *Returning Home,* 193–97, observes that such an interpretation requires that "idols" in 6:16 carry a non-literal metaphorical sense. Also, Furnish, *II Corinthians,* 383.

13. David Rensberger, "2 Corinthians 6:14–7:1—A Fresh Examination," *StBibTh* 8 (1978): 41–42. Following Dahl's argument, Rensberger maintains that the "unbelievers" in 6:14 refers to Paul's opponents. More recently in support of the Dahl-Rensberger position is Paul Brooks Duff, "The Mind of the Redactor: 2 Cor. 6:14–7:1 In Its Secondary Context" *NovT* 35 (1993): 160–80.

was incorporated by the apostle himself as he wrote this letter";[14] and Ralph Martin concludes that "it seems more probable that Paul borrowed a writing of Essene origin, placed the finishing touches on it and added it to this letter because of a specific intention."[15]

More recently, interpreters seek to demonstrate the contextual compatibility of 6:14–7:1 by employing the rhetorical categories of *inventio*. In this approach, 2 Cor 6:14–7:1 functions as a Pauline "digression," which was a standard rhetorical strategy in Paul's day.[16] However, another approach in establishing the contextual compatibility of the passage focuses on the use of scriptural themes that link it to the surrounding context. This approach looks closely at the scriptural catena (6:16c–18) that provides the framework for contextual integration. The work of G. K. Beale and William Webb are representative of this approach; they maintain that the contextual compatibility of 2 Cor 6:14–7:1 derives from the scriptural themes of new covenant and exilic return found in the scriptural catena.[17] Beale focuses on the catena's themes of Israel's exilic return and restoration, which are also prominent in 2 Cor 5:17–6:2. Beale, then, is able to view "vv. 16–18 as a continuation of restoration promises to Israel quoted by Paul in 6.2 and even 5.17...."[18]

Webb advances Beale's work and focuses on the catena's scriptural themes as a source for contextual integration. Webb, however, recognizes in the catena the themes of new covenant in addition to those of exilic return. He traces new covenant and exilic return theology throughout 2 Cor 2:14–7:4 and concludes that "these traditions have been woven into the fabric of

---

14. Furnish, *II Corinthians*, 383.

15. Martin, *2 Corinthians*, 195.

16. Ben Witherington III, *Conflict and Community in Corinth: A Socio-Rhetorical Commentary on 2 Corinthians* (Grand Rapids: Eerdmans, 1995), 402–6. J. D. H. Amador, "Revisiting 2 Corinthians: Rhetoric and the Case For Unity," *NTS* 46 (2000): 101–5.

17. G. K. Beale, "The Old Testament Background of Reconciliation in 2 Corinthians 5–7 and Its Bearing on the Literary Problem of 2 Corinthians 6:14–7:1," *NTS* 35 (1989): 550–81. Developing the work of Beale is Webb, *Returning Home: New Covenant and Second Exodus as the Context for 2 Corinthians 6:14–7:1*.

18. Beale, "The Old Testament Background of Reconciliation in 2 Corinthians 5–7," 569.

Paul's understanding of his role in apostolic ministry."[19] In the remote context of 2:14–5:10 "new covenant traditions lie at the heart of Paul's portrayal of his ministry," and in the immediate context of 5:11–7:4 there are "significant points of contact with the fragment through exilic return traditions" that include material in 5:17, 6:1–2, 6:3–4a, and 6:11–13.[20] The result is that 2 Cor 6:14–7:1 is firmly linked to the context of 2:14–7:4 on the basis of new covenant and exilic return traditions.

My approach in the following discussion will be similar to Beale and Webb's thematic approach, except that it depends on a different thematic link: living God theology. Living God theology is an important factor for integrating 2 Cor 6:14–7:1 into the wider framework of 2 Cor 2:14–7:4. Further, unlike Beale and Webb, I will focus not simply on a part of 6:14–7:1 that links up with the surrounding context, but rather on the whole passage to show contextual compatibility. In showing the contextual compatibility of the passage, I will focus on the close and special link between 2 Cor 2:14–3:6 and 6:14–7:1, both of which employ the epithet living God. Interpreters typically fail to account for the epithet living God in discussing the contextual compatibility of 2 Cor 6:14–7:1, a failure that will be redressed in the following discussion.

My primary focus in the following discussion concerns questions on the internal coherence of 2 Cor 6:14–7:1. Clearly 2 Cor 6:14–7:1 is a tightly woven literary unit. The question, however, concerns how the outer shell stands in thematic relation to the ensuing catena.[21] The outer shell would seem to have little in common with the catena on the thematic level. The former is devoid of new covenant and exilic return themes that inform the catena, and so one wonders how the two sub-units cohere on the thematic level. The need for investigation in this area is illustrated in the work of Beale and Webb; they are success-

---

19. Webb, *Returning Home,* 157.

20. Ibid., 157–58.

21. Rensberger, "2 Corinthians 6:14–7:1," 41, observes "the transition in v. 16 from the contrasts to the catena is problematic. The entire matter of the temple of God could be Paul's addition to the originally symmetrical four-membered set of oppositions."

ful in establishing new covenant and exilic return themes in catena (6:16c–18) that enable them to link the catena to the surrounding context. However, their treatment of the outer shell (6:14–16a) is less convincing because they leave it thematically unintegrated with the catena.[22] The themes of new covenant and exilic return are, at best, marginal in 6:14–16a and so the latter do not seem to cohere on the thematic level with the catena.

This inability to address how the outer shell stands integrally related with the catena means that nagging questions remain about the thematic coherence of 2 Cor 6:14–7:1. The literary integrity of the passage is not in question here, but one wonders exactly how the outer shell hangs together with the catena on the thematic level. What precisely is the function of the outer shell, with its antithetical couplets, in relation to the scriptural catena?

2 Cor 6:16b: Its Pivotal Role and Significance

Second Corinthians 6:16b offers a crucial hint on resolving the issue of how the outer shell stands in thematic relation to the catena. The affirmation in 6:16b, "for we are the temple of the living God," stands at a pivotal point in the whole passage and discloses the thematic link between the outer shell and the catena. 6:16b offers a kind of nodal point in which there is a shift from the rhetorical questions of 6:14–16a to the scriptural catena of 6:16c–18. The pivotal role of 6:16b is clear from its function within the wider framework of the passage. In terms of literary structure, 2 Cor 6:14–7:1 has three basic parts.[23] The

---

22. Beale, "The Old Testament Background of Reconciliation," 569, observes of the antithetical questions in 6:14a–16a that they "assume a context of peaceful restoration," and this context links the questions to the scriptural themes in the catena. Webb, *Returning Home,* 59–71, concedes the "lexical ambiguity" of the language in 2 Cor 6:14–16b and the "lack of explicit Old Testament material" in these verses. Nonetheless, he still argues that this language has "affinities" with the theology of the scriptural catena.

23. The subdivisions follow Furnish, *II Corinthians,* 371–75 (6:14–16a; 6:16b–18; 7:1). Fee, "II Corinthians VI.14–VII.1 and Food Offered to Idols," 156, offers a similar structural outline: 6:14a is closely related to 6:14b–16a, the latter functioning as a rhetorical expansion of the former; 6:16b is supported by a biblical base in

first part is the outer shell found in 6:14–16a, consisting of an initial exhortation supported by five rhetorical questions: "Do not be misyoked with unbelievers. For what partnership have righteousness with iniquity? Or what fellowship light with darkness? What accord has Christ with Belial? Or what has a believer in common with an unbeliever? What agreement has the temple of God with idols?" Following the fifth and last rhetorical question comes the central affirmation of 6:16b, supported by an ensuing scriptural catena: "For we are the temple of the living God;[24] as God said, 'I will live in them and move among them, and I will be their God and they shall be my people. Therefore, come out from them, and be separate from them, says the Lord, and touch nothing unclean; then I will welcome you, and I will be a father to you, and you shall be my sons and daughters, says the Lord Almighty" (6:16c–18). The passage concludes with a final appeal in 7:1, which is part of the outer shell: "Since we have these promises, beloved, let us cleanse ourselves from every defilement of body and spirit, and make holiness perfect in the fear of God." The phrase "these promises" refers to the preceding catena, specifically, the promises of 6:16c and 6:17c–18.[25]

The different sections in 2 Cor 6:14–7:1 stand together as an integral literary unit and consist of closely interrelated elements from beginning to end. The scriptural catena, for example, was either composed to go with the outside shell or it has been "heavily redacted from pre-existing material to fit within the shell."[26] The opening exhortation in 6:14a ("Do not be misyoked with unbelievers") corresponds closely with the scriptural admonitions of 6:17 ("Therefore, come out from them, and be separate from them, says the Lord . . .").[27] Further, there is

---

6:16c–18; and 7:1 is a concluding paraenesis. See also Lambrecht, *Second Corinthians*, 123–24, whose outline is similar to Fee's.

24. There is a variant reading with ὑμεῖς . . . ἐστε, but this variant is most likely an assimilation to the second person of vv. 14, 17, and to the wording of 1 Cor 3:16. Metzger, *A Textual Commentary on the Greek New Testament*, 580. See also Martin, *2 Corinthians*, 202; and Furnish, *II Corinthians*, 373.

25. Furnish, *II Corinthians*, 375.

26. Webb, *Returning Home*, 69.

27. Furnish, *II Corinthians*, 371, 374; Webb, *Returning Home*, 67; and Beale, "The Old Testament Background of Reconciliation," 573.

a close correspondence between the thought of 6:17 and the closing appeal of 7:1.[28]

Despite this close interconnection of elements in the passage, the nagging question about thematic coherence remains, particularly the thematic relation of the outer shell (6:14–16a) to the central affirmation and scriptural catena (6:16b–18). What made the author of the passage combine the antithetical language of 6:14–16a with the scriptural catena? In addressing this question, the expression "for we are the temple of the living God" in 2 Cor 6:16b offers the crucial insight. The relation of 6:16b to the preceding antithetical questions is clear from its close link to the fifth and final rhetorical question in 6:16a. It follows immediately upon the question of 6:16a: "And what agreement has God's temple with idols?" This question climaxes the preceding series of rhetorical questions and "forms the climax and transition, for here we have the confrontation between God's temple and idols."[29] To be sure, this final rhetorical question serves as a climax to the preceding series of questions. However, it is not, by itself, the climax of the whole passage. 6:16a cannot be viewed as climactic or transitional apart from the affirmation of 6:16b to which it leads. A close link between 6:16a and 6:16b is established from the logical connective "for" at the beginning of 6:16b, which draws out the implication of the preceding question.[30] The rhetorical question of 6:16a, then, leads to the affirmation of 6:16b that serves as the key point of transition in the whole passage.[31]

Further, the pivotal character of 6:16b is also evident in the way that it stands out from the preceding questions as an affir-

28. Furnish, *II Corinthians*, 371, 375; and Beale, "The Old Testament Background of Reconciliation," 572–73.

29. Gnilka, "2 Cor 6:14–7:1," 51. Fee, "II Corinthians VI.14–VII.1 and Food Offered to Idols," 158, also takes a similar view noting that the fifth question "is the great question to which the others lead. . . . "

30. Furnish, *II Corinthians*, 373, observes that the questions in 6:14–16a " . . . are here [6:16b] grounded in the indicative: believers are to avoid any alliance with the world that would be unworthy of a community which understands itself as the temple of the living God." See also Beale, "The Old Testament Background of Reconciliation," 570; and Fee, "II Corinthians VI.14–VII.1," 158.

31. R. J. McKelvey, *The New Temple: The Church in the New Testament* (Oxford: Oxford University Press, 1969), 94–95.

mation in the first person plural: "for we are the temple of the living God" (ἡμεῖς γὰρ ναὸς θεοῦ ἐσμεν ζῶντος). Verse 6:16b serves to discontinue the preceding rhetorical questions and represents a development in the line of thought. What was implicit in 6:14–16a is here made explicit in the bald assertion that the readers are the "temple of the living God," stressing a specific ecclesial identity. The affirmation in 6:16b thus draws out the issue of ecclesial identity that forms the basis of the exhortations in the passage. The importance of 6:16b also appears in the way that it generates the ensuing scriptural catena in 6:16c–18 and signals a shift to the scriptural themes of new covenant and exilic return: "the dignity of the Christians as 'temple of the living God' is so considerable that it requires detailed scriptural proof."[32] The living God's indwelling of the temple " . . . is the basis upon which the following ethical themes of separation and holiness are developed."[33]

The close connection between the affirmation of 6:16b and the scriptural catena is also evident in the wording of 6:16b. In Greek, the attribute "living" is placed in isolation from the word it modifies, "God," and comes at the end of the affirmation. It could be rendered, "for we are the temple of God (who is) living" (ἡμεῖς γὰρ ναὸς θεοῦ ἐσμεν ζῶντος). This word order places the attribute "living" at the end of the affirmation and in proximity to the first scriptural citation in 6:16c: "as God said, I will dwell in them and move among them, and I will be their God and they shall be my people." The inference here is that the verbs in 6:16c, "I will live and move among them," both serve to define the sense of "living" in 6:16b.[34] The use of the epithet "living God" in 6:16b is closely integrated with the scriptural quotation in 6:16c.

Second Corinthians 6:16b, then, functions as a kind of nodal point in which the outer shell finds transition to the ensuing

---

32. Gnilka, "2 Cor 6.14–7.1," 51. For similar thoughts, see Fee, "II Corinthians VI.14–VII.1," 156; and Stenger, "Die Gottesbezeichnung," 66.

33. Everding, "The Living God," 325. Fee, "2 Corinthians VI.14–VII.1," 158, notes that 6:16b "derives its meaning from the contrasts of the fifth question but also serves in turn as the premise on which the rest of the argument rests."

34. Everding, "The Living God," 324–25.

scriptural catena. As the key transitional point in the passage, 6:16b serves to link the outer shell to the scriptural catena. Viewed in this way, 2 Cor 6:16b is undoubtedly pivotal for the wider interpretation of 2 Cor 6:14–7:1. It is, however, precisely at this point where the lack of scholarly insight into the expression "temple of the living God" inhibits any movement forward. Verse 6:16b is a *hapax legomenon* that remains far from clear among interpreters. In general, scholarly treatments of the expression "temple of the living God" remain cursory and incomplete. For example, some interpreters view the living God in 2 Cor 6:16b as generally equivalent to "God" and thus lacking in any special significance.[35] Other interpreters neglect the living God altogether and focus their attention on the temple motif, discussing the admittedly rich image of the Corinthian community as God's "temple."[36] There is much discussion on the parallel temple imagery of 1 Cor 3:16–17 and 6:19 that serves to clarify the "temple of the living God" as a figure expressing the holiness of the Corinthian community.

However, almost invariably, interpreters fail to account for the living God in 2 Cor 6:16b and neglect the epithet's function in alluding to early Christian kerygma of the living God.[37] A few interpreters, however, do recognize this function based upon the antithesis between idols and the living God in 2 Cor 6:16a and 16b. The pattern of language in 6:16a and 6:16b reflects the convert's experience of making "a complete break with his religious past, which was one of idol worship . . .";[38] also, "the

---

35. For example, Collange, *Énigmes*, 309, observes that "for Paul, the important term here is θεοῦ (repeated and qualified by ζῶντος, cf. 3:3)." Many commentators pass over the epithet in silence, e.g., Bultmann, *The Second Letter to the Corinthians*, 180; Plummer, *Second Epistle of St. Paul to the Corinthians*, 208–9; and Barrett, *The Second Epistle to the Corinthians*, 199–200.

36. Everding, "The Living God," 324; Stenger, "Die Gottesbezeichnung 'lebendiger Gott,'" 66; Kraus, "Der lebendige Gott," 198; Gnilka, "2 Cor 6:14–7:1," 61–62; and Bertil Gärtner, *The Temple and the Community in Qumran and the New Testament* (SNTSMS; Cambridge: Cambridge University Press, 1965), 50–51.

37. Numerous commentators cite 1 Thess 1:9 and Acts 14:15 as parallels to 2 Cor 6:16 with no comment clarifying the significance of the parallel (Everding, "The Living God," 324; Hans Joseph Klauck, *2. Korintherbrief* [Kommentar zum Neuen Testament; Echter, 1986], 61; and Victor C. Pfitzner, *Strength in Weakness: A Commentary on 2 Corinthians* [Adelaide, South Australia: Chi Rho, 1992], 103).

38. Philip E. Hughes, *Paul's Second Epistle to the Corinthians* (Grand Rapids: Eerdmans, 1973), 251–251.

God/idols dualism marks the coming out of paganism...and the turning to the living God of Christianity";[39] and "the living God, the one who provides the only way to life—through rebirth—is in Paul's mind and is conveyed by a favorite element of his apostolic teaching."[40] In short, the antithesis in 6:16a and 6:16b resembles Pauline kerygmatic formulations and suggests an underlying kerygmatic substratum in 2 Cor 6:16a–b.

While the latter observations are insightful, they are, however, too brief and do not demonstrate what they assert. What is needed, then, is a fuller analysis which gathers together all the evidence and demonstrates the kerygmatic significance of the expression "temple of the living God." The evidence that supports a kerygmatic interpretation of 2 Cor 6:16a–b is of three types: (1) the biblical Jewish evidence of Dan 4:19; 5:23 LXX; (2) the post-Pauline evidence of 1 Tim 3:15; and (3) the Pauline kerygmatic texts of 1 Thess 1:9 and Acts 14:15. The first type of evidence emerges in Dan 4:19; 5:23 LXX, both of which have been earlier examined and use the expression "house of the living God" in referring to the Jerusalem temple.[41] Daniel 5:23, in particular, offers a significant parallel to 2 Cor 6:16 through its use of a similar pattern of motifs involving the temple, the living God, and idols. Nowhere else in biblical or Jewish literature is there found this antithesis of idols and the temple/house of the living God.

In my earlier discussion of Dan 5:23 LXX I showed that the expression reflects a traditional biblical view which closely linked the living God to temple worship. The "house of the living God" was God's special dwelling place, and this divine indwelling marks Israel as a special people defined by a covenantal relation to the living God. The link between the living God and the Jerusalem temple functions as a sign of God's covenantal faithfulness. More significantly, however, Dan 5:23 LXX also expresses the distinctive views of Hellenistic Jews living in a polytheistic milieu. The expression "house of the living God" is part

---

39. Webb, *Returning Home,* 193.
40. Martin, *2 Corinthians,* 203.
41. Everding, "The Living God," 324 n. 2, and Furnish, *II Corinthians,* 363, cite Daniel 5:23 LXX as a key parallel to the "temple of the living God" in 2 Cor 6:16b.

of a text that promotes the superior worship of the living God in a polytheistic milieu.[42] In the text, Daniel represents the Jewish community that devotes itself in praise to the living God, and Belshazzar represents the idolatrous Gentile who foolishly refuses to praise the living God. The "house of the living God" in Dan 5:23 LXX presupposes a Hellenistic Jewish community that defines itself through the rejection of idols as false worship.

The parallel of Dan 5:23 LXX therefore suggests that the expression "temple of the living God" in 2 Cor 6:16b reflects a Gentile Christian community that has forsaken pagan ways and converted to the exclusive worship of the one living God. The expression, in other words, points to Gentile converts who have accepted the living God as the one true God who alone is worthy of reverence and worship. As a "temple of the living God," the Gentile community distinguishes itself by rejecting the polytheistic worship of the surrounding environment and by devoting itself to the worship of the living God.

First Timothy 3:15 offers a second type of evidence that supports the "temple of the living God" as an allusion to Gentile conversion, and again, the fruits of an earlier discussion are relevant.[43] First Timothy 3:15 describes the Christian community as "the house of God which is the church of the living God, the pillar and bulwark of truth." The ecclesial motifs in this verse offer parallels to the "temple of the living God" in 2 Cor 6:16b. For example, 1 Tim 3:15 characterizes the community as the "house of God," a traditional expression for the Jerusalem temple, which echoes the temple image in 2 Cor 6:16b. Also 1 Tim 3:15 describes the community using the same genitive expression that is found in 2 Cor 6:16b, "of the living God." Further, the expression "church of the living God" in 1 Tim 3:15 functions in a hortatory setting and serves to clarify the

---

42. In chapter 3 I observed that Dan 5:23 LXX embodies Jewish traditions of the living God in which the latter was employed in stylized formulations of idol polemic. Other examples of such formulations are found in Dan 6:26–27 LXX; Bel 5 Th; *Sib. Or.* 3:763; and *Jos. Asen.* 8:5.

43. Commentators on 2 Cor 6:16b often cite 1 Tim 3:15 as a parallel and vice versa. For example, Stenger, "Die Gottesbezeichnung 'lebendiger Gott,' " 68, discusses 1 Tim 3:15 by referring to 2 Cor 6:16. See also Knight, *Commentary on the Pastoral Epistles,* 181.

solemn identity of the readers as the basis for the exhortation on how they are to "behave" in Paul's absence. A similar hortatory function characterizes the "temple of the living God" in 2 Cor 6:16b and serves to clarify the identity of the readers as a basis for exhortation.

The suggestion is that 1 Tim 3:15 offers a hint about how to interpret the "temple of the living God" in 2 Cor 6:16b. As previously discussed, the genitive expression "of the living God" in 1 Tim 3:15 functions as a subjective genitive, designating the origins of a community in the living God. The expression "church of the living God" designates a community that belongs to the living God because its origins go back to the living God (cf. 1 Thess 1:1). The expression alludes to a community whose origins are rooted in conversion to the living God. Viewed in this light, then, the "temple of the living God" in 2 Cor 6:16b also serves as an allusion to the foundational experience of conversion and designates a community whose origins go back to the living God.

A final observation clinches the claim that the "temple of the living God" alludes to Gentile conversion, and it has already been expressed by the commentators cited earlier in this section. Second Corinthians 6:16a and 6:16b, taken together, form an antithesis between the living God and idols.[44] The close syntactical relation between 6:16a and 6:16b results in an antithesis of the living God and idols, recalling Paul's kerygmatic formulations in 1 Thess 1:9; Acts 14:15; and *Acts Paul* 7:2. In 6:16a the "temple of God" stands in direct antithesis to idols and 6:16b extends this opposition by clarifying the nature of the "temple" in 6:16a.[45] The "temple" of 6:16b is none other than the writer and readers themselves who, together, are the "temple of the living God." The antithesis, then, is between idols and the temple-community, and the latter is defined by its monotheistic worship of the living God, having renounced its former idolatry.

---

44. Everding, "The Living God," 324; Furnish, *II Corinthians,* 373; and Windisch, *Der zweite Korintherbrief,* 211.

45. In both 2 Cor 6:16b and 1 Cor 3:16–17 the term ναός is used as the term for temple. ναός specifically designates the holy of holies in the temple (Barrett, *The Second Epistle to the Corinthians,* 199; Martin, *2 Corinthians,* 202–3; and Furnish, *II Corinthians,* 363, 373).

Second Corinthians 6:16a–b thus employs a pattern of language that is similar to the kerygmatic language found in 1 Thess 1:9 and Acts 14:15, as commentators note. This similarity in language suggests that 2 Cor 6:16a–b has its roots in kerygmatic language of the living God. The antithetical patterning of language of 2 Cor 6:16a and 6:16b is rooted in what Nils Dahl calls "the soteriological contrast pattern," a pattern characterized by a "once you were/now you are" sequence.[46] Dahl observes that "this preaching type is intended to help believers understand what the existence newly offered to them in Christ really means and entails, in contrast to their former life as pagans or Jews."[47] This language of opposition to idols, of course, is directed to Gentile converts who renounced their idols at conversion and, as a result, became God's "temple," a community committed to the exclusive worship of the one God. The expression "temple of the living God" thus serves to allude to a Gentile community that had its origins in conversion to the living God, as some interpreters perceptively conclude. The mention of "idols" in 2 Cor 6:16a refers "to the false gods or no-gods from whom the Corinthians were delivered at conversion."[48] The expression "temple of the living God" in 6:16b reflects "the concept of a new beginning to Christian existence.... The living God, the one who provides the only way to life—through rebirth—is in Paul's mind...."[49]

There is, however, a serious objection to this claim that the "temple of the living God" alludes to Gentile conversion. The language of 2 Cor 6:14–7:1 is not explicitly kerygmatic since it is addressed to those who are already believing Christians. In fact, the hortatory function of the language in 2 Cor 6:16a and 6:16b is distinguishable from the kerygmatic language of 1 Thess 1:9 and Acts 14:15. Second Corinthians 6:16a–b is not kerygma per se, but rather is "paraenesis for cultic holi-

---

46. Nils Dahl, "Form-Critical Observations On Early Christian Preaching," *Jesus in the Memory of the Early Church* (Minneapolis: Augsburg, 1976), 33–34. Bultmann, *Theology of the New Testament*, 1:105–6.

47. Dahl, "Form-Critical Observations," 33–34.

48. R. J. McKelvey, *The New Temple*, 94.

49. Martin, *2 Corinthians*, 203.

ness."[50] While these observations are undeniable, they do not preclude the validity of attributing a kerygmatic character to 2 Cor 6:16a–b. While the expression "temple of the living God" may not function explicitly as kerygma, it is nonetheless rooted in kerygmatic language that has been recast for purposes of paraenesis. The author-redactor of 2 Cor 6:14–7:1 composed the passage by drawing upon the language of early Christian kerygma, using this language as the basis for exhortation. The underlying language of kerygma in 6:16a–b serves to ground the primary paraenetic thrust of the entire passage. It is therefore possible to think of 2 Cor 6:16 as grounded in the language of early Christian kerygma that has been subsequently recycled for paraenesis. Second Corinthians 6:16a–b, in other words, is based upon an underlying substratum of conversion language.

The likelihood of 2 Cor 6:16 reflecting a substratum of kerygmatic language is bolstered by the following observation. Gentile conversion has an intrinsic ethical dimension, entailing not only the renunciation of idols, but also the renunciation of pagan immorality. Gentile converts, in turning to the living God, embrace a new life of holiness. The expression "temple of the living God" is thus an effective ground for exhortation because it reminds the readers of the ethical implications of their conversion and provides the basis for the exhortation in the passage (6:14a; 6:17; 7:1). The "temple" image itself is essential in conveying to the readers their responsibility for living a holy life as converts, similar to Paul's exhortation in 1 Cor 3:16–17.[51] The language of 2 Cor 6:16a–b calls the readers back to their conversion roots and the holiness ideals that came with conversion. The expression "temple of the living God" thus serves as an effective reminder that the readers, as Gentile converts, are expected to live holy lives in service to the living God.

---

50. Everding, "The Living God," 324–25.

51. McKelvey, *The New Temple*, 102, observes that the thought of 1 Cor 3:16–17 is very similar to that of 2 Cor 6:16b: "the only difference lies in the nature of the danger to which the church is exposed; here it is internal (divisiveness), whereas at 2 Cor. 6. 16–17 it is external...."

Allusions to Gentile Conversion in the Outer Shell (6:14–16a, 7:1) and Scriptural Catena (6:16c–18)

The foregoing insights hold ramifications for interpreting 2 Cor 6:14–7:1. In alluding to Gentile conversion, 2 Cor 6:16b furnishes an important clue about how to interpret the surrounding material in the outer shell and ensuing catena. The suggestion here is that all the elements in 2 Cor 6:14–7:1 can be viewed as alluding to the root experience of Gentile conversion.[52] More specifically, I propose that the outer shell is grounded in a substratum of kerygmatic language that is recast for paraenetic purposes, and that the scriptural catena uses scriptural texts to allude to Gentile conversion in the manner of Rom 9:25–26. Second Corinthians 6:14–7:1, therefore, has an internal thematic coherence based upon motifs that allude to Gentile conversion.

I begin with the language in the outer shell that remains in need of further investigation. My previous analysis of 6:16a–b, however, suggests that the linguistic roots of the outer shell lie in early Christian kerygma. Three observations support this claim. First, there is the close formal connection between the rhetorical questions in 6:14b–16a and the pivotal affirmation of 6:16b. The latter is "a metaphorical summary of the preceding antitheses"[53] and thus stands in thematic connection with them. The inference, then, is that the substrate of kerygmatic language in 6:16b also informs 6:14–16a. Second, the pattern of antithetical language in 6:14b–16a reflects the same antithetical logic expressed in Pauline kerygmatic formulations such as 1 Thess 1:9 and Acts 14:15.

Third, an examination of individual terms in the outer shell indicates numerous parallels with conversion language found in Paul's letters and Acts.[54] The linguistic background of 6:14–16

---

52. Rensberger makes a similar suggestion: "Very possibly the text itself [=2 Cor 6:14–7:1], like other elements in Paul's letters, came to him from the early Christian 'kerygma' described by Bultmann and identified as sectarian-influenced by Flusser" ("2 Corinthians 6:14–7:1—A Fresh Examination," 41).

53. Beale, "The Old Testament Background of Reconciliation in 2 Corinthians 5–7," 570.

54. Rensberger, "2 Corinthians 6:14–7:1," 41; and Klauck, *2. Korintherbrief,* 61.

and 7:1 supports the presence of a kerygmatic substratum. The outer shell commences in 6:14a with the exhortation, "Do not be misyoked with unbelievers," and then a series of rhetorical questions in 6:14b–16a serve to reinforce the thought of 6:14a. Each question consists of a pair of opposites that stress the exclusive character of Christian life in contrast to former pagan existence: "For what partnership have righteousness and iniquity? Or what fellowship has light with darkness? What accord has Christ with Belial? Or what has a believer in common with an unbeliever? What agreement has the temple of god with idols?" (6:14b–16a). These questions represent a variation on Dahl's soteriological contrast pattern and serve to remind the readers of the radical change that came with conversion to the living God. As converts the readers have left behind their lawlessness, darkness, Belial, unbelief, and idolatry for a new life characterized by righteousness, light, Christ, faith, and holiness as God's temple.[55]

In 2 Cor 6:15, for example, the term "believer" is used in antithesis with "unbeliever" and suggests the technical sense of conversion faith.[56] The antithesis of "faith" and "unbelief" stresses the chasm that exists between former pagan life and the new life of faith.[57] Further, this conversion faith in 6:15 also reflects a monotheistic faith in the living God, as it also does in 1 Thess 1:8. The exclusive opposition between pagan lawlessness and Christian righteousness in 6:14b reflects the contrast between pre-conversion existence and the new life characterized by righteousness.[58] Conversion entails a movement from lawlessness to a life of righteousness. A similar opposition is described by Paul in Rom 6:19: "For just as you once yielded your members

---

55. Gnilka, "2 Cor 6:14–7:1," 50–51, observes that "the contrasts have been chosen in such a way that they are appropriate for denoting the particular spheres to which the Christian or heathen belongs."

56. Rudolf Bultmann, "πιστεύω," *TDNT* 6:218–19. For this technical sense of πίστις in 2 Cor 6:15b see Gnilka, "2 Cor 6:14–7:1," 57; Furnish, *II Corinthians*, 362–63; and Martin, *2 Corinthians*, 201.

57. 1 Cor 6:6; 7:12–15. Barrett, *The Second Epistle to the Corinthians*, 199, observes that "Christian faith is exclusive, and the question is intended rather to make the point that one cannot be a believer and unbeliever at the same time."

58. Dahl, "Form-Critical Observations," 33, identifies 6:14b as illustrative of the soteriological contrast pattern in early Christian preaching.

to impurity and to greater and greater lawlessness, so now yield your members to righteousness for sanctification." In 2 Cor 3:9 Paul can describe his ministry as a "ministry of righteousness," that is, a ministry that brings justification by faith.

Conversion to the living God is also like a movement from darkness to light.[59] Through conversion, Gentiles are brought from their former pagan darkness into the light of monotheistic truth (Acts 26:18; 1 Pet 2:9; 1 Thess 5:4–5; Rom 2:19). Gentile Christians "have been called out of darkness into [God's] marvelous light" (1 Pet 2:9); and, God has called them "that they may turn from darkness to light and from the power of Satan to God" (Acts 26:18). Against this background the light/darkness opposition in 2 Cor 6:14c recalls the status of Christian believers who have been illumined by the knowledge of the one true God. Conversion also involves a change of lordship for the converts, bringing about a liberation from spiritual powers and entities to which the converts were formerly enslaved (cf. Gal 4:8–9; 1 Cor 8:4–5). The Christ/Belial couplet in 6:15a thus reflects this aspect of conversion in which the convert has moved from bondage to Satan to God (cf. 2 Cor 4:4; Acts 26:17–18).

Finally, the exhortation of 2 Cor 7:1 draws on conversion language, expressing the holiness requirements entailed by conversion to the living God: "Since we have these promises, beloved, let us cleanse ourselves from every defilement of body and spirit and make holiness perfect in the fear of God."[60] Conversion entails for Gentiles a new life of holiness as an ethical requirement. In practical terms this means the renunciation of idolatry and the immoral practices associated with idolatry. The movement from the convert's former paganism to the new life of service to the living God entails holiness and sanctification, as in 1 Thess 4:3–8. Paul also describes the Corinthians as "those sanctified in Christ Jesus, called to be saints . . . (1 Cor 1:2; cf. 2 Cor 1:1).

In sum, then, the outer shell in 2 Cor 6:14–16a; 7:1 employs a substratum of kerygmatic-conversion language that has been

---

59. Bultmann, *Theology of the New Testament*, 1:66–67.
60. Heb 9:14 offers a parallel here: "How much more shall the blood of Christ, who through the eternal spirit offered himself without blemish to God, *purify your conscience from dead works to serve the living God*" [italics mine].

taken up and reworked for purposes of exhortation. The antithetical questions in 6:14b–16a serve to recall the exclusive dynamics of Gentile conversion in which converts renounced their idolatry and committed themselves to the living God.

In turning to 2 Cor 6:16c–18, the scriptural catena works a little differently in the way that it alludes to Gentile conversion. It uses scriptural motifs and language to speak metaphorically about Gentile conversion, much in the manner of Rom 9:25–26. At first glance, this claim appears to go beyond the evidence, since the catena would seem to say nothing about Gentile conversion and everything about the new covenant and exilic return. However, my earlier discussion of Rom 9:25–26 has suggested that scriptural texts can and do refer to Gentile conversion. In Rom 9:24–26 Paul uses the prophetic language of Hos 2:25 and 2:1 LXX, addressed originally to Israel, to show that God's call of Gentiles fulfills new covenant promises. Through conversion, Gentiles have become "my people" (9:25) and "sons of the living God" (9:26). The catena in 2 Cor 6:16c–18, then, can also be viewed as using new covenant language to allude to Gentile conversion. The scriptural language in 2 Cor 6:16c–18 employs the language of exilic return and new covenant to speak about Gentile Christians. Like Rom 9:25–26, 2 Cor 6:16c–18 describes Gentile converts as covenantal "sons" (6:18) and "people," using the new covenantal formula "and they shall be my people" (6:16c). The parallels also extend to the use of the epithet living God in both passages. In 2 Cor 6:16b, Gentile converts are the "temple of the living God."

Moreover, the literary placement of 2 Cor 6:16c–18 also suggests that it has something to do with Gentile conversion. The outer shell, with its substrate of conversion language, frames the scriptural catena and thereby provides a significant framework for its interpretation. Moreover, the catena is closely linked to the preceding affirmation of 6:16b that it serves to document and support. The catena thus documents the assertion that the readers are a temple-community whose identity is rooted in conversion to the living God.[61] The scriptural catena of 6:16c–18,

---

61. Second Corinthians 7:1, the concluding appeal of the outer shell, summarizes

then, stands in continuity with a substratum of kerygmatic language in the outer shell, suggesting its function in alluding to Gentile conversion.

A perusal of individual components in the catena further bears out its function in alluding to Gentile conversion. The catena consists of four scriptural texts, each of which has been modified in varying degrees: Ezek 37:27 (6:16c); Isa 52:11–12 (6:17a–c); Ezek 20:31 (6:17d); and 2 Sam 7:14 (6:18). The first scriptural text comes in 6:16c, is from Ezek 37:27, and is conflated with elements from Lev 26:11–12: "as God said, 'I will live in them and move among them, and I will be their God and they shall be my people'" (ἐνοικήσω ἐν αὐτοῖς καὶ ἐμπεριπατήσω καὶ ἔσομαι αὐτῶν θεὸς καὶ αὐτοὶ ἔσονταί μου λαός).[62] This paraphrase serves to document the preceding affirmation of 6:16b and is a fitting prooftext since Ezek 37:26–28 envisions the restoration of future Israel in terms of a new temple, described as "my sanctuary among them" and "my dwelling place with them." The promise that God would live and move among his people is fulfilled in the existence of a Gentile Christian community in whom the divine Spirit dwells.[63]

The allusion to Gentile conversion emerges in the new covenant formula at the end of 6:16c, "and I will be their God and they shall be my people" (cf. Ezek 11:20; 14:11; 34:24, 30; 36:28; 37:23, 27).[64] As in Rom 9:25–26 and 1 Pet 2:9–10, this formula serves to clarify the newfound status of Gentile converts as God's "people."[65] For example, in Rom 9:25–26 the formula is used in a reversal scheme to show that Gentiles, who were "not my

---

the content of the catena as "these promises." Furnish, *II Corinthians*, 365. Beale, "The Old Testament Background of Reconciliation in 2 Corinthians 5–7," 569, 572.

62. Beale, "The Old Testament Background," 570, describes the wording as a conflation of the two texts; however, Webb, *Returning Home*, 33–40, prefers the view of Ezek 37:27 as the primary text "with influence from Leviticus 26.11–12." See also Furnish, *II Corinthians*, 363–64, 374, and Webb, *Returning Home*, 37.

63. Furnish, *II Corinthians*, 374. McKelvey, *The New Temple*, 95, observes that 'God no longer dwells *with* his people in a sanctuary which they make for him; he dwells *in* them and they are his temple."

64. Webb, *Returning Home*, 68.

65. Striking here is the application of the covenantal term λαός to the Gentile Corinthian community, a term that was traditionally reserved for Israel (cf. Rom 9:25).

people," are now "my people." The new covenant formula in
6:16c thus serves as an allusion to Gentile converts who become
God's "people" through conversion.

The scriptural texts in 2 Cor 6:17–18 employ the language
of exilic return (Isa 52:11) and restoration (Ezek 20:34; 2 Sam
7:14), and they are arranged in a sequence that corresponds
metaphorically to the dynamics of Gentile conversion. The sequence involves a separation from an idolatrous environment
(=Babylon; 6:17a–c); God's ingathering and acceptance of exilic returnees (6:17d); and the restoration of the exiles to filial
status (6:18). The sequence begins in 2 Cor 6:17 with the citation of Isa 52 (6:17a–c): "therefore come out from them, and be
separate from them, says the Lord, and touch nothing unclean"
(διὸ ἐξέλθατε ἐκ μέσου αὐτῶν καὶ ἀφορίσθητε, λέγει κύριος, καὶ
ἀκαθάρτου μὴ ἅπτεσθε). Since the readers are God "people"
(6:16c), they should separate themselves from the "uncleanness" of Babylon. In its original context Isa 52:11 expresses the
notion of exilic return in which Israel departs from "Babylon"
and its worship of pagan gods. The Isaian text relates Israel's
"purification from cultic uncleanness" following its departure
from Babylon, and the reference to "uncleanness" likely refers
to pollution associated with idolatry.[66]

In 2 Cor 6:17, however, Isa 52:11 no longer refers to a literal
return of exiled Israel from Babylon but to Gentile Christians.
The new metaphorical referent of Isa 52:11 is that of Gentile
believers who have left "Babylon" and arrived at "the temple of
the living God." In its present context this reference to Babylon
becomes "a representation of humanity's alienation from God,
since Paul is applying Isaiah's message for Israel to Gentiles."[67]
Second Corinthians 6:17, in other words, exhorts Gentile Christians to remove themselves from a pagan (idolatrous) sphere
signified as "Babylon."[68] Isaiah 52:11 is thus suited as an allu-

---

66. Furnish, *II Corinthians,* 365; and Martin, *2 Corinthians,* 209.
67. Beale, "The Old Testament Background of Reconciliation in 2 Corinthians
5–7," 558–59.
68. Gnilka, "2 Cor 6:14–7:1," 52, observes, " . . . this O.T. background means that
God himself sanctions and guides the separation of the Christians from the heathen,
although it is not clear, from the passage considered in itself, whether this Exodus
is meant in a real or moral sense."

sion to the repentance that accompanied the process of Gentile conversion to the living God.[69] It serves to remind the Gentile readers of their original conversion experience that involved a separation from pagan ways. In conversion Gentiles turned "from idols." Second Corinthians 6:17a–c thus exhorts Gentile readers to complete the process of separation begun in conversion.

Second Corinthians 6:17d expresses the result of the readers separating themselves from Babylon: "then I will welcome you" (κἀγὼ εἰσδέξομαι ὑμᾶς).[70] God "welcomes" the readers after their return from Babylon.[71] Verse 6:17d draws upon the text of Ezek 20:34 LXX, although other scriptural texts are sometimes cited (e.g., Ezek 11:17 and Zeph 3:20). In its original setting Ezek 20:34 refers to exilic return in which God's ingathers the Jewish exiles from Babylon: "... I will bring you out from the nations and gather you from the countries over which you are scattered...." Ezekiel 20:34 expresses the initiating of an exilic return that culminates in God receiving Israel from its exilic estrangement. Having separated themselves from "Babylon" and its idols, the returnees (=converts) will be welcomed by God.

Finally, 2 Cor 6:18 alludes to God's act of receiving his converts, as a father would receive lost children. Second Corinthians 6:18 represents a modified version of 2 Sam 7:14, and it expresses the powerful transforming effect of conversion: "and I will be your father, and you shall be my sons and daughters, says the Lord Almighty" (καὶ ὑμεῖς ἔσεσθέ μοι εἰς υἱοὺς καὶ θυγατέρας, λέγει κύριος παντοκράτωρ). The God who gathers "exiles" from the nations is a loving father with whom converts can find a warm reception. Like the other citations in the catena, 2 Sam 7:14 LXX is significantly modified. The original "son" has been pluralized into "sons" in a process that interpreters typically describe as a democratizing of the origi-

---

69. Beale, "The Old Testament Background of Reconciliation in 2 Corinthians 5–7," 558.

70. The expression is found nine times in a promise formula: Mic 4:6; Zeph 3:19, 20; Jer 23:3; Ezek 11:17; 20:34, 41; Zech 10:8, 10.

71. The motif of divine welcome may go back to the idea of converts being warmly received into relationship with God the father (cf. *Jos. Asen.* 11:13; 12:8).

nal promise. The original promise to individual Davidic kings is transferred to corporate Israel (cf. Isa 55:3–5).[72]

Another significant modification in 6:18 involves the addition of "and daughters," not attributable to 2 Sam 7, and it likely stems from Isa 43:6 (cf. 49:22; 60:4). Interpreters customarily clarify this addition in one of two ways. Either the writer shows egalitarian concerns in mentioning "daughters" or the mention of "daughters" is a direct borrowing from Isa 43:6.[73] However, both these explanations do not consider the possibility that "sons and daughters" functions as an allusion to Gentile conversion. The key to recognizing this allusion is the sonship motif, an attribution of Gentile converts. For example, in Rom 8:14–17, 9:56–26, Paul describes the effects of conversion in terms of converts attaining a close filial relationship with God. The new covenant identity of peoplehood expressed earlier in 6:16c is here given a personal filial twist and stresses the new status of Gentile converts as God's children.

The sonship motif in 2 Cor 6:18 is, perhaps, best understood in connection with the idea of eschatological sonship found in *Jub.* 1:24–25. The latter is a prophecy that envisions a future eschatological Israel in terms of the sonship motif derived from 2 Sam 7:14 and Hos 2:1 LXX [1:10].[74] The *Jubilees* passage is similar to 2 Cor 6:18 in using the prophecy of 2 Sam 7:14 in democratized form to speak about eschatological sonship.[75] Further, the Jubilees passage envisions eschatological sonship in explicit connection with God's identity as "father." These "sons"

---

72. Webb, *Returning Home,* 54. Also, Beale, "The Old Testament Background of Reconciliation," 571–72.

73. On the former, see Martin, *2 Corinthians,* 206–7. Barrett, *The Second Epistle to the Corinthians,* 201, observes: "to Paul it was an essential feature of Christian existence that by faith and in Christ there could be neither male nor female could be otherwise expressed by speaking of daughters as well as sons of God." However, Beale, "The Old Testament Background of Reconciliation in 2 Corinthians 5–7," 572, and Webb, *Returning Home,* 56–58, consider the expression "sons and daughters" to align with exilic return theology deriving from Isa 43:6, 49:22, 60:4.

74. *Jub.* 1:24–25: "And they will do my commandments. And I shall be father to them, and they will be sons to me. And they will all be called 'sons of the living God,' And every angel and spirit will know and acknowledge that they are my sons and I am their father in uprightness and righteousness. And I shall love them."

75. Webb, *Returning Home,* 54–56. See also Brendan Byrne, *"Sons of God"—"Seed of Abraham": A Study of the Idea of the Sonship of All Christians in Paul Against the Jewish Background* (Analecta biblica 83; Rome: Biblical Institute, 1979), 193–95.

stand in a close filial relation to the divine "father" who "loves" them: "and I am their father in uprightness and righteousness. And I shall love them" (*Jub.* 1:25). The *Jubilees* passage, then, suggests an interpretive tradition in which the sonship motif in 2 Sam 7:14 is linked to Hos 2:1 LXX and the "sons of the living God." That 2 Cor 6:18 covertly alludes to Hos 2:1 LXX and "sons of the living God" is supported by the proximity of the epithet in 6:16. In 2 Cor 6:18, then, the expression "sons and daughters" likely serves as an allusion to the new filial identity brought about by conversion.

In sum, the scriptural catena in 2 Cor 6:16c–18 uses a collection of scriptural language in alluding to Gentile conversion and stands in thematic continuity with the outer shell (6:14–16b). The primary elements in the allusion are separation from idolatry and reception by the divine father into covenantal relation. The catena urges converts to leave behind their idolatrous "Babylon" (6:17) and return home to their God who, as "father," promises to receive them as covenantal sons and daughters (6:17d-18). Through conversion, the Corinthians have become God's new covenantal "people" (6:16c) and beloved "sons and daughters" in fulfillment of God's earlier promises (2 Sam 7:14 and Hos 2:1 LXX [1:10]).

2 Cor 3:3 and 6:16b:
Thematic Correspondences

The foregoing discussion holds implications for understanding the internal coherence of 2 Cor 6:14–7:1 and its contextual compatibility within 2 Cor 2:14–7:4. The central affirmation of 6:16b, "for we are the temple of the living God," consists of a substrate of kerygmatic language that has been recast for paraenetic purposes. It functions to remind the readers that their identity is rooted in the foundational experience of conversion to the living God. This substratum of kerygma in 6:16b also extends to the whole outer shell (6:14–16a; 7:1) that draws upon kerygmatic language recast for paraenetic purposes. In this way, the outer shell calls the readers to their origins in conversion to the living God. Further, the scriptural catena in 6:16c–18 coheres well with the material in the outer shell because it uses biblical texts that allude to conversion. Second Corinthians 6:14–7:1 is thus characterized by a thematic coherence that derives from an underlying substratum of missionary kerygma and scriptural texts which allude to Gentile conversion.

These observations suggest that 2 Cor 6:14–7:1, in its original pre-Pauline form, functions to exhort Gentile Christians on the basis of their foundational experience of conversion. This foundational experience carried ethical demands and entailed holiness ideals that the unknown composer wishes to impress upon his readers. Although the situation in Corinth remains far from clear, the use of 2 Cor 6:14–7:1 implies that the Gentile Christian addressees have strayed from their conversion ideals by relapsing into pagan associations. The readers have either relapsed into a literal idolatry of some kind or they are participating in social associations that are tantamount to idolatry. Either way, Paul (or a disciple) finds the exhortation of 2 Cor 6:14–7:1 relevant to the situation in Corinth. The Corinthians have also relapsed into pagan associations and fallen away from the living God. They thus stand in need of the admonitions in 6:14–7:1. As wayward Israel had gone astray in worshiping other gods and had to be exhorted by the prophets to return to covenant, so too the Corinthians have fallen away from their original call by some behavior that Paul considers idolatrous. Through 2 Cor 6:14–7:1 Paul was able to urge the Corinthians to complete the process of return to the living God that began in conversion. The Corinthians should complete their "return" to God and his apostle.

That 2 Cor 6:14–7:1 aligns well with Paul's wider epistolary aims is suggested from several observations. Many of the terms in the outer shell in 2 Cor 6:14–7:1 resonate with Paul's missionary language: the use of the living God in antithesis to idols (1 Thess 1:9); the antitheses of righteousness/lawlessness (Rom 6:19) and light/darkness (Rom 2:19; 1 Thess 5:4–5); the notion of the community as a "temple" (1 Cor 3:16–17); and the attribute of the readers as "beloved" (2 Cor 12:19; 1 Thess 2:8).[76] The language in the outer shell not only links up with

---

76. Fee, "II Corinthians VI.14–VII.1 And Food Offered to Idols," 147.

Paul's missionary language, but it also serves to recall Paul's role in bringing about conversion in Corinth. Second Corinthians 6:14–7:1 offers a useful summary of Paul's own work in Corinth where he had proclaimed the living God, turning the Corinthians from darkness to light and Beliar (Satan) to Christ, and from unbelief to the living God.[77]

Second Corinthians 6:14–7:1 thus fits Paul's wider epistolary aims in 2 Cor 2:14–7:4 of recalling the Corinthians to his missionary role of introducing them to the living God and founding the Corinthian community. That 2 Cor 6:14–7:1 serves these aims is strengthened by the parallel between 6:16b and the "Spirit of the living God" in 3:3. It seems that 2 Cor 6:16b intentionally echoes and supplements the earlier mention of the "Spirit of the living God." The correspondences between 3:3 and 6:16 are numerous and substantial, beginning with the common use of the epithet living God. The expressions "Spirit of the living God" (3:3) and "temple of the living God" (6:16) correspond not only in their use of the epithet, but also in the motifs of Spirit and temple that are already closely correlated in 1 Cor 3:16–17. In the latter, Paul identifies the Corinthians as God's temple because the Holy Spirit dwells in them; this establishes a close link between the temple and Spirit motifs. For the Corinthians, then, the temple motif is already correlated with the Spirit—they are God's temple marked by the Spirit's indwelling. In this light, the mention of the "temple of the living God" in 2 Cor 6:16b certainly evokes the earlier "Spirit of the living God" and goes together with the motif of the Spirit found in 2 Cor 3:3.

In fact, a covert allusion to the Spirit is present through the scriptural language of 6:16c, "I will dwell in them (ἐνοικήσω) and move among them." This language of indwelling characterizes the Spirit in both 1 Cor 3:16 (οἰκεῖ) and Rom 8:11 (ἐνοικοῦντος), indicating that "indwelling" is one of the Spirit's characteristic activities. Second Corinthians 6:16c, then, conveys

---

77. Perhaps the material in 6:14–7:1 was already familiar to the Corinthians. If so, then Paul, by employing this pericope, was able to ground his claims of apostolic authority in a fragment of early Christian tradition, adding traditional authority to his claims.

the idea that the living God moves and dwells in the Corinthian community through the Spirit, and this further bolsters the alignment of 2 Cor 3:3 with 6:16. Explicitly or implicitly, the motif of God's Spirit is present in 2 Cor 3:3 and 6:16. The Corinthians are a "temple of the living God" because the living God's Spirit "wrote" the Corinthian letter.

The "Spirit of the living God" and the "temple of the living God" correspond in other ways as well. Both expressions point the Corinthians back to the foundational experience of conversion. The mention of the living God serves as an allusion to Paul's missionary kerygma and the resulting conversion. The Spirit motif, as discussed earlier, functions as conversion language in Paul's vocabulary. In 2 Cor 3:3 Paul's reference is to the Spirit who accompanied his preaching in the mission field (1 Cor 2:5; cf. 1 Thess 1:5–6). The Spirit of the living God is instrumental in converting the Corinthians (1 Cor 2:4–5). Similarly, in 2 Cor 6:16 the "temple of the living God" designates a Gentile community that: (a) has its origins in conversion to the living God; and (b) has received the Spirit upon conversion, marking the community as God's holy people, that is, his temple. As in 1 Tim 3:15, the genitive expression "of the living God" designates communal origins through conversion.

Finally, both expressions utilize the language of Ezekiel's new covenant prophecy. Both 2 Cor 3:3 and 6:16 are similar in linking the existence of the Corinthian community to the fulfillment of Ezekiel's new covenant. In 3:3 the Spirit of the living God is active in "writing" upon the Corinthian hearts, described as "tablets of fleshy hearts," an expression deriving from Ezek 11:19; 36:26. Similarly, in 2 Cor 6:16, the existence of the Corinthian community as the temple of the living God fulfills Ezekiel's promises of a new covenant "people" and a new "sanctuary" (Ezek 37:26–28). The use of the new covenant formula in 2 Cor 6:16c derives from Ezek 37:27 and is paralleled in 2 Cor 3:3 by an implicit allusion to the new covenant formula there; the explicit references to Ezek 11:19; 36:26 in 2 Cor 3:3 carry the association of the new covenant formula found in Ezek 11:20 and 36:28. Both 2 Cor 3:3 and 6:16 are therefore closely aligned in describing the origins of the Corinthian community in tandem with the new covenant language of Ezek 36–37. Both verses link the foundations of the Corinthian community with Ezekiel 's vision of a new Israel.

These correspondences between 2 Cor 3:3 and 6:16, then, are substantial and suggest reasons why Paul or a redactor employed 2 Cor 6:14–7:1 in the argument of 2 Corinthians. Second Corinthians 6:14–7:1 furnishes a significant parallel to 2 Cor 2:14–3:6 and indicates the redactor's compositional intent of arranging the discourse into a circular or concentric arrangement. The inclusion of 6:14–7:1 serves to round off the line of thought begun in 2:14–3:6, specifically recalling the earlier thought of 2 Cor 3:3. Second Corinthians 6:14–7:1 reiterates the ideas of 3:3 by stressing Paul's role in the missionary foundations of the community. However, 2 Cor 6:14–7:1 also serves to develop the thought of 2 Cor 3:3 and advance it. Where 2 Cor 3:3 stresses the Spirit as the divine means of conversion, 2 Cor 6:16b stresses the results of that conversion by focusing the readers' attention on their own identity as a point for reflection. Through the temple image in 2 Cor 6:16b Paul is able to shift attention to the Corinthian community and stress its commitments and responsibilities as God's holy people. Second Corinthians 6:14–7:1 fits the general shift of tenor that begins in 2 Cor 6 where Paul begins to directly exhort the Corinthians.

The question remains, however, why 6:14–7:1 was incorporated exactly at the point between 6:11–13 and 7:2–4. How does 6:14–7:1 fit its immediate literary context? In general the issue of the passage's integration in the immediate literary setting remains without satisfactory resolution.[78] In particular, the abrupt introduction of "unbelievers" in 6:14 remains difficult in transition from 6:11–13, and could refer either to false apostles or pagans.[79] However, the foregoing discussion does shed some light on the issue. The central affirmation of 6:16b, "for we

---

78. Some recent discussions, however, merit consideration. For example, Jerome Murphy-O'Connor, "Relating 2 Corinthians 6.14–7.1 to Its Context," *NTS* 33 (1987): 272–75; Belleville, *Reflections of Glory,* 98–103; and Duff, "The Mind of the Redactor," 160–80.

79. The presence of a substratum of kerygmatic language in the outer shell may weigh in favor of taking "unbelievers" in 6:14 in the usual Pauline sense and "idols" in 6:16a in the literal sense. This is the position of Martin, *2 Corinthians,* 193–94;

are the temple of the living God," offers specific links to the surrounding material in 6:11–13 and 7:2–4. The affirmation of 6:16b is in the first person plural "we" and stresses Paul's solidarity with the Corinthians. In affirming that "we are the temple of the living God," Paul makes a statement of his solidarity with the Corinthians. He and the Corinthians together are the "temple of the living God." The implication is that without Paul the Corinthians are not "the temple of the living God," but with Paul they are. Their status of being God's "temple" and God's "people" depends on their relationship to Paul.

This emphatic "we" of 6:16b, along with the cohortative of 7:1, links up with the themes and language of 6:11–13 and 7:2–4. In the former, Paul assures the readers of his affection for them. He asserts that "our mouth is open to you, Corinthians; our heart is wide," and he calls upon them affectionately as his "children" (6:13; cf. 1 Cor 4:14–15). The stress here is on Paul's affection for the Corinthians and their need to be mutual in returning his affection. Further, the language in 7:2–4 shows even stronger affinities with the emphatic "we" of 6:16b. After defending himself against claims that he wronged and took advantage of them (7:2), Paul says "I do not say this to condemn you, for I said before that you are in our hearts, to die together and to live together" (7:3). The latter is a powerful expression of Paul's solidarity with the Corinthians and it offers a useful commentary on the affirmation of 6:16b. Together Paul and the Corinthians are the "temple of the living God"; they die and live together in Christ. Their identity as God's temple, then, is inextricably tied up with their founding apostle.

Fee, "II Corinthians VI.14–VII.1," 140–61; and others. See also Webb, *Returning Home*, 197–99, for a summary of this view.

Chapter Nine

Implications for Interpreting 2 Corinthians 2:14–7:4

🙢🙢🙢🙢🙢🙢🙢🙢🙢🙢🙢

The foregoing discussion provides a clearer picture of what the epithet living God meant to Paul, and it also illumines his discourse in 2 Cor 2:14–7:4. Paul inherits rich traditions of the living God that took shape in the centuries before the Christian era. These traditions came to him from scripture and from Diaspora Jewish circles in the Hellenistic world. These Jewish traditions of the living God are particularly significant in providing Paul with formulations for his monotheistic kerygma. In continuity with Jewish tradition Paul proclaims the living God as the one true God over against idol-gods who were dead and dumb. It was the living God alone who was worthy of worship and to whom Gentiles should convert. However, Paul also inherited living God tradition *via* early Christian kerygma that had reformulated earlier Jewish traditions. Early Christian kerygma transformed Jewish traditions by identifying the living God as the one who raised Jesus from the dead, thus giving Paul's monotheistic kerygma a specifically Christian twist. For Paul and other early Christians, God's "living" character manifested itself definitively in the life-giving act of raising Jesus.

Paul, however, was not simply a passive recipient of living God tradition. Romans 9:25–26; 2 Cor 2:14–3:6 and 6:14–7:1 show that he was innovative and used it in creative ways by impressing it with his own distinctive stamp. The Pauline significance of the living God is characterized by a complexity and richness that distinguishes it from earlier Jewish and Christian formulations. For Paul, the significance of the living God involves a wide spectrum of associations, beginning with the epithet's association with and function in his missionary preaching. In 2 Cor 3:3 and 6:16 Paul's use of the epithet presupposes his proclamation of the living God in Corinth. Corresponding to this kerygmatic function of the epithet is its association with Gentile conversion. Upon hearing Paul's gospel Gentiles often responded by turning to the living God. The living God for Paul thus functions as conversion language, designating the foundational experience of conversion.

Further, the epithet's function as a term signifying conversion also designates a divine initiative that gives life, as in Rom 9:25–26; 2 Cor 3:3 and 6:16. Conversion is the work and initiative of the living God who reaches out to Gentiles, calling them into a new life as God's children. For example, in 2 Cor 3:3 the Spirit of the living God "writes" the Corinthian letter, thus indicating the origins of the Corinthian community in divine life-giving. The Spirit of the living God is the same Spirit of 2 Cor 3:6 who "gives life" in association with Paul's ministry. Through conversion the living God transforms the Corinthian converts into sons and daughters of the living God and brings them into a close filial relation with the divine father (Rom 9:25–26; 2 Cor 6:18). Moreover, conversion to the living God is a divine life-giving act, viewed on analogy with Jesus' resurrection. Through conversion, the living God "raises" Gentile communities to life and recreates them as a "people" where no (covenantal) people had previously existed (Rom 9:25–26; 2 Cor 6:16). This divine initiative of conversion results in the creation of Gentile communities that are described as "churches" or "temples" of the living God (1 Tim 3:15; 2 Cor 6:16).

The Pauline use of the living God thus carries a rich spectrum of associations that have been melded together into something distinctively Pauline. These associations include: the one God proclaimed in his missionary kerygma; the God who raised Jesus from the dead; the God who initiates conversion in the mission field through the gospel and the Spirit; and the creator God who gives life in converting Gentiles and establishing Gentile communities of faith. What distinguishes the living God from other divine appellations is the epithet's significance in designating the life-giving creator who stands in antithesis to the idol-gods of the Hellenistic world. In Paul's kerygma, the living God serves to designate God's superior character as the source and giver of life. This life-giving character is definitively manifested in Jesus' resurrection which signals the dawn of a new creation and this new creation is further manifested in the Pauline mission.

Moreover, the rich significance of the Pauline living God holds implications for the interpretation of Paul's epistolary discourse, especially that of 2 Cor 2:14–3:6 and 6:14–7:1. In these passages, living God theology supplies underlying theological and literary threads that unify disparate aspects of the discourse. Living God theology provides the theological foundation from which Paul's discourse works. More specifically, in 2 Cor 2:14–3:6 Paul argues from the presupposition that he is an apostle of the living God, called and commissioned by the living God to be a vehicle of eschatological life in Corinth. Key motifs in 2:14–3:6 can thus be read in terms of a theocentric conception of Paul's apostleship in which Paul's ministry is closely interrelated with the divine action of the living God acting through the Spirit. Paul's ministry is grounded in and closely linked to the divine action of the living God. Paul's ministry goes back to a call from the living God and is informed by a presupposition that is given articulation in *Acts Paul* 3:17, where Paul says that the living God has "sent" him to preach and bring salvation to Gentiles. In 2 Cor 2:14–3:6 Paul is thus led by "God" in triumphal procession (2:14); he proclaims the gospel as one commissioned "from God" (2:17; cf. 4:1); and he is made "competent" by God as a minister of the new covenant (3:5–6).

Living God theology also informs those motifs in 2:14–3:6 that express the life-giving effects of Paul's ministry. Paul's role as apostle of the living God entails the mediation of divine life in Corinth, where Paul worked as a vehicle of divine life-giving. In Corinth, Paul's proclamation of the gospel means salvation and life for those who accept it (2:15–16). Through Paul the Corinthians come to know the living God's Spirit, who "gives life" through conversion (3:3, 6). The very existence of the Corinthian community itself manifests the life-giving effect of Paul's ministry. The existence of the Corinthian community serves to confirm Paul's role as apostolic mediator of eschatological divine life since it is nothing short of a new creation (4:6; 5:17).

Living God theology also supplies a theological foundation for interpreting 2 Cor 6:14–7:1. The latter derives its theological coherence from a substratum of kerygmatic language that alludes to Gentile conversion to the living God. Many of the motifs in 6:14–7:1 go back to root notions of conversion theology. For example, the two formulations in 2 Cor 6:16b and 6:16c reflect a substratum of missionary kerygma antithetically opposing the living God and idols. The Corinthians are a "temple of the living God," alluding to their origins in conversion to the living God. Further, the formulations in 6:16b and 6:16c are closely integrated with the surrounding material and thus indicate the presence of conversion language throughout the passage. The passage employs kerygmatic language recast as exhortation that serves to remind Gentile Christian readers of their foundational conversion experience. Through conversion, the Corinthians left behind their former unbelief, darkness, lawlessness, and Belial for a new life of faith (6:14–16a). The catena in 6:16c–18 uses scripture to allude to conversion and the dynamics of separation from idolatry. As a result of conversion the living God receives them as covenantal sons and daughters (6:16c–18). By rooting 6:14–7:1 in living God theology, the pre-Pauline composer of the passage is able to draw out the ethical implications of conversion to the living God and the need for converts to live as God's holy people.

Much of the discourse in 2 Cor 2:14–3:6 and 6:14–7:1 can be interpreted in connection with living God theology and the root idea that Paul is an apostle of the living God who has been, and continues to be, a mediator of the living God's creative activity in Corinth. Paul's ministry is a manifestation of the living God's initiative of eschatological new creation that began with the death and resurrection of Jesus. This divine initiative aims at the restoration of eschatological Israel envisioned by the prophets Hosea, Jeremiah, and Ezekiel. Paul's ministry effects a new creation that transforms Gentiles into covenantal sons and daughters (Rom 9:25–26; 2 Cor 3:3 and 6:16). Through

Paul's ministry the Spirit of the living God is active in Corinth as Ezekiel's divine Spirit that restores dead Israel to new life (Ezek 37:1–14). Through Paul's ministry the Corinthians have become a temple of the living God in whom the living God dwells and moves. The Corinthians have covenantal identity in relation to the living God because Paul came to Corinth proclaiming the gospel.

By using living God theology, Paul is thus able to construe his ministry within a broader salvation-historical framework by using the language of scriptural prophecy in Rom 9:25–26; 2 Cor 3:3 and 6:16. Paul construes his ministry in connection with a broader divine initiative in which the living God forms a new covenant people in a manner consonant with his past action of forming Israel on Horeb. As the living God formed Israel on Horeb, speaking as a voice from fire without visible form (Deut 4–5 LXX), so now he establishes a new covenantal people by speaking through Paul's gospel and the accompanying activity of the Spirit. As the living God had formerly created a people through a manifestation of fire and word through the mediation of Moses, so now the living God establishes eschatological Israel by means of the gospel and Spirit that are mediated through Paul's ministry. Further, as the living God once dwelled in the Jerusalem temple as a sign of covenantal faithfulness, so now he indwells the Corinthian temple-community as a sign of covenantal love for Gentile converts. Paul thus makes creative use of living God theology in 2 Cor 2:14–3:6 and 6:14–7:1 to clarify for the Corinthians the significance of his apostolic role in connection with an eschatological new creation.

Finally, Paul's use of living God tradition can also be detected in the wider epistolary framework of 2 Cor 2:14–7:4 and, again, living God theology serves his aims of establishing and clarifying his apostolic credentials to the Corinthians.[1] Some general ob-

---

1. In recent scholarly discussions more interpreters are paying attention to the internal coherence that characterizes the discourse in 2 Cor 2:14–7:4. For example, Furnish, *II Corinthians*, 242; Fitzgerald, *Cracks in an Earthen Vessel*, 148–53; and Frances Young and David Ford, *Meaning and Truth in 2 Corinthians* (Grand Rapids: Eerdmans, 1987), 14.

servations suggest the presence of living God theology in 2 Cor 2:14–7:1, most notably, the dual use of the epithet in 3:3 and 6:16. Can it be a coincidence that 2 Cor 6:14–7:1 presents a second usage of the living God that corresponds to the first usage in 3:3? The thematic correspondence between the two uses is striking. Both expressions—the "Spirit of the living God" (2 Cor 3:3) and the "temple of the living God" (2 Cor 6:16)—allude to the foundational experience of conversion to the living God in Corinth. Second Corinthians 3:3 stresses the means by which the Corinthians were brought to conversion: Paul's ministry acting in concert with the living God's Spirit. Second Corinthians 6:16 stresses the results of that conversion: the Corinthians are God's holy temple and have the Spirit in their midst.

The two occurrences of the living God in 2 Cor 3:3 and 6:16 would thus seem to reflect an epistolary design that involves an inclusio arrangement. The result of framing 2 Cor 2:14–7:4 with two references to the living God in thematically corresponding formulations is a concentric arrangement of material that is characteristic of Pauline style. Recent proponents of rhetorical criticism have observed that Paul has a penchant for arranging his epistolary materials concentrically. "Circularity and repetition were characteristic of Paul's rhetoric," as in 1 Thess 2:13–16, which corresponds to the earlier passage in 1:2–10.[2] Also, Paul employs "framing structures as a means of organizing and developing his argumentation," as in 1 Cor 6:12–11:1 where the expression "all things are lawful but not all things are beneficial" functions as a framing device for the intervening material.[3]

This stylistic penchant of Paul in using repetition and inclusio also characterizes the material in 2 Cor 2:14–7:4. For example, Paul's use and placement of two hardship catalogues in 4:7–12 and 6:3–10 reflects such an arrangement. The second catalogue

2. John L. White, *The Apostle of God: Paul and the Promise of Abraham* (Peabody, Mass.: Hendrickson, 1999), 74–75. Handbooks on ancient rhetoric refer to this circularity and repetition as *"commutatio."* See Heinrich Lausberg, *Handbook of Literary Rhetoric: A Foundation for Literary Study* (trans. M. Bliss, A. Jansen, and D. Orton; Leiden: E. J. Brill, 1998), 354–57.

3. Amador, "Revisiting 2 Corinthians: Rhetoric and the Case for Unity," 101–2.

serves to repeat and supplement the earlier one.[4] Inclusio arrangement is also evident in the thematic correspondence of material in 2 Cor 2:15–16 and 6:14–16. The latter passages employ a similar antithetical style of language that points to an inclusio arrangement.[5] These observations suggest that the relation between 2 Cor 2:14–3:6 and 6:14–7:1 reflects a compositional arrangement formulated along the lines of an inclusio. The use and placement of 2 Cor 6:14–7:1 in the latter part of the argumentative unit (2 Cor 2:14–7:4) serves to round out and balance the earlier argument.

My thesis, then, is that Paul (or a redactor) decided to frame 2 Cor 2:14–7:4 with two uses of the living God in 2 Cor 3:3 and 6:16, suggesting that living God theology plays an important role in the intervening argument. Paul, in other words, employs an epistolary strategy that draws upon living God theology in the intervening argument. More specifically, I am suggesting that living God theology informs the intervening argument as a theological presupposition and that 2 Cor 5, for example, can be interpreted in the light of this theology. The material in 2 Cor 5 is particularly interesting because it is the focal point of the wider argument and uses motifs that are easily related to living God theology. A perusal of 2 Cor 5:11–20 shows to what extent it parallels and reiterates themes from 2:14–3:6. Verbal links emerge in the expressions of self-commendation in 3:1 and 5:12 and also in the references to Paul's "ministry" in 3:3, 5–6, 8 and 5:18–20. Paul's activity of "ministering" the Corinthian letter and in having a new covenant ministry (3:3, 5–6) is closely linked to his "ministry of reconciliation" in 2 Cor 5:18–20. Paul is entrusted by God with the "ministry" and "message of reconciliation" (5:18–19).

The verbal links between 2 Cor 2:14–3:6 and 5:11–21 suggest

4. Fitzgerald, *Cracks In An Earthen Vessel*, 192, notes of the second hardship catalogue: "by the repetition of items from a previous catalogue and the introduction of new ones, an author not only reminds his readers of the previous catalogue but suggests to them that what follows is to be understood as a supplement to that initial list."

5. Dahl, "A Fragment and Its Fragment: 2 Corinthians 6:14–7:1," 66. Lambrecht, "Structure and Line of Thought in 2 Cor 2,14–4,6," 347–50, observes a concentric arrangement in 2 Cor 2:14–4:6 that is arranged according to "a concentric A-B-A' pattern."

the presence of living God theology in the latter, and this theology emerges in the theme of new creation (5:17). The living God's initiative of establishing an eschatological new creation begins in 5:14–15 with the death and resurrection of Christ: "And he died for all, that those who live might no longer live for themselves but for him who for their sake died and was raised" (5:15). Moreover, in 5:17, the eschatological effect of Christ's death and resurrection is made clear in subsequent verses; in 5:17, for example, God's act in Jesus' death and resurrection is the basis for an eschatological new creation: "Therefore, if anyone is in Christ, there is a new creation; the old has passed away; behold, the new has come!" (cf. Isa 43:18–19). The living God, who raised Jesus from the dead, now operates through Paul's ministry and message of reconciliation. Paul's ministry of reconciliation helps to bring about an eschatological new creation that transforms and recreates the world through conversion. Paul's role as mediator of divine eschatological life in Corinth is clarified in terms of an eschatological new creation. The living God, working through Paul (5:20), converts Gentiles, reconciles them to God, and establishes them as a new creation. Similarly, in 6:1, Paul exhorts the Corinthians: "working together with him, then, we entreat you not to accept the grace of God in vain." Paul continues to "work together" with God as the vehicle of divine life among the Gentiles. Living God theology, then, is present here in Paul's theocentric conception of his ministry and in the theme of eschatological new creation.

Paul's wider epistolary strategy in 2 Cor 2:14–7:4 is thus bound up with the aim of promoting his continuing apostolic role among the Corinthians, and living God theology is instrumental in achieving this aim. Paul came to Corinth as a missionary proclaiming the living God and subsequently converted the Corinthians to faith. Through Paul the Corinthians were introduced to the living God and came into relationship with him, attaining an ecclesial identity as sons and daughters of the living God. This foundational event of conversion serves to attest and verify Paul's role as mediator of eschatological life. In connection with Paul the Corinthians became a "temple of the living God," a community that had renounced pagan ways and devoted itself to the worship of the one living God. Paul thus commends himself as an apostle of the living God and the ambassador of Christ through whom the Corinthians have been recreated as God's people.

However, what had begun through Paul in Corinth was now in danger of failing. The formerly close relation between Paul and his community was jeopardized in connection with certain outsiders who had come into the Corinthian church. In response, Paul reminds the Corinthians in 2 Cor 2:14–7:4 that they should have no doubts about Paul's continuing role in their salvation. Paul was and still is the vehicle of the living God's eschatological life to the Corinthians. Through Paul, God's work of eschatological new creation had begun in Corinth and it was still bound up with him. Paul remains the living God's apostle, as is clear from the way that God sustains him in his trials and sufferings (6:3–10); and to turn away from Paul the apostle is tantamount to falling away from the living God. Put another way, the Corinthians, apart from Paul their founding apostle, would jeopardize their relationship with the living God. It is only in relationship with Paul that the Corinthians are a "temple of the living God," as the assertion in 2 Cor 6:16b makes clear: "for we (Paul and the Corinthians) are the temple of the living God." Therefore, relationship to Paul remains essential in the life of the Corinthian community. A relationship with the living God entails a relationship with the living God's apostle.

Bibliography

Aland, Kurt, M. Black, C. M. Martini, B. M. Metzger, and A. Wikgren, editors, *Novum Testamentum Graece*. 26th ed. Stuttgart: Deutsche Bibelstiftung, 1979.

Allo, P. E. B. *Saint Paul: Seconde épître aux Corinthiens*. 2d ed. Études Bibliques. Paris: Librairie Lecoffre, 1956.

Amador, J. D. H. "Revisiting 2 Corinthians: Rhetoric and the Case For Unity." *NTS* 46 (2000): 92–111.

Andersen, F. I., and D. N. Freedman. *Hosea*. AB 24. Garden City, N.Y.: Doubleday, 1980.

Anderson, H. "3 Maccabees." *The Old Testament Pseudepigrapha*. Edited by James Charlesworth. Garden City, N.Y.: Doubleday, 1983. 2:509–29.

Aptowitzer, Victor. "Aseneth, the Wife of Joseph: A Haggadic Literary-Historical Study." *HUCA* 1 (1924): 239–306.

Aubin, Paul. *Le Problème de la Conversion. Étude sur une terme commun a l'hellénisme et au christianisme des trois premiers siècles*. Paris: Beauchesne, 1963.

Aune, David E. *The New Testament in Its Literary Environment*. Philadelphia: Westminster, 1987.

Baird, William. "Letters of Recommendation: A Study of 2 Cor 3:1–3." *JBL* 80 (1961): 166–72.

Barrett, C. K. *A Commentary on the Epistle to the Romans*. HNTC. New York: Harper, 1957.

———. *The Second Epistle to the Corinthians*. HNTC. Peabody, Mass.: Hendrickson, 1973, 1987.

Bassler, Jouette M. *Divine Impartiality*. SBLDS 59. Chico, Calif.: Scholars Press, 1982.

Bauckham, Richard, "The Acts of Paul as a Sequel to Acts." In *The Book of Acts in Its First Century Setting*. Edited by Bruce W. Winter and Andrew D. Clark. Grand Rapids: Eerdmans, 1993. 1:105–52.

Beale, G. K. "The Old Testament Background of Reconciliation in 2 Corinthians 5–7 and Its Bearing on the Literary Problem of 2 Corinthians 6.14–7.1." *NTS* 35 (1989): 550–81.

Belleville, Linda L. *Reflections of Glory: Paul's Polemical Use of the Moses-Doxa Tradition in 2 Corinthians 3:1–18*. JSNTSup 52. Sheffield: JSOT Press, 1991.

————. "Paul's Polemic and Theology of the Spirit in 2 Corinthians," *CBQ* 58 (1996): 281–304.

Berger, Klaus. "Jüdisch-hellenistische Missionsliteratur und apokryphe Apostelakten." *Kairos* 17 (1975): 232–48.

Best, Ernest. *A Commentary on the First and Second Epistles to the Thessalonians.* BNTC. Repr., London: A. & C. Black, 1986.

Betz, Hans D. "2 Cor 6:14–7:1: An Anti-Pauline Fragment?" *JBL* 92 (1973): 88–108.

————. *Galatians: A Commentary on Paul's Letter to the Churches in Galatia.* Hermenia. Philadelphia: Fortress Press, 1979.

Bevan, E. *Holy Images: An Inquiry into Idolatry and Image-Worship in Ancient Paganism and in Christianity.* Repr., London: George Allen & Unwin, 1940. 1971.

Bornkamm, Günther. *Early Christian Experience.* Translated by P. L. Hammer. New York: Harper & Row, 1969.

————. *Paul.* Translated by D. M. C. Stalker. New York: Harper and Row, 1971.

Bousset, Wilhelm, and Hugo Gressmann. *Die Religion des Judentums im spät-hellenistischen Zeitalter.* 3d ed. Handbuch zum Neuen Testament 21. Tübingen: J. C. B. Mohr, 1966.

Brown, Raymond. *An Introduction to the New Testament.* New York: Doubleday, 1997.

Bruce, F. F. *1 and 2 Thessalonians.* WBC 45. Waco, Tex.: Word Books, 1982.

Bultmann, Rudolf. *The Second Letter to the Corinthians.* Translated by R. A. Harrisbille. Minneapolis: Augsburg, 1985.

————. "πιστεύω," *TDNT.* Edited by G. Kittel. Translated by Geoffrey Bromiley. Grand Rapids: Eerdmans, 1968. 6. 217–22.

————. *Theology of the New Testament.* Translated by K. Grobel. New York: Charles Scribner's Sons, 1951, 1955.

Burchard, Christoph. *Untersuchungen zu Joseph und Aseneth. Überlieferung-Ortbestimmung.* WUNT 8. Tübingen: J. C. B. Mohr, 1963.

————. "Joseph and Aseneth." In *The Old Testament Pseudepigrapha.* Edited by James Charlesworth. Garden City, N.Y.: Doubleday, 1985. 2.177–247.

————. "Liber Aseneth." In Albert-Marie Denis. *Concordance Grecques des Pseudépigraphes d'Ancien Testament.* Louvain: Université Catholique de Louvain, 1987. 851–59.

Bussmann, Claus. *Themen der paulinischen Missionspredigt auf dem Hinter-grund der spätjüdisch-hellenistischen Missionsliteratur.* Europäische Hochschulschriften XXIII. 3. Bern: Peter Lang, 1971.

Byrne, Brendan. *"Sons of God"—"Seed of Abraham": A Study of the Idea of the Sonship of All Christians in Paul against the Jewish Background.* Analecta biblica 83. Rome: Biblical Institute, 1979.

Charles, R. H., editor, *The Apocrypha and Pseudepigrapha of the Old Testament.* 2 vols. Oxford: Clarendon, 1913.

Charlesworth, James H., editor. *Old Testament Pseudepigrapha*. 2 vols. Garden City, N.Y.: Doubleday, 1983.

Chestnutt, Randell, "From Text to Context: The Social Matrix of Joseph and Aseneth," *Society of Biblical Literature 1996 Seminar Papers*. Atlanta: Scholars Press, 1996.

Cohen, Shaye, D. "Crossing the Boundary and Becoming a Jew." *HTR* 82 (1989): 13–33.

Collange, J. F. *Énigmes de la deuxième épître de Paul aux Corinthiens. Étude exégétique de 2 Cor. 2:14–7:14*. SNTSMS 18. Cambridge: Cambridge University Press, 1972.

Collins, John J. *Between Athens and Jerusalem: Jewish Identity in the Hellenistic Diaspora*. New York: Crossroad, 1986.

———. *The Sibylline Oracles in Egyptian Judaism*. SBLDS 13. Missoula: University of Montana Press, 1974.

Collins, John J. *Daniel*. Hermeneia. Minneapolis: Fortress Press, 1993.

Collins, Raymond F. *Studies on the First Letter to the Thessalonians*. Bibliotheca Ephemeridum Theologicarum Lovaniensium 61. Leuven: Peeters, 1984.

Cranfield, C. E. B. *A Critical and Exegetical Commentary on the Epistle to the Romans*. ICC. 2 vols. Edinburgh: T. & T. Clark, 1979.

Dahl, Nils A. *Studies in Paul: Theology for the Early Christian Mission*. Minneapolis: Augsburg, 1977.

———. "Form-Critical Observations on Early Christian Preaching." In *Jesus in the Memory of the Early Church: Essays by Nils Alstrup Dahl*. Minneapolis: Augsburg, 1976. 30–36.

———. "A Fragment in Its Context: 2 Corinthians 6:14–7:1." In *Studies in Paul: Theology for Early Christian Mission*. Minneapolis: Augsburg, 1977. 62–69.

Dalbert, Peter. *Die Theologie der Hellenistisch-Jüdischen Missionsliteratur unter Ausschluss von Philo und Josephus*. Hamburg: Herbert Reich, 1954.

Davenport, G. L. *The Eschatology of the Book of Jubilees*. Studia Postbiblica. Leiden: E. J. Brill, 1971.

Davies, Witton. "Bel and the Dragon," *The Apocrypha and Pseudepigrapha of the Old Testament in English*. Edited by R. H. Charles. 2 vols. Oxford: Clarendon, 1983. 1: 652–57.

Delcor, M. *Le Livre de Daniel*. Paris: Gabalda, 1971.

Delling, G. "Einwirkungen der Sprache der Septuaginta in 'Joseph und Aseneth.' " *JSJ* 9 (1978): 29–56.

———. "Die Kunst des Gestaltens in 'Joseph und Aseneth.' " *NovT* 26 (1984): 1–29.

———. "Partizipiale Gottesprädikationen in den Briefen des Neuen Testaments." *Studia Theologica* 17 (1963): 1–59.

Denis, Albert M. *Concordance grecque des pseudépigraphes d'Ancien Testament*. Louvain-la-Neuve: Université Catholique de Louvain, 1987.

———. *Concordance latine du Liber Jubilaeorum sive Parva Genesis*. Louvain: Université Catholique, 1973.

Dibelius, Martin. *The Pastoral Epistles: A Commentary on the Pastoral Epistles.* Translated by P. Buttolph and A. Yarboro. Hermeneia. 2d rev. ed. Philadelphia: Fortress Press, 1972.

———. *Studies in the Acts of the Apostles.* Translated by M. Ling. Edited by H. Greeven. London: SCM, 1956.

Dinkler, Erich. "Die Verkündigung als eschatologisch-sakramentales Geschehen. Auslegung von 2 Kor 5,14–6,2." In *Die Zeit Jesu. Festschrift für Heinrich Schlier.* Edited by G. Bornkamm and K. Rahner. Freiburg: Herder, 1970: 169–89.

Dodd, Charles H. *The Apostolic Preaching and Its Developments.* Repr., Grand Rapids: Baker, 1980.

Donaldson, Terence. *Paul and the Gentiles: Remapping the Apostle's Convictional World.* Minneapolis: Fortress Press, 1997.

Doran, Robert. *Temple Propaganda: The Character and Purpose of 2 Maccabees.* CBQMS 12. Washington, D.C.: Catholic University Press, 1981.

Duff, Paul Brooks, "The Mind of the Redactor: 2 Cor. 6:14–7:1 in Its Secondary Context." *NovT* 35 (1993): 160–80.

Dunn, James D. G. *Romans.* WBC 38. 2 vols. Dallas: Word Books, 1988.

Dupont, Dom J. *The Salvation of the Gentiles: Essays on Acts of the Apostles.* Translated by J. Keating. New York: Paulist, 1979.

Ellis, Earl E. *Paul's Use of the Old Testament.* Edinburgh: Oliver & Boyd, 1957.

Endres, John C. *Biblical Interpretation in the Book of Jubilees.* CBQMS 18. Washington, D.C.: Catholic Biblical Association of America, 1987.

Everding, Edward H. *The Living God: A Study in the Function and Meaning of Biblical Terminology.* Ph.D. diss., Harvard, 1968.

Fee, Gordon D. "II Corinthians VI.14–VII.1 and Food Offered to Idols." *NTS* 23 (1977): 140–61.

Feldman, Louis H. *Jew and Gentile in the Ancient World: Attitudes and Interactions from Alexander to Justinian.* Princeton: Princeton University Press, 1993.

Fiensy, D. A., and D. R. Darnell. "Hellenistic Synagogal Prayers." In *Old Testament Pseudepigrapha.* Edited by James H. Charlesworth. Garden City, N.Y.: Doubleday, 1985. 2:671–97.

Fischer, Thomas. "Maccabees, Books of." *ABD.* 4:442–50.

Fitzgerald, John T. *Cracks in an Earthen Vessel: An Examination of the Catalogues of Hardships in the Corinthian Correspondence.* SBLDS 99. Atlanta: Scholars Press, 1988.

Fitzmyer, Joseph A. *Essays on the Semitic Background of the New Testament.* London: Geoffrey Chapman, 1971.

———. *Romans.* AB 33. New York: Doubleday, 1993.

———. *To Advance the Gospel.* New York: Crossroad, 1981.

———. *Essays on the Semitic Background of the New Testament.* SBLSBS 5; Missoula: Scholars Press, 1974.

Freed, Edwin D. *The Apostle Paul, Christian Jew: Faithfulness and the Law.* Lanham, Md.: University Press of America, 1994.

Friedrich, Gerhard. "Ein Tauflied hellenistischer Judenchristen, I Thess 1., 9f." *Theologische Zeitschrift* 21 (1965): 502–16.

Furnish, Victor P. *II Corinthians*. AB 32A. Garden City, N.Y.: Doubleday, 1984.

Gaventa, Beverly R. *From Darkness to Light: Aspects of Conversion in the New Testament*. Overtures to Biblical Theology. Philadelphia: Fortress Press, 1986.

Gärtner, Bertil. *The Temple and the Community in Qumran and the New Testament: A Comparative Study in the Temple Symbolism of the Qumran Texts and the New Testament*. SNTSMS 1. Cambridge: Cambridge University Press, 1965.

Geffcken, Johannes, *Die Oracula Sibyllina*. Die Griechischen Christlichen Schriftsteller der ersten drei Jahrhunderte. Leipzig: J. C. Hinrichs, 1902.

Georgi, Dieter. *The Opponents of Paul in Second Corinthians*. Philadelphia: Fortress Press, 1986.

Goldstein, Jonathan. *II Maccabees*. AB 41A. Garden City, N.Y.: Doubleday, 1983.

Goodman, Martin. *Mission and Conversion: Proselytizing in the Religious History of the Roman Empire*. Oxford: Clarendon, 1994.

Goodenough, Edwin. *Jewish Symbols in the Greco-Roman Period*. 11 vols. Princeton: Princeton University Press, 1953.

Goodwin, Mark J. "The Pauline Background of the Living God As Interpretive Context for 1 Timothy 4.10." *JSNT* 61 (1996): 65–85.

Goulder, Michael D. *The Psalms of the Sons of Korah*. JSOTSup 20. Sheffield: JSOT Press, 1982.

Gnilka, Joachim. "2 Cor 6:14–7:1 in the Light of the Qumran Texts and the Testaments of the Twelve Patriarchs." In *Paul and the Dead Sea Scrolls*. Edited by J. Murphy O'Connor and J. Charlesworth. New York: Crossroad, 1990. 48–68.

Grant, Frederick C. *Hellenistic Religions: The Age of Syncretism*. Indianapolis: Bobbs-Merrill, 1953.

Grant, Robert M. *Gods and the One God*. LEC 1. Philadelphia: Westminster, 1986.

Guerra, Anthony J. "The One God Topos in Spec. Leg. 1.52." *Society of Biblical Literature 1990 Seminar Papers*. Edited by D. Lull. Scholars Press, 1990. 148–57.

Guillet, Jacques, "Le Titre Biblique *Le Dieu Vivant*," *L'Homme Devant Dieu: Mélanges offerts au Père Henri De Lubac*. Théologie: Etudes Publiées sous la direction de l Faculté Théologie S.J. de Lyon-Fourvière 56. Aubier, 1963.

Habicht, Christian. *Historische und legendarisch Erzählungen: 2. Makkabäerbuch*. Judische Schriften aus hellenistisch-römischen Zeit. Gerd Mohn, 1976.

Hadas, Moses. *Aristeas to Philocrates (Letter of Aristeas)*. Jewish Apocryphal Literature. New York: Harper & Brothers, 1951.

————. *The Third and Fourth Book of Maccabees.* Jewish Apocryphal Literature. New York: Ktav, 1953.

Haenchen, Ernst. *The Acts of the Apostles: A Commentary.* Philadelphia: Westminster, 1971.

Hafemann, Scott. *Suffering and Ministry in the Spirit: Paul's Defense of His Ministry in II Corinthians 2:14–3:3.* Grand Rapids: Eerdmans, 1988.

Hahn, Ferdinand. *Mission in the New Testament.* SBT 47. London: SCM, 1981.

Harnack, Adolf von. "Κόπο (Κοπιᾶν, οἱ Κοπιῶντες") im frühchristlichen Sprachgebrauch." *ZNW* 28 (1928): 1–10.

————. *The Mission and Expansion of Christianity in the First Three Centuries.* Translated by J. Moffatt. Gloucester, Mass.: Peter Smith, 1972. Based on *Die Mission und Ausbreitung des Christentums in den ersten drei Jahrhunderten.* 4th ed. Leipzig: Hinrischs, 1924.

Hartman, L. F., and A. A. DiLella. *The Book of Daniel.* AB 23. Garden City, N.Y.: Doubleday, 1977.

Hays, Richard B. *Echoes of Scripture in the Letters of Paul.* New Haven: Yale University Press, 1988.

Heinrici, C. F. G. *Der zweite Brief an die Korinther.* Kritisch exegetischer Kommentar über das Neue Testament. Göttingen: Vandenhoeck & Ruprecht, 1890.

Hengel, Martin. *Judaism and Hellenism: Studies in their Encounter in Palestine during the Early Hellenistic Period.* Translated by J. Bowden. 2 vols. Philadelphia: Fortress Press, 1974.

————. *The Pre-Christian Paul.* Translated by J. Bowden. London: SCM; Philadelphia: Trinity Press International, 1991.

Héring, Jean. *The Second Epistle of Saint Paul to the Corinthians.* Translated by A. W. Heathcote and P. J. Allcock. London: Epworth, 1967.

Hermann, Ingo. *Kyrios und Pneuma: Studien zur Christologie der paulinischen Hauptbriefe.* Munich: Kösel, 1961.

Holladay, Carl. "Acts." In *Harper's Bible Commentary.* Ed James L. Mays. San Francisco: Harper & Row, 1988. 1077–1118.

Hommel, Hildebrecht. *Schöpfer und Erhalter. Studien zum Problem Christentum und Antike.* Berlin: Lettner, 1956.

Hughes, Philip E. *Paul's Second Letter to the Corinthians.* Grand Rapids: Eerdmans, 1973.

Humphreys, Lee W. "A Lifestyle for the Diaspora." *JBL* 92 (1973): 211–23.

Hurtado, Larry. *One God, One Lord: Early Christian Devotion and Ancient Jewish Monotheism.* Philadelphia: Fortress Press, 1988.

Jackson, F. J. F., and K. Lake. *The Beginnings of Christianity. Part 1: The Acts of the Apostles.* 5 vols. Repr., Grand Rapids: Baker Book House, 1979.

Jellicoe, Sidney. *The Septuagint and Modern Study.* Oxford: Clarendon, 1968.

Käsemann, Ernst. *Commentary on Romans.* Edited and translated by Geoffrey Bromiley. Repr., Grand Rapids: Eerdmans, 1990.

————. *Perspectives on Paul.* Translated by M. Kohl. Philadelphia: Fortress Press, 1971.

Kelly, James N. D. *A Commentary on the Epistles of Peter and Jude.* HNTC. New York: Harper & Row, 1969.

Kim, C. H. *Form and Structure of the Familiar Letter of Recommendation.* SBLDS 4. Missoula: University of Montana Press, 1970.

Kittel, G., and G. Friedrich. *Theological Dictionary of the New Testament.* Translated by and rev. by G. W. Bromiley. 10 vols. Grand Rapids: Eerdmans, 1964–76.

Klauck, Hans Joseph. *2. Korintherbrief.* Kommentar zum Neuen Testament. Würzburg: Echter Verlag, 1986.

Koch, Dietrich A. *Die Schriften als Zeuge des Evangeliums. Untersuchungen zur Verwendung und zum Verständnis der Schrift bei Paulus.* Beiträge zur historischen Theologie 69. Tübingen: J. C. B. Mohr, 1986.

Koester, Helmut. *Introduction to the New Testament: History and Literature of Early Christianity.* Philadelphia: Fortress Press, 1982.

Knight, George W. *Commentary on the Pastoral Epistles.* NIGTC. Grand Rapids: Eerdmans, 1992.

Kraus, Hans J. *Psalms 1–59: A Commentary.* Translated by H. C. Oswald. Minneapolis: Augsburg, 1988.

————. "Der lebendige Gott." *Evangelische Theologie* 27 (1967): 169–201.

Kuhn, K. G. "The Lord's Supper and the Communal Meal at Qumran." In *The Scrolls and the New Testament.* Edited by K. Stendahl. New York: Harper, 1957. 65–93.

Lake, K., and H. J. Cadbury. *The Beginnings of Christianity. Part I: The Acts of the Apostles.* Edited by K. Lake and F. J. F. Jackson. 5 vols. Repr., Grand Rapids: Baker, 1979.

Lambrecht, Jan. "Structure and Line of Thought in 2 Cor 2, 14–4.6." *Biblica* 64 (1983): 344–80.

————. *Second Corinthians.* Sacra Pagina 8. Collegeville, Minn.: Michael Glazier/Liturgical Press, 1999.

Langevin, Paul É. *Jésus Seigneur et l'eschatologie. Exégèse de textes prépauliniens.* Paris: Desclée de Brouwer, 1967.

Lausberg, Heinrich. *Handbook of Literary Rhetoric: A Foundation for Literary Study.* Translated by M. Bliss, A. Jansen, and D. Orton. Leiden: E. J. Brill, 1998.

Lerle, E. "Die Predigt in Lystra." *NTS* 57 (1960): 46–55.

Levine, Lee I. *Judaism and Hellenism in Antiquity: Conflict or Confluence?* Peabody, Mass.: Hendrickson, 1998.

Liddell, H. G., and R. Scott. *A Greek-English Lexicon.* 9th ed. Revised and augmented by H. S. Jones and R. McKenzie, with supplement by E. A. Barber. Oxford: Clarendon, 1940, 1968.

Lull, David. *The Spirit in Galatia: Paul's Interpretation of Pneuma as Divine Power.* SBLDS 49. Chico, Calif.: Scholars Press, 1980.

MacDonald, Dennis R. *The Legend and the Apostle: The Battle for Paul in Story and Canon.* Philadelphia: Westminster, 1983.

McKelvey, R. J. *The New Temple: The Church in the New Testament.* Oxford Theological Monographs. Oxford: Oxford University Press, 1969.

McKnight, Scot. *A Light among the Gentiles: Jewish Missionary Activity in the Second Temple Period.* Minneapolis: Fortress Press, 1991.

Malherbe, Abraham J. *Paul and the Thessalonians: The Philosophic Tradition of Pastoral Care.* Philadelphia: Fortress Press, 1987.

Marshall, P. "A Metaphor of Social Shame: ΘPIAMBEYEIN in 2 Cor 2:14." *NovT* 25 (1983): 302–17.

Martin, Ralph P. *2 Corinthians.* WBC 40. Waco, Tex.: Word Books, 1986.

Mays, James L. *Hosea: A Commentary.* Old Testament Library. Philadelphia: Westminster, 1969.

Meeks, Wayne A. *The First Urban Christians. The Social World of the Apostle Paul.* New Haven: Yale University Press, 1983.

———. *The Moral World of the First Christians.* Philadelphia: Westminster, 1986.

Metzger, Bruce M. *A Textual Commentary on the Greek New Testament.* 3d ed. London and New York: United Bible Societies, 1975.

Moore, Carey A. *Daniel, Esther, and Jeremiah: The Additions.* AB 44. Garden City, N.Y.: Doubleday, 1977.

Montgomery, J. A. *A Critical and Exegetical Commentary on the Book of Daniel.* ICC. Repr., Edinburgh: T. & T. Clark, 1959.

Moore, George F. *Judaism in the First Centuries of the Christian Era: The Age of the Tannaim.* 3 vols. Cambridge, Mass.: Harvard University Press, 1927–30.

Moxnes, Halvor. *Theology in Conflict: Studies of Paul's Understanding of God in Romans.* Leiden: E. J. Brill, 1980.

Munck, Johannes. "I Thess. 1.9–10 and the Missionary Preaching of Paul." *NTS* 9 (1962–63): 95–110.

Murphy-O'Connor, Jerome. *2 Corinthians.* Cambridge: Cambridge University Press, 1991.

———. "Relating 2 Corinthians 6.14–7.1 to Its Context." *NTS* 33 (1987): 272–75.

Nickelsburg, George W. E. *Jewish Literature Between the Bible and the Mishnah: A Historical and Literary Introduction.* Philadelphia: Fortress Press, 1981.

———. "Joseph and Aseneth." In *Jewish Writings of the Second Temple Period. Apocrypha, Pseudepigrapha, Qumran Sectarian Writings, Philo, Josephus.* CRINT 2.2. Edited by M. Stone. Philadelphia: Fortress/Van Gorcum, 1984. 65–71.

———. "Jubilees." In *Jewish Writings of the Second Temple Period. Apocrypha, Pseudepigrapha, Qumran Sectarian Writings, Philo, Josephus.* CRINT 2.2. Edited by M. Stone; Philadelphia: Fortress/Van Gorcum, 1984. 97–103.

———. "Stories of Biblical and Early Post-Biblical Times." In *Jewish Writings of the Second Temple Period. Apocrypha, Pseudepigrapha, Qumran Sectarian Writings, Philo, Josephus.* CRINT 2.2. Edited by M. Stone. Philadelphia: Fortress/Van Gorcum, 1984. 33–88.

Nock, Arthur D. *Conversion. Essays on Religion in the Ancient World.* Edited by Zeph Stewart. Cambridge, Mass.: Harvard University Press, 1972.

————. *Conversion. The Old and the New in Religion from Alexander the Great to Augustine of Hippo.* Brown Classics in Judaica. Repr., Lanham, Md.: University Press of America, 1988.

Oepke, A. *Die Missionspredigt des Apostels Paulus. Eine biblisch-theologische und religionsgeschichtliche Untersuchungen.* Missionswissenschaftliche Forschungen 2. Leipzig: J. C. Hinrichs, 1920.

Pak, James Yeong-Sik. *Paul as Missionary: A Comparative Study of Missionary Discourse in Paul's Epistles and Selected Contemporary Jewish Texts.* European University Studies XXIII. 410. Frankfurt: Peter Lang, 1991.

Pate, C. Marvin. *Adam Christology as the Exegetical and Theological Substructure of 2 Corinthians 4:7–5:21.* Lanham, Md.: University Press of America, 1991.

Pax, Elpidius. "Beobachtungen zur Konvertitensprache im ersten Thessalonicherbrief." *Studii Biblici Franciscani Analecta* 21 (1971): 220–61.

Pervo, R. I. "Joseph and Aseneth and the Greek Novel." In *Society of Biblical Literature 1976 Seminar Papers.* Edited by G. MacRae. Missoula: University of Montana Press, 1976. 171–81.

Pfitzner, Victor C. *Strength in Weakness: A Commentary on 2 Corinthians.* Adelaide, South Australia: Chi Rho, 1992.

Philo. Translated by F. H. Colson and G. H. Whitaker 10 vols. LCL. Cambridge, Mass.: Harvard University Press, 1956–62.

Philonenko, Marc. *Joseph et Aséneth: Introduction, texte critique, traduction et notes.* Studia Post-Biblica. Leiden: E. J. Brill, 1968.

Plummer, A. *A Critical and Exegetical Commentary on the Second Epistle of St. Paul to the Corinthians.* ICC. Edinburgh: T. & T. Clark, 1985.

Preuss, Horst D. *Old Testament Theology.* Translated by G. Perdue. 2 vols. Louisville: Westminster/John Knox. 1995.

Provence, Thomas E. " 'Who Is Sufficient for These Things?' An Exegesis of 2 Corinthians ii 15–iii 18." *NovT* 24 (1982): 54–81.

Quasten, Johannes. *Patrology.* 3 vols. Repr., Westminster, Md.: Christian Classics, 1990.

Quinn, Jerome D. *The Letter to Titus.* AB 35. New York: Doubleday, 1990.

Rahlfs, Alfred, editor. *Septuaginta.* 4th ed. Repr., Stuttgart: Deutsche Bibelgesellschaft, 1979.

Räisänen, Heikki. *Paul and the Law.* Philadelphia: Fortress Press, 1986.

Rensberger, D. "2 Corinthians 6:14–7:1—A Fresh Examination." *StBibTh* 8 (1978): 25–49.

Richard, Earl. "Polemics, Old Testament, and Theology: A Study of II Cor. III,1–IV,6." *RB* 88 (1981): 340–67.

————. *First and Second Thessalonians.* Sacra Pagina. Collegeville, Minn.: Michael Glazier/Liturgical Press, 1995.

Richardson, Neil. *Paul's Language about God.* JSNTSup 99. Sheffield: Sheffield Academic Press, 1994.

Rigaux, Beda. *Saint Paul. Les épîtres aux Thessaloniciens.* Études Bibliques. Paris: Librairie Lecoffre/J. Gabalda, 1956.

Ringgren, Helmer. *Israelite Religion.* Translated by David Green. Philadelphia: Fortress Press, 1966.

Roloff, Jürgen. *Der erste Brief an Timotheus.* Evangelisch-Katholischer Kommentar zum Neuen Testament. Neukirchener: Benziger, 1988.

Rordorf, Willy. "Tradition and Composition in the Acts of Thecla: The State of the Question." *Semeia* 38 (1986): 43–52.

Rosner, Brian S., editor. *Understanding Paul's Ethics: Twentieth-Century Approaches.* Grand Rapids: Eerdmans, 1995.

Roth, W. M. W. " 'For Life, He Appeals to Death' (Wis 13:18): A Study of Old Testament Idol Parodies." *CBQ* 37 (1975): 21–42.

Safrai, S. "Relations Between the Diaspora and the Land of Israel." In *The Jewish People in the First Century: Historical Geography, Political History, Social, Cultural, and Religious Life and Institutions.* CRINT. Edited by S. Safrai and M. Stern. Amsterdam: Van Gorcum, 1974.

Sanday, W., and A. C. Headlam. *The Epistle to the Romans.* ICC. 5th ed. Repr., Edinburgh: T. & T. Clark, 1902, 1962.

Sanders, Edward P. *Paul and Palestinian Judaism. A Comparison of Patterns of Religion.* Philadelphia: Fortress Press, 1977.

———. *Judaism: Practice and Belief: 63 B.C.E.–66 C.E.* Philadelphia: Trinity Press International, 1992.

Sänger, Dieter. *Antikes Judentum und die Mysterien. Religionsgeschichte Untersuchungen zu Joseph und Aseneth.* WUNT 2.5. Tübingen: J. C. B. Mohr, 1980.

Schmidt, Carl, editor. ΠΡΑΞΕΙΣ ΠΑΥΛΟΥ: *Acta Pauli.* Glückstadt: J. J. Augustin, 1936.

Schmoller, A. *Handkonkordanz zum griechischen Neuen Testament.* Repr., Münster/Westfalen: Deutsche Bibelgesellschaft, 1989.

Schneemelcher, Wilhelm, *New Testament Apocrypha.* Translated by R. McL. Wilson. 2 vols. Louisville: Westminster/John Knox, 1991.

Schneider, Gerhard. *Die Apostelgeschichte.* HTKNT 5. 2 vols. Freiburg: Herder, 1982.

———. "Urchristliche Gottesverkündigung in hellenistischer Umwelt," *Biblische Zeitschrift* 13 (1969): 59–75.

Scholz, Anton. *Commentar über das Buch Judith und über Bel und Drache.* Würzburg: Leo Woerl, 1896.

Schröter, Jens. *Der versöhnte Versöhner: Paulus als unentbehrlicher Mittler im Heilsvorgang zwischen Gott und Gemeinde nach 2 Kor 2.14–7.4.* Tübingen: Francke, 1993.

Schubert, Paul. *Form and Function of the Pauline Thanksgivings.* Berlin: Töpelmann, 1939.

Schürer, Emil. *The History of the Jewish People in the Age of Jesus Christ (175 B.C.–A.D. 135).* Revised and edited G. Vermes, F. Millar and M. Goodman. 3 vols. Edinburgh: T. & T. Clark, 1986.

Schütz, J. H. *Paul and the Anatomy of Apostolic Authority.* SNTSMS 26. Cambridge: Cambridge University Press, 1975.

Schweizer, Eduard. "Concerning the Speeches in Acts." In *Studies in Luke-Acts.* Edited by L. Keck and J. L. Martyn. Philadelphia: Fortress Press, 1980. 208–16.

Soards, Marion L. *The Speeches in Acts: Their Content, Context, and Concerns.* Louisville: Westminster/John Knox, 1994.

Stenger, W. "Die Gottesbezeichnung 'lebendiger Gott' im Neuen Testament." *Trierer Theologische Zeitschrift* 87 (1978): 61–69.

———. "Romans 9:6–29–A Midrash." *JSNT* 22 (1984): 37–54.

Steussy, Marti J. *Gardens in Babylon: Narrative and Faith in the Greek Legends of Daniel.* SBLDS 141. Atlanta: Scholars Press, 1993.

Strathmann, H. "λαός." In *TDNT.* Edited by G. Kittel. Translated by Geoffrey W. Bromiley. Grand Rapids: Eerdmans, 1967. 4. 50–57.

Stuhlmacher, Peter. *Das Paulinische Evangelium.* FRLANT 95. 2 vols. Göttingen: Vandenhoeck & Ruprecht, 1968.

Sumney, Jerry. *Identifying Paul's Opponents: The Question of Method in 2 Corinthians.* JSNTSup 40. Sheffield: Sheffield Academic Press, 1990.

Tacitus: The Histories. Translated by C. H. Moore, and J. Jackson. LCL. 5 vols. Cambridge, Mass.: Harvard University Press, 1969.

Tedesche, Sidney. *The Second Book of Maccabees.* Edited by S. Zeitlin. New York: Harper & Brothers, 1954.

Tcherikover, Victor. "Jewish Apologetic Literature Reconsidered." *Eos* 48 (1956): 169–93.

Testuz, Michel. *Les Idées Religieuses du Livre des Jubilés.* Paris: Ménard, 1960.

Thrall, Margaret. "The Problem of II Cor. VI. 14–VII. 1 in Some Recent Discussions." *NTS* 24 (1977): 132–48.

von Rad, Gerhard. *Wisdom in Israel.* Nashville: Abingdon, 1972.

Vouaux, Leon. *Les Actes de Paul et ses lettres apocryphes.* Les Apocryphes du Nouveau Testament. Paris: Librairie Letouzey, 1913.

Webb, William J. *Returning Home Covenant and Second Exodus as the Context for 2 Corinthians 6.14–7.1.* JSNTSup 85. Sheffield: JSOT, 1993.

Weinfeld, Moshe. *Deuteronomy 1–11.* AB 5. New York: Doubleday, 1991.

———. "Deuteronomy, Book of." In *ABD.* New York: Doubleday, 1992. 2:168–82.

Weiss, Johannes. *The History of Primitive Christianity.* Translated and edited by F. C. Grant. 2 vols. New York: Wilson-Erickson, 1937.

Wenham, David. "Acts and the Pauline Corpus II: The Evidence of Parallels." In *The Book of Acts in Its First Century Setting.* Edited by Bruce W. Winter and Andrew D. Clark. Grand Rapids: Eerdmans, 1993. 1:215–58.

Wevers, Jan W., editor. *Deuteronomy. Deuteronomium.* Septuaginta. Academie Scientarum Gottengensis III. 2. Göttingen: Vandenhoeck & Ruprecht, 1977.

White, John L. *The Apostle of God: Paul and the Promise of Abraham.* Peabody, Mass.: Hendrickson, 1999.

Wilckens, Ulrich. *Die Missionsreden der Apostelgeschichte: Form- und traditions-geschichtliche Untersuchungen.* WMANT 5. Neukirchen-Vluyn: Neukirch-ener Verlag, 1974.

———. *Der Brief und die Römer.* 3 vols. EKKNT VI. 2. Neukirchener: Benziger, 1987.

Wills, Lawrence M. *The Jewish Novel in the Ancient World.* Ithaca, N.Y.: Cornell University Press, 1995.

Windisch, Hans. *Der zweite Korintherbrief.* MeyerK 6. Göttingen: Vandenhoeck & Ruprecht, 1924.

Wintermute, O. S. "Jubilees." In *The Old Testament Pseudepigrapha.* Edited by James Charlesworth. Garden City, N.Y.: Doubleday, 1985. 35–142.

Witherington, Ben III. *Conflict and Community in Corinth: A Socio-Rhetorical Commentary on 2 Corinthians.* Grand Rapids: Eerdmans, 1995.

Wolff, Hans W. *Hosea.* Hermeneia. Translated by G. Stansell. Philadelphia: Fortress Press, 1974.

Young, Frances, and David F. Ford. *Meaning and Truth in 2 Corinthians.* Grand Rapids: Eerdmans, 1987.

Ziegler, Joseph, editor. *Daniel. Susanna, Daniel, Bel et Draco.* Septuaginta. Societatis Litterarum Gottingensis XVI. 2. Göttingen: Vandenhoeck & Ruprecht, 1954.

———. *Ezekiel. Ezechiel.* Septuaginta. Societatis Litterarum Gottingensis XVI. 1 Göttingen: Vandenhoeck & Ruprecht, 1952.

———. *Hosea. Duodecim prophetae.* Septuaginta. Societatis Litterarum Got-tingensis XIII. Vandenhoeck & Ruprecht, 1943.

———. *Jeremiah. Ieremias. Baruch. Threni. Epistulae Ieremiae.* Septuaginta. Societatis Litterarum Gottingensis XV. Göttingen: Vandenhoeck & Ruprecht, 1957.

———. *Sirach. Sapientia Iesu Filii Sirach.* Septuaginta. Societatis Litterarum Gottingensis XII. 2. Vandenhoeck & Ruprecht, 1965.

Zimmermann, F., editor. *Tobit. The Book of Tobit.* Jewish Apocryphal Literature. New York: Harper, 1958.

Index of Ancient Sources

𐰃𐰃𐰃𐰃𐰃𐰃𐰃𐰃𐰃𐰃

EARLY CHRISTIAN WRITINGS

General Index